Library of
Davidson College

BURT FRANKLIN: RESEARCH & SOURCE WORKS SERIES 812
American Classics in History and Social Science 205

THE

POLITICAL WRITINGS

OF

JOEL BARLOW

THE
POLITICAL WRITINGS
OF
JOEL BARLOW

NEW EDITION
With

Joel Barlow: A Bibliographical List

Prepared by
Division of Bibliography
Library of Congress

BURT FRANKLIN
NEW YORK

Published by LENOX HILL Pub. & Dist. Co. (Burt Franklin)
235 East 44th St., New York, N. Y. 10017
Originally Published: 1796
Reprinted: 1971
Printed in the U.S.A.

S.B.N.: 8337-01665
Library of Congress Card Catalog No.: 70-135175
Burt Franklin: Research and Source Works Series 812
American Classics in History and Social Science 205

Library of Congress
Division of Bibliography
JOEL BARLOW, 1754-1812:
A BIBLIOGRAPHICAL LIST

Compiled by

Florence S. Hellman
Acting Chief Bibliographer
May 1935

WRITINGS

We have not attempted to give the location of the various editions. If a copy is in the Library of Congress other copies are not listed. These are indicated by the call numbers at the end of the entries. The star * indicates the work is located in the Rare Book Room.

1. **(Barlow, Joel)** Advice to the privileged orders in the several states of Europe, resulting from the necessity and propriety of a general revolution in the principle of government. London, J. Johnson, 1792-93. 2 v.

    Pt. II (with author's name) has imprint: Paris, Printed at the English press, and sold by Barrois, senior, 1793. JC211.B25*

    Same. Part I. 2d ed. London, J. Johnson, 1792. 1 p.l., 156 pp., 1l. (Miscellaneous pamphlets, v. 681, no. 1)
    AC901.M 5,v.681*

    Same. Reprinted at New York, 1792. 178 p. Sabin.

Same. London—printed: New York—Reprinted by Childs and Swaine, 1792-94. 2 v.

Pt. II has imprint: Paris, printed; New York—Reprinted for Francis Childs & co. and J. Fellows, by George Forman, 1794. JC211.B23*

Same. London, J. Johnson, 1793. 2 v. JC211.B252*

Vol. I, 3rd ed.; v. 2 has imprint: Paris, Printed at the English press, and sold by Barrois, senior.

Same. London, J. Johnson, 1793-95. 2 v. in 1. NN

Avis aux ordres privilegies... Paris, Barrois l'aine, 1794. 2 v. JC211.B28*

Same. Advice to the privileged orders... Part II. London, D. I. Eaton, 1795. 4 p.l., 64 pp. (Miscellaneous pamphlets, v. 681, no. 2) AC901.M5,v.681*

Same. _____ 2d ed. London, D. I. Eaton, 1795. 4 p.l., 64 pp. (Miscellaneous pamphlets, v. 605, no. 2)

AC901.M5,v.605*

Same. ——— 3d ed. London, Printed and sold by Daniel Isaac Eaton, 1795. 4 p.l., 64 pp. NN

2. **Barlow, Joel.** (The chapter of *Chronicles*.) American historical magazine (New Haven) Jan. 1836, v. 1: 23-25.

E171.A52,v.1*

3. ——— The Columbiad, a poem. Philadelphia, C. and A. Conrad, 1807. xvi, 454 pp. Bib. Nat.

Same. Philadelphia, 1808. 2 v. I

Same. Philadelphia: Published by C. and A. Conrad and Co. Philadelphia; Conrad, Lucas and Co. Baltimore. Fry and Kammerer, Printers. 1809. 2 v. E120.B256

An amplification of the author's "Vision of Columbus."

Same. London, Printed for R. Phillips, 1809. xxxiii, (2), 426 pp.   E120.B257

Same. With the last corrections of the author. Paris, Printed for F. Schoell, 1813. xl, (2), 448 pp.   E120.B258

Same. Washington (D.C.) J. Milligan, 1825. xl, (2), 448 pp.   E120.B259*

Same. Printed for the booksellers, (n.d.) xl, 448 pp.
  CoFcA

Reviews:

The Port folio (Philadelphia) Jan. 1809, n.s.v.l: 61-70.   AP2.P85,n.s.v.l*

The Port folio (Philadelphia) May, 1809, n.s.v.l: 434-450
  From the London monthly magazine
  AP2.P85,n.s.v.l*

Critical observations on the poem of Mr. Joel Barlow, the Columbiad, by Mr. (H.) Gregoire, formerly Bishop of Blois, Senator, Member of the National Institute, &c., &c., Paris, Mar. 15, 1809. The Port folio (Phila.) July, 1809, n.s.v.2: 463-471   AP2.P85,n.a.v.2*

F. Jeffrey in Edinburgh review, Oct. 1809, v. 15: 24-40.   AP4.E3, v.15

Eclectic review (London) Apr. 1810, v. 11: 403-417.
  AP4.E17, v.11

Historical magazine (Boston) Mar., Dec. 1857, v. 1: 92-93. 375.   E171.H64,v.1

4. ——— The conspiracy of kings; a poem: addressed to the inhabitants of Europe, from another quarter of the world. London, J. Johnson, 1792. 20 p.   PS704.C6 1792*

Same. Paris: Printed at the English press; and sold by Barrois, senior, 1793. xi (2) 14-32 p. (Duane pamphlets, v. 128, no. 9)   AC901.D8,v.128*

Same. (*In his* Letter to the National convention of France, on the defects of the constitution of 1791. New York (179-) p. 75-87.) JC211.B23

Same. (*In his* Vision of Columbus. Paris, 1793. p. (277)-304) El20.B254

Same. Printed and sold by Robinson & Tucker: Newburyport–1794. 1 p.1.,(v)-viii,(9)-30 p.

"Note on Mr. Burke": p. 25-30. PS704.C6 1794*
Same 3d ed. London, 1796. Brit. Mus.

5. **Barlow, Joel.** Copy of a letter from Joel Barlow, Esq., to John Fellows, dated Hamburgh, May 23, 1795. Connecticut journal, v. 32, Aug. 28, 1799, p. 1. *

6. (———) An elegy on the late Honorable Titus Hosmer, esq; one of the counsellors of the state of Connecticut, a member of Congress, and a judge of the Maritime court of appeals for the United States of America. Hartford: Printed by Hudson & Goodwin (1780) 15 p.

E302.6.H8B2*

7. (———) Guter rath an die volker Europens, etc. bei der nothwendighk die regierrungsgrundsatze. (Pt. I) London, 1792. MH

8. (———) The hasty-pudding: a poem, in three cantos. Written at Chambery, in Savoy, January, 1793. (New-Haven: Printed by T. and S. Green, for Tiebout and O'Brien, New-York, 1796) 15 p.

"Written by Mr. Barlow." –p.2.

CSmH; MWA;NN;NNHist

Previously printed in the New York weekly magazine, Jan. 1796, p. 41-49.

Same. Catskill, T. & M. Croswell (1796) 12 p..   MWA

Same. (New Haven, 1796) 12 p.

Same. New York: Printed (by John Bull) for Fellows and Adams, 1796. 22 p.   Evans 30023

Same. New York, Printed for the purchaser (1796) 12 p.   MBBC

Same. New London, Printed and sold by Charles Holt, 1797. 23 p.   MH

Same. Printed and sold at the Printing-Office in Fairhaven (*ca.* 1797) 16 p.   PS704.H24*

Same. Printed by Rosseter & Willard, Stockbridge, 1797. 16 p.   PS704.H25*

Same. Poughkeepsie, Re-printed by N. Power (1798) 12 p.   NNHist

Same. Salem: Printed by Joshua Cushing, 1799. 1 p.1.,(v)-vi, (7)-21 p.   PS704.H3*

Same. Sag-Harbor, N.Y., Printed by Alden Spooner, 1807. 16 p. Photostat reproduction.   NN

Same. Boston, Printed: and for sale at the book stores, 1810. 16 p. (Bailey pamphlets, v. 69, no.7)

  AC901.B3,v.69*

Same. Canandaigua: Printed and sold by J.D. Bemis & co., (*ca.* 1815) 23 p.   MWA

Same. Together with The ruling passion. By Robert T. Paine, jun, Esq. Hallowell, Me., Published by Ezekiel Goodale. Printed by Goodale & Burton, 1815. 32 p.

  PS704.H35*

Same. Exeter, N.H., A. Brown (182-?) 24 p.

  PS704.H4*

Same. Caldwell, W. Storer, jr., printer, 1821. 18 p.
MB
Canandaigua, J.D. Bemis & co., (1822 ?) Brinley Cat. 6790

Same. Exeter, 1826. Nh

Same. Hallowell: Printed and sold by Glazier & co., 1826.

Same. New Haven, W. Storer, 1838. 12 p. MH

Same. With a memoir on maize or Indian corn. Comp. by D.J. Browne... New York, W. H. Graham, 1847. 56 p.
PS704.H4 1847

Same. New York, C. M. Saxton (1850?) 48 p. DA

Same. New York, 1856. 48 p. (Saxton's rural handbooks) MBHo

9. **Barlow, Joel.** Joel Barlow to his fellow citizens, of the United States of America. Letter I. On the system of policy hitherto pursued by their government. (Philadelphia? 1799?) 55 p.

Dated: Paris 4 March, 1799. E323.B25

Same. (Philadelphia: Reprinted at the Aurora office, March 8, 1800) 27 p. (Misc. pamp.v.962,no.3)
AC901.M5,v.962*

Same. (Philadelphia? 1800) 32 p. E323.B25 Toner

10. ——— (Letter II) On certain political measures proposed to their consideration. (Philadelphia, W.Duane, 1801) 70 p., 1 1. JK2263.1799.B25*

Letter dated: Paris, 20th December, 1799.
AC901.M5,v.690*

Same. (Philadelphia, 1801) 102 p.

Appendix: Memoir on certain principles of public maritime law. Written for the French government: p. 78-102. JK2263.1799.B24

Same. New-York, Printed by D. Denniston, 1801. 40 p. JK2263.1799.B26
Republished in England with title: Letters from Paris, to the citizens of the United States of America, ... London, Printed for James Ridgway by A. Wilson, 1800. 116 p. (Duane pamphlets, v. 66, no.1) AC901.D8,v.66*

11. ——— A letter, addressed to the people of Piedmont, on the advantages of the French revolution, and the necessity of adopting its principles in Italy. Translated from the French by the author. London, Printed and sold by D.I. Eaton, 1795. 48 p. DC138.B25

Same. New-York: Printed at the Columbian press, by Robertson and Gowan, for J. Fellows, bookseller, Waterstreet. 1795. iv,(5)-45p. (Miscellaneous pamphlets, v. 14, no.4) AC901.M5,v.14*

Same. New York, 1796. MBAt

Lettre adressee aux habitants du Piemont, sur les avantages de la Revolution francaise et la necessite d'en adopter les principes en Italie. (Chambery, 29 decembre an Ier.) (n.p., n.d.) 32 p. Bib. Nat.

An Italian version was printed at Nice in the winter of 1792-93. Dexter.

12. **Barlow, Joel.** (A letter to Ezra Stiles, president of Yale college. Dated, Hamburgh, 27 May, 1794) MS. MH

13. ——— Letter to Henry Gregeirs ... in reply to his letter on The Columbiad. Washington, Printed by R. C. Weightman, 1809. 14 p. (Miscellaneous pamphlets, v. 799, no.7) AC901.M5,v.799*

14. ——— A letter to the National convention of France, on the defects in the constitution of 1791, and the extent of the amendments which ought to be applied. To which is added, The conspiracy of kings, a poem. New-York: Printed by Thomas Greenleaf, for J. Fellows, no. 192, Water-street (179-) 87 p. front. (port.)

With this are bound the author's Advice to the privileged orders, New-York, 1792-94, 2 parts, and his Letter . . . to the people of Piedmont, N.Y., 1795.

JC211.B23* JN2475.Z5 1790*

Same. New York, Printed by D. Greenleaf, for J. Fellows (1791) 85 p. (Miscellaneous pamphlets, v. 14)

AC901.M5,v.14*

Same. London: Printed for J. Johnson, 1792. 70 p. (Miscellaneous pamphlets, v. 599) AC901.M5,v.599*

Same. Dublin, P. Byrne, 1792. 46 p. (Duane pamphlets, v.135) AC901.D8,v.135*

Same. Lettre at la Convention nationale de France sur les vices de la Constitution de 1791 et sur l'etendue des amendemens a y porter . . . traduite de L'anglais (par Wilh. E. Ludger). Paris, Nee de La Rochelle, 1792. 68 p.

Bib. Nat.
Br.Mus. NIC

15. ——— An oration, delivered at the North church in Hartford, at the meeting of the Connecticut society of the Cincinnati, July 4th, 1787. In commemoration of the independence of the United States. Hartford, Printed by Hudson and Goodwin (1787) 20 p. E286.H32 1787*

Same. (*In* The American museum or repository (Philadelphia) Aug. 1787, v. 2: 135-142.) AP2.A2A8,v.2* xiii

Same. (*In* Niles, Hezekiah. Principles and acts of the revolution in America. Baltimore, Printed and pub. for the editor, by W.O. Niles, 1822. p 384-389.)   E203.N69

Same. (*In* Niles, Hezekiah. Centennial offering. Republication of the Principles and acts of the revolution in America. New York, Chicago, etc. A.S. Barnes & co., 1876. p. 145-150.)   E203.N71

16. ——— Oration delivered at Washington, July fourth, 1809; at the request of the Democratic citizens of the District of Columbia. Washington city, Printed and published by R.C. Weightman, 1809. 14 p.   E286.W22 1809*

    Same. Newburyport, Gilman (n.d.) 16 p.   MB
    Same. (Washington city, 1809) 8 p.   MB

17. **(Barlow, Joel)** A poem, spoken at the public commencement at Yale college, in New-Haven; September 12, 1781. Hartford: Printed by Hudson & Goodwin (1781) 16 p.

"Mainly in theme a prior study of the author's Vision of Columbus, as that in its turn is of his Columbiad." —Dexter, Yale biog. and annuals, v. 4, p. 9.

    PS704.P6*

18. ——— The political writings... Printed at New-York, by Mott & Lyon for Fellows & Adam, Thomas Greenleaf, and Naphtati Judah, 1796. 258 p.   MH MWA NN

Same. A new ed. cor. New York, Printed and sold by Mott & Lyon, 1796. xvi, (17)-258 p.   JC211.B27*

19. ——— The prospect of peace. A poetical composition, delivered in Yale-college, at the public examination, of the candidates for the degree of bachelor of arts; July

23, 1778. New-Haven: Printed by Thomas and Samuel Green, 1788. 12 p. (Hazard pamphlets, v. 38, no.17)

AC901.H3,v.38*

20. (———) Prospectus of a national institution, to be established in the United States. Washington city, Printed by S.H. Smith, 1806. 44 p. Q11.S64B2

Same. (*In* American historical association. Papers, 1890, v. 4, pt. 2, p. 175-187. E172.A65,v.4

Same. Extracts in National intelligencer, Washington, D.C., Aug. 1, 1806, p. 2; Nov. 24, 1806, p.2; Nov. 26, 1806, p. 1-2.

21. (——— and William Playfair) Prospectus pour l'etablissement sur les rivieres d'Ohio et de Scioto en Amerique. (Paris, Prault, 1789) 15 p. *

Imperfect. Wanting title, appendix and supplement, also map and table.

Barlow was the agent of the Scioto company and arrived in Paris in the summer of 1789. Playfair was a friend of Barlow, and interested in the Company also.

22. (———) The second warning, or strictures on the speech delivered by John Adams, president of the United-States of America at the opening of the Congress of said states in November last. Paris: At the printing-office of the Social-circle, 1798. 28 p. NN

23. ——— Six letters of Joel Barlow to Oliver Wolcott. Edited by Theodore A. Zunder. New England quarterly, July, 1929, v. 2: 475-489.

Manuscripts in Connecticut Historical Society.
Foot-note references. F1.N62, v. 2.

Same. (Portland, Me.) The Southworth press, 1929. 1 p.l.,475-489 p.   CtY

Reprinted from the New England quarterly.

24. **(Barlow, Joel)** Strictures on Bishop Watson's "Apology for the Bible." By a citizen of New York. New York: Printed for J. Fellows, 1796. 1 p.l., 48 p.   BL2740.W4S7*

25. ——— A translation of sundry psalms which were omitted in Doctor Watts' version; to which is added, a number of hymns. Hartford, Barlow & Babcock, 1785. 14 p.   Sabin 3432

26. ——— Two letters to the citizens of the United States, and one to General Washington, written from Paris in the year 1799, on our political and commercial relations. New-Haven, Sidney's press, 1806. v, (7)- 119 p.

JK2263.1799.B27*

27. ——— A view of the public debt, receipts, and expenditures of the United States. London, 1800. 67 p.

Dexter

28. ——— The vision of Columbus; a poem in nine books. Hartford, Printed by Hudson and Goodwin, for the author, 1787. xxi, (4) 26-258, (12) p.

This poem formed the basis of the author's "Columbiad." First edition; second edition published the same year. "Subscribers' names": (12) p. at end.

E120.B25*

Same. 2d ed. Hartford, Printed by Hudson and Goodwin, for the author, 1787. xxi (4) 26-258 p.

E120.B251*

Same. London, C. Dilly, 1787. xx, 244 p.
                                    KU MB NN RPJCB
Same. 5th ed., cor. . . . To which is added, The conspiracy of kings: a poem, by the same author. Paris, Printed at the English press, and sold by Barrois, senior, and R. Thomson, 1793. 2 p. l., 304 p. front. (port.) E120.B254

Same. With explanatory notes. From a revised edition of the author. Baltimore, W.D. Bell and J.D. Fry, 1814. 288 p.   MH MBBC Nh

29. **American State Papers**. Class I, Foreign relations, vol. III. Washington, Gales & Seaton, 1832. 753,xlii p.

Mr. Barlow appointed Minister to France, July 27, 1811: p. 422. For instructions to him and his correspondence, see Index, p. iv-v.   J33 For. rel.v.3

30. **U.S.** *Dept. of state.* Message from the President of the U. States, transmitting copies and extracts from the correspondence of the Secretary of State, and the minister plenipotentiary of the United States at Paris. Washington city: Printed by R. C. Weightman, 1812. 51 p. (Wolcott pamphlets, v 44, no.4)

James Monroe, Secretary of state; Joel Barlow, minister to France.   AC901.W7,v.44*

31. **Bible** *O. T. Psalms. English. Paraphrases.* Doctor Watts Imitation of the Psalms. . .corr. and enl. by Joel Barlow. To which is added a collection of hymns. Hartford, Printed by Barlow & Babcock, 1785. 348 p.
                                        BS1440.W4B3 1785*
Same. The 2d ed. Hartford: Printed for Hudson and Goodwin, and Nathaniel Patten (1785) 356 p.
                                        BS1440.†4B3 1785a*

Same. 4th ed. Hartford: Printed by Nathaniel Patten (1785) 332 p. BS1440.W4B3 1785c*
Same. Glasgow, 1786. NNHist
Same. 4th ed. Hartford (1790) 360 p. MWA
Same. New-York, Printed by R. Durell, 1791. 314,(7) p. BS1440.W4B3 1791n*
Same. Psalms carefully suited to the Christian worship in the United States of America. Being an improvement of the old version of the Psalms of David. Allowed by the reverend Synod of New York and Philadelphia. Philadelphia: Printed by Francis Bailey, 1787. 307 p.
BS1440.B4B3 1787*
Barlow's revision of Watts' metrical version.
Same. Elizabethtown (Pa.) S. Kollock, 1791. 314,(10) p. BS1440.W4B3 1791e*
Same. Wilmington, Printed and sold by Peter Brynberg, 1797. (2), 287. (21) p. BS1440.W4B3 1797*

32. **Barlow, Joel,** *ed.* American Mercury, Hartford, Conn. Edited with Elishe Babcock, July 12, 1784- Nov. 14, 1785.

33. **Barlow, Joel,** *tr.* (Brissot de Warville, Jacques Pierre) His travels in the United States of America: including The commerce of America with Europe; particularly with France and Great Britain. (London, J.S. Jordan, 1794) 2 v.
E164.B892
Tr. from the last French ed., rev. by Brissot. With the life of Brissot, and an appendix, by the translator.

Volney, Constantin Francois Chasseboeuf, *comte* de. A new translation of Volney's Ruins, or Meditations on the revolution of empires. Made under the inspection of the author. (Joel Barlow) Paris, Levrault, 1802. 2 v. in 1.   NN

We have been unable to locate all editions of Barlow's translations of this work, but through the Union catalogue have found the following:

>New York, C. Blanchard, (18--) 216 p.   MiU
>New York, Blanchard, 1857.   NL
>New York, P. Eckler, 1890. 219 p.   NN
>New York, Peter Eckler publ co., 1926. xxii, 225 p. (see esp. p.xii)   D16.7.V8 1926

34. **Barlow, Joel.** Contributed to the following publications:

(Alsop, Richard) The echo, with other poems. (New York, Printed at the Porcupine press of Pasquin Petronius) 1807. xv, 331, (10) p.   PS703.A5E4 1807

The Anarchiad, a New England poem. Written in concert by D. Humphreys, Joel Barlow (and others) Edited by L.G. Briggs. New Haven, J.H. Pease, 1861.

>Reprinted from the New-Haven Gazette, 1786-87.
>PS700.A1A5

Pigott, Charles. (Extracts from Pigott's Political dictionary) 8 tracts. (London) Printed for Citizen Lee (1795?) (Duane pamphlets, v. 81, no. 9-16)   AC901.D8,v.81*

Some numbers contain also extracts from Barlow, Gerrald, and others.

Trumbull, John. M'Fingal: a modern epic poem, in four cantos. New-York: Printed by John Buel, 1795. vii, 136 p.

>The notes are in part taken from the London edition of 1792 ascribed to Joel Barlow.   PS852.M3 1795*

Same. The 2d ed., with plates, and explanatory notes. New-York: Printed and published by E. Low, 1810. vii, 136 p. PS852.M3 1810*

Same. (Hallowell, Me.) Published and sold by Ezekiel Goodale, at the Hallowell bookstore, 1813. v, (6)- 138 p. PS852.M3 1813*

SYMBOLS:

Bib.Nat.	Bibliotheque Nationale, Paris.
Br.Mus.	British Museum, London.
CSmH	Henry Huntington Library, San Marino, Cal.
CoFcA	Colorado State Agricultural College, Fort Collins, Col.
CtY	Yale University, New Haven, Conn.
DA	U.S. Dept. of Agri. Library, Washington, D. C.
I	Illinois State Library, Springfield, Ill.
KU	University of Kansas, Lawrence, Kans.
MB	Boston Public Library, Boston, Mass.
MBAt	Boston Athenaeum, Boston, Mass.
MBBC	Boston College Library, Boston, Mass.
MBHo	Mass. Horticultural Society, Boston, Mass.
MH	Harvard University, Cambridge, Mass.
MWA	American Antiquarian Society, Worcester, Mass.
MiU	University of Michigan, Ann Arbor, Mich.
NL	Newberry Library, Chicago, Ill.
NN	New York Public Library, New York, N.Y.
NNHist	New York Historical Society, New York, N.Y.
Nh	New Hampshire State Library, Concord, N.H.
RPJCB	John Carter Brown Library, Providence, R.I.
*	Rare Book Room, Library of Congress.

SELECTIONS

35. American poems, selected and original. v. 1. Litchfield, Conn., Printed by Collier and Buel (1793) viii 304 p., 4 l.
    No more published.
    Contains Barlow's Prospect of peace: p. 85-93; Poem at the commencement in 1781: p. 94-107; Elegy on Titus Hosmer: p. 108-117.   PS601.A5*

36. **Boynton, Percy H.**, **ed**. American poetry. New York, C. Scribner's sons, 1918. 721 p.
    Extracts from Vision of Columbus and Hasty pudding: p. 125-135; Critical comments: p. 621-624.
    PS507.B6

37. **Bronson, Walter C.**, *ed*. American poems (1625-1892) selected and ed., with illustrative and explanatory notes and a bibliography. Chicago, Ill., The University of Chicago press (1912) 669 p.
    Joel Barlow: p. 116-133. Selections from Vision of Columbus, Columbiad and Hasty pudding.   PS386.B8

38. **Burton, William E.**, *ed*. The cyclopaedia of wit and humor; ... New York, D. Appleton and co., 1858. 2 v.
    PN6153.B8
    Joel Barlow: The Hasty pudding: v 1, p. 19-22.

39. **Cairns, William B.**, *ed*. Selections from early American Writers, 1607-1800. New York, The Macmillan co., 1917. 493 p.

Joel Barlow: Brief sketch, followed by extracts from his works: p. 421-430.　　　PS531.C3 1917

40.　**Griswold, Rufus W**. The poets and poetry of America, to the middle of the nineteenth century. 10th ed., rev. and enl. Philadelphia, Carey and Hart, 1850. 550 p.

Joel Barlow: p. 52-58. Brief sketch followed by The Hasty pudding, and extracts from Columbiad.

L.C. has other editions.　　　PS583.G7 1850

41.　**Howe, John W. S.**, *comp.* Golden leaves from the American poets. New York, G. Routledge and sons (1864) 532 p. (The Golden leaves series. II)

Joel Barlow: The Hasty pudding: p. 29-41.

42.　**Kettell, Samuel**. Specimens of American poetry, with critical and biographical notices. Boston, S. G. Goodrich and co., 1829. 3 v.

Joel Barlow: v. 2, p. 1-13; followed by The Hasty pudding and Embassy of Rocha. p. 14-27.　　　PS586.K3

43.　**Miller, Edwin L.**, *ed.* Explorations in literature. v I. American writers. Chicago, Philadelphia, J.B. Lippincott co., (1933)

Joel Barlow: p. 111-113.　　　PS507.M47, v. 1.

44.　**Morris, Charles**, *comp.* Half-hours with the best American authors. Philadelphia, J.B. Lippincott co., 1887. 4 v.

Joel Barlow: The Hasty pudding (extracts): v. 1. p. 186-193.　　　PS507.M6,v.1

45. **Newcomer, Alphonso G.**, *and others, eds.* Three centuries of American poetry and prose. Rev. ed. Chicago, Atlanta, etc., Scott, Foresman & co., (1929) 907 p.
    Joel Barlow: p. 132-136.   PS507.N4 1929

46. **Pattee, Fred L.**, *ed.* Century readings in American literature. The 4th ed. New York, The Century co., (1932) 1185 p.
    Joel Barlow: p. 145, 173-177, 184, 227.
    PS507.P25 1932

47. **Shafer, Robert**, *ed.* American literature. (Complete ed.) Garden City, N.Y., Doubleday, Page & co., 1926. 758 p.
    Joel Barlow: p. 182; The Hasty pudding: p. 182-187.   PS507.S45

48. **Smith, Huntington**, *comp.* A century of American literture; Benjamin Franklin to James Russell Lowell; selections from a hundred authors. New York, T.Y. Crowell & co. (1889) 390 p.
    Joel Barlow. Extracts from The Hasty pudding and Columbiad: p. 31-33.   PS507.S6

49. **Snyder, Franklyn B.** *and* **Edward D. Snyder**, *eds.* A book of American literature. New York, The Macmillan co., 1927. 1245 p.
    The Hasty pudding, Joel Barlow: p. 200-226.
    PS507.S65

50. **Spiller, Robert E.**, *ed.* The roots of national culture; American literature to 1830. New York, The Macmillan co., 1933. 758 p. (American literature: a period anthology;

Oscar Cargill, general editor. v. 1)

Joel Barlow, Hasty pudding: p. 307-316; Notes: p. 718-719.   PS504.A6,v. 1

51. **Van Doren, Mark,** *ed.* American poets, 1630-1930. Boston, Little, Brown, and co., 1932. 698 p.

Joel Barlow: The Hasty pudding: p. 25-33; Advice to a raven in Russia: p. 34-35.   PS586.V3

BIOGRAPHICAL AND CRITICAL

(No attempt has been made to give all the editions of the publications listed below.)

52. **Adams, Henry**. History of the United States of America. New York, C. Scribner's sons, 1921. 9 v.

Vol. V-VI. The first administration of James Madison. Joel Barlow: v. 5, p. 299-300, 359, 427; v. 6, p. 53-57, 61, 245-266.   E302.1.A23

53. **Adams, John**. The works of John Adams, second president of the United States. Boston, Little, Brown and co., 1850-56. 10 v.

Joel Barlow: v. 6, p. 453; v. 8, p. 624, 625; v. 9, p. 241-244, 307.   E302.A26

54. **Adams, John Quincy**. Memoirs of John Quincy Adams, comprising portions of his diary from 1795 to 1848. Ed. by Charles Francis Adams. Philadelphia, J. B. Lippincott & co., 1874-77. 12 v.

Joel Barlow: v. 1, p. 361; At Wilna, p. 441; Death of, at Cracow, p. 444, 493; Archives of the Russian Embassy deposited with; correspondence relating to, p. 444-446.   E377.A19

55. **Alden, Timothy.** Zarnowich, Poland: [Joel Barlow] (*In his* Collection of American epitaphs and inscriptions with occasional notes. New York, 1814. v. 4, p. 159-162.)
E176.A35, v.4

56. **Bacon-Foster, Corra.** The story of Kalorama [the home of Barlow in Washington, D.C.]. Columbia historical society. Records, 1910, v. 13, p. 98-118. Port. opp. p. 108)
F191.C72,v.13

57. **Baldwin, A. C.** Joel Barlow. New Englander (New Haven) July, 1873, v. 32: 415-437.   AP2.N5, v. 32

58. **Barlow [meaning and origin of surname].** Notes and queries (London) Jan. 23, 1915, 11th ser., v. 11, p. 78.
AG305.N7,11th a. v.11

59. **Beers, Henry A.** The Connecticut wits. Yale review (New Haven) Jan. 1913, n.s.v.2: 242-256.   AP2.Y2,n.s.v.2

"Account of that literary coterie in Connecticut during the latter part of the 18th century, which included Joel Barlow, John Trumbull, Timothy Dwight, David Humphreys, Lemuel Hopkins, Richard Alsop and Theodore Dwight."

60. ——— Same. *In his* The Connecticut wits, and other essays. New Haven, Yale university press, 1920. p. 7-29.
PR99.B35

61. **Benson, Adolph B**. An American poet-enemy of Gustavus III of Sweden. Scandinavian studies and notes (Menasha, Wis.) Nov. 1928, v. 10: 104-110.

                                                PD1505.S6,v.10

"A sketch of Joel Barlow (1754-1812), poet, philosopher and radical, whose poem, 'The conspiracy of kings' (London, 1792) contains an invective against the Swedish king."

62. **Best, Mary A**. Thomas Paine, prophet and martyr of democracy. New York, Harcourt, Brace & co. [1927] 413 p.

    Joel Barlow: p. 313, 330-331.   JC178.V2B45

63. **Blankenship, Russell**. American literature as an expression of the national mind. New York, H. Holt and co. [1931] 731 p.

    Joel Barlow (1754-1812): p. 188-189.   PS38.B6

64. **Bolton, Charles K**. The Elizabeth Whitman mystery at the old Bell tavern in Danvers; a study of "Eliza Wharton," the heroine of a famous New England romance. Peabody, Mass., Peabody historical society, 1912. 155 p.

                                                     CT275.W55B6

"Notes on various editions of 'The coquette' ": p. 147-155.

65. **Breck, Samuel**. Recollections of Samuel Breck, with passages from his note-books. (1771-1862.) Ed. by H. E. Scudder. London, S. Low, Marston, Searle, & Rivington, 1877. 318 p.

    See p. 171-172.   E164.B825

66. **Bronson, Walter C.** A short history of American literature. Rev. and enl. Boston, New York, D. C. Heath & co. [1919] 490 p.
    Joel Barlow: p. 59, 62-63, 377, 442, 450.

                                                PS92.B7 1919

67. **Brown, Solyman.** An essay on American poetry, with several miscellaneous pieces on a variety of subjects, sentimental, descriptive, moral, and patriotic. New-Haven, Published by Hezekiah Howe, Flagg & Gray, printers, 1818. 191 p.   PS1139.B7E7 1818*
    Barlow: p. 44-45, 183.

68. [**Bryant, William Cullen**] Essay on American poetry. B. Brown. [Review] North American review (Boston) July, 1818, v. 7: 198-211.
    Joel Barlow: p. 202-203.   AP2.N7,v.7

69. **Cairns, William B.** A history of American literature. Rev. ed. New York, Oxford university press, 1930. 569 p.
    Joel Barlow: p. 123, 124, 129, 130-132, 133.

                                                PS92.C3 1930

70. **Calverton, Victor F.** The liberation of American literature. New York, C. Scribner's sons, 1932. 500 p.
    Joel Barlow: p. 21, 159, 206n.   PS88.C26

71. The Cambridge history of American literature, edited by William P. Trent, and others. New York, G. P. Putnam's sons; Cambridge, Eng., University press [1927] 4 v.

                                                PS88.C3 1927
    Joel Barlow: v. 1, p. 164, 169-171, 174, 261.

72. **Chambers, Robert.** Chamber's cyclopaedia of English literature. New ed., by David Patrick. Philadelphia, J. B. Lippincott co., 1902-04. 3 v.
>Joel Barlow: v. 3, p. 740. PR83.C4 1902

73. **Channing, Edward.** A history of the United States. New York, The Macmillan co., 1927-30. 6 v. E178.C442
>Joel Barlow: v. 3, p. 468; sent to Paris to seek settlers: p. 549; on the American commissioners: v. 4, p. 188; and peace overtures: p. 202-203; appointed Minister at Paris: p. 448; arrives at Paris (1811) p. 449; account of: v. 5, p. 280; his *Columbiad* and other writings appraised: p. 280-281.

74. **Chapman, Henry L.** Joel Barlow and the Columbiad. Maine historical society. Collections and proceedings, 2d ser., v. 4. Portland, 1893. p. 50-61. F16.M33,2d s.v.4

75. **Columbia university course in Literature.** v. XVI. Early days in America. New York, Columbia university press, 1929. 515 p.
>Joel Barlow: p. 206-208; Extracts from The Hasty pudding: p. 208-211. PN6013.C5 1928, v. 16

76. **Connecticut.** *Adjutant-general's office.* Record of service of Connecticut men in the I.–War of the revolution. ... Hartford, [The Case, Lockwood & Brainard co., printers,] 1889. 779 p.
>Joel Barlow: p. 144, 314, 376. E263.C5C5

77. **Crawford, Mary C.** The romance of old New England churches. Boston, L. C. Page & co., [1907] 377 p.
>Joel Barlow and Ruth Baldwin: p. 23-26.
>F5.C91 1907

78. ——— Romantic days in the early republic. Boston, Little, Brown, and co., 1912. 438 p.
    Joel Barlow: p. 188.   E164.C89

79. ——— Social life in old New England. Boston, Little, Brown, and co., 1914. 513 p.
    Joel Barlow: p. 80, 81, 425-426.   F5.C913

80. [**Crosby, W. P.**] Joel Barlow. (*In* Herring, James *and* James B. Longacre, *eds.* National portrait gallery. v. 1. New York, M. Bancroft, 1834. 6 p. port.)   E176.H56,v.1
    Same. v. 1. Philadelphia, D. Rice & A. N. Hart, 1854. [p. 255-260] port.   E176.H564,v. 1.
    Same. v. 1. Philadelphia, Rice, Rutter & co. [1868. p. 429-432].   E176.H566,v.1

81. **Cutler, William P.** Life, journals and correspondence of Rev. Manasseh Cutler, LL.D. By his grandchildren, William Parker Cutler and Julia Perkins Cutler. Cincinnati, R. Clarke & co., 1888. 2 v. "The Scioto purchase" [by E. C. Dawes] :v. 1, p. 494-524. Joel Barlow: p. 498-518. See also p. 327 n, 381; v. 2, p. 330.   F483.C93

82. **Dall,** *Mrs.* **Caroline Wells (Healey)** A centennial "posie". Unitarian review (Boston) Aug. 1876, v. 6: 157-189.   BX9801.U7,v.6

83. ——— The romance of the Association; or, One last glimpse of Charlotte Temple and Eliza Wharton. A curiosity of literature and life. Cambridge [Mass.] Press of J. Wilson and son, 1875. 102 p.
    Joel Barlow: p. 77-78; Letters of Eliza Wharton to Barlow: p. 80-102.   CT275.W4D3

──── The "Romance of the Association" for the last time. [n.p.,1875?] p. 103-114.

A supplement, paged continuously with the preceding, disclosing the real name of Eliza Wharton, to be Elizabeth Whitman, daughter of the Rev. Elnathan Whitman and Abigail Stanley.   CT275.W4D32

84. **Dell'Isola, Maria.** Joel Barlow, precurseur de la Societe des nations. Revue de litterature comparee (Paris) Apr.-June, 1934, v. 14: 283-296.   PN851.R4,v.14

85. **Dexter, Franklin B.** Joel Barlow. (*In his* Biographical sketches of the graduates of Yale college, v. 4, July, 1778-June, 1792. New York, Henry Holt & co., 1907. p. 3-16.)   LD6323.D5,v.4

86. [**Du Pont de Nemours, Pierre Samuel**] Notice sur la vie de M. Barlow, ministre plenipotentiaire des Etats-Unis d'Amerique aupres de S. M. l'Empereur et Roi, lue a la Societe d'encouragement pour l'industrie national par un des vice-presidens. Paris, Impr. de Mme. Hazard, 1813. 13 p. p.   Bib. Nat.
    Same. Mercure de France, April 10, 1813.

87. **Duyckinck, Evert A.** Joel Barlow. (*In his* National portrait gallery of eminent Americans. New York, 1862. v. 1, p. 378-384.)   E176.D98, v. 1.

88. ──── *and* **George L. Duyckinck.** Cyclopaedia of American literature. New York, C. Scribner, 1856. 2 v.
    PS85.D62
    Joel Barlow, biographical sketch, followed by extracts from his works: v. 1, p. 391-403.

89. **Dwight, Benjamin W.** The history of the descendents of Elder John Strong, of Northampton, Mass. Albany, N.Y., J. Munsell, 1871. 2 v.   CS71.S923 1871

    Family of Ruth Baldwin, wife of Joel Barlow: v. 1,p. 760-761.

90. **Everest, Charles W.** The posts of Connecticut; with biographical sketches. Hartford, Cass, Tiffany and Burnham, 1843. 468 p.

    Joel Barlow: p. 73-81. Followed by extracts from Hasty pudding and Columbiad: p. 81-92.

                                       PS548.C8E8 1843

91. [**Everett, A. H.**] Irving's life of Columbus. Review. North American review (Boston) Jan. 1829, v. 28: 103-134.

    Poetical genius of Barlow: p. 106-107.

                                       AP2.N7,v.28

92. [**Everett, Edward**] Claims on France. North American review (Boston) Oct. 1826, v. 23, 385-414.

    Joel Barlow: p. 398-399.   AP2.N7,v.23

93. [———] On the complaints in America against the British press. An essay in the New London monthly magazine for February 1821. North American review (Boston) July, 1821, v. 13: 20-47.

    Barlow's Columbiad, how regarded in the U.S.: p. 29.   AP2.N7,v.13

94. [———] Poems by James G. Percival [Review]. North American review, Jan. 1822, v. 14: 1-15.

    Character of Barlow's Columbiad: p. 7.

                                       AP2.N7,v.14

95. **Foster, Cora Bacon**. Joel Barlow's oration and how they celebrated the Fourth of July a century ago. Americana (New York) May, 1910, v. 5: 451-463.   E171.A53,v.5
   Celebration at Washington, July 4, 1809.

96. [**Foster, Mrs. Hannah (Webster)**] The coquette; or, The history of Eliza Wharton; a novel; founded on fact. By a lady of Massachusetts. Charlestown, Printed by S. Etheridge, for E. and S. Larkin, 1802. 261,[1] p.
   PS744.F7C6 1802*
   Second edition; 1st edition, 1797.
   Same. New ed. With an historical preface, and a memoir of the author [by Jane E. Locke]. Boston, W. P. Petridge and co., 1855. 286 p.   PS744.F7C6 1855*

97. **France**. Reimpression de l'ancien Moniteur, seule histoire authentique et inalteree de la revolution francaise depuis la reunion des Etats-generaux jusqu'au Consulat (mai 1789-novembre 1799) avec des notes explicatives. Paris, H. Plon, 1858-63. 32 v.
   Bestowing on Joel Barlow the title and rights of a French citizen: Feb. 19, 1793: v. 15, p. 491.
   DC140.A15,v.15

98. [**French, Benjamin F.**] Biographia americana; or, A historical and critical account of the lives, actions, and writings of the most distinguished persons in North America ... By a gentleman of Philadelphia. New York, D. Mallory, 1825. 356 p.
   Joel Barlow: p. 30-32.   E176.F78

99. **Fullerton, Bradford M.** Selective bibliography of

American literature, 1775-1900; a brief estimate of the more important American authors and a description of their representative works. New York, W. F. Payson, 1932. 327 p.

    Joel Barlow: p. 18-19.   Z1224.F97

100. **Goode, George B**. The origin of the national scientific and educational institutions of the United States. New York & London, G. P. Putnam's sons [1890] 112 p. (Papers of the American historical association, vol. IV, pt. 2. 1 p.l., p. 93-202)   E172.A63,v.4

    Joel Barlow's project for a national institution of learning: p. 116-119, 158; Appendix C. Prospectus ... of Barlow: p. 175-187.   LC173.C7

    Also issued in Annual report of American historical association, 1889, p. 33-161.   E172.A60 1889

    Also issued in Annual report of the National Museum, 1897, Washington, Govt. print. off., 1901. v. 2, p. 263-354.   Q11.U5, 1897, v.2

101. **Gould, Frederick J**. Thomas Paine (1737-1809) London, L. Parsons; Boston, Small, Maynard and co. [1925] 192 p. (The roadmaker series)

    Joel Barlow: p. 89, 104, 115.   JC178.V2G6

102. **Greene, George W**. Historical view of the American revolution. Boston, Ticknor & Fields, 1865. 459 p.

    Joel Barlow: p. 393-397.   E208.G79

103. **Gregoire [Henri]** *constitutional bp. of Blois.* Critical observations on the poem of Mr. Joel Barlow, The Columbiad. Washington, Printed by R. C. Weightman, 1809. 15 p. (Miscellaneous pamphlets, v. 799, no. 6)

    Translated from the French.   AC901.M5,v.799*

104. **Grumman, William E.** The revolutionary soldiers of Redding, Connecticut, and the record of their services; . . . [Hartford, Conn.] Hartford press: The Case, Lockwood & Brainard co., 1904. 208 p.
    Joel Barlow: p. 111-117. Port. opp. p. 111.
                                              F104.R3G8

105. **Guppy, Henry B.** Homes of family names in Great Britain. London, Harrison and sons, 1890. 601 p.
    Barlow: p. 453.   CS2505.G85

106. **Haney, John L.** The story of our literature; an interpretation of the American spirit. New York, Chicago, C. Scribner's sons [1923] 399 p.
    Joel Barlow: p. 49, 343.   PS88.H3

105. **Harrison, Henry,** *and* **G. Pulling.** Surnames of the United Kingdom; a concise etymological dictionary. London, The Eaton press, 1912-18. 2 v.
    Barlow: p. 21.   CS2505.H3

108. **Hatfield, Edwin F.** The poets of the church. A series of biographical sketches of hymn-writers with notes on their hymns. New York, A. D. F. Randolph & co. [1884] 719 p.
    Joel Barlow: p. 41-45.   PR508.R4H3

109. **Headley, Joel T.** The chaplains and clergy of the revolution. New York, C. Scribner, 1864. 402 p.
    Joel Barlow: p. 206-216.   E206.H33

110. [**Hill, Moses**] Genealogy of the Hill family from 1632, including a biographical sketch of Joel Barlow. Norwalk, The Hour steam print [1879] 29 p.

CS71.H647 1879

The Barlow family: p. 12-16; Joel Barlow: p. 17-23, 25-29.

111. **Hinman, Royal R.** A catalogue of the names of the early Puritan settlers of the colony of Connecticut;... Hartford, Press of Case, Tiffany and co., 1852-56. 884 p.

Hon. Joel Barlow: foot-note, p. 131-132.

F93.H66

112. **Howe, Henry**. Historical collections of Ohio... Cincinnati, O., Derby, Bradley & co., 1847. 581 p.

F491.H82 1847

Joel Barlow and the Scioto company: p. 177-179.

113. **Humphreys, Frederick**. The Humphreys family in America. New York, Humphreys print, 1883. 1115 p.

CS71.H926 1883

Letter of David Humphreys to Nathaniel Greene, dated April 10, 1780, relating to genius of Joel Barlow: p. 155-156.

114. **Jefferson, Thomas**. The writings of Thomas Jefferson. Definitive ed. Washington, D.C., Issued under the auspices of the Thomas Jefferson memorial association of the United States, 1905. 20 v. in 10.   E302.J474

Barlow, Joel, letter of Jefferson introducing, v. 6, p. 423; arrival of, in Paris, v. 7, p. 65; "Conspiracy of

Kings" by, v. 8, p. 382; principles of v. 10, p. 222; plan of, for Territory of the United States, v. 10, p. 321, his "Columbiad" v. 11, p. 430; oration by, v. 12, p. 231; mission to France, v. 13, p. 44; request for national hymn to be written by, v. 19, p. 161; death of, p. 189. Letters to, See Index, v. 20, p. 23.

115. ——— Interesting letter of Jefferson to Joel Barlow, in 1802, with comments. Historical magazine (Boston) Mar. 1861, v. 5: 89-90.   E171.H64,v.5

116. **Joel Barlow.** (*In* Allibone, S. Austin. A critical dictionary of English literature, & British and American authors. v. 1. Philadelphia, Childs & Peterson, 1858. p. 122.)   Z1224.A43,v. 1.

117. **Joel Barlow.** (*In* Enciclopedia universal ilustrada Europeo-Americana. Barcelona [n.d.] v. 7, p. 837-838.)
    AE61.E6, v.7

118. **Joel Barlow.** (*In* Encyclopedia americana. v. 3. New York, Americana corp., 1927. p. 259.)   AE5.E333 1927,v.3

119. **Joel Barlow.** (*In* Encyclopaedia britannica. 14th ed. v. 3. London, New York, 1929. p. 117.)   AE5.E363 1929, v.3

120. **Joel Barlow.** (*In* The National cyclopedia. v. 2. New York, P.F. Collier & son corp., 1935. p. 5.)
    AE5.N278 1935,v.2

121. **Joel Barlow.** (*In* The New international encyclopaedia. 2d ed. v.2. New York, Dodd, Mead & co., 1914. p. 683.)   AE5.N553 1914,v.2

122. **Joel Barlow, A.M.** (*In* Public characters of 1806. London, Printed for Richard Phillips, 1806. p. 152-180. port.)   CT770.P8,v.8

123. **Johnston, Henry P.** Yale and her honor-roll in the American revolution, 1775-1783; including original letters, record of service, and biographical sketches. New York, Priv. print. [press of G. P. Putnam's sons] 1888. 357 p.
    Class of 1778–Joel Barlow: p. 338-339.
                                                 E270.Y2J7

124. **Jones, Abner D.** The American portrait gallery;... New York, J.M. Emerson and co., 1853. 768 p.
    Joel Barlow, LL.D.: p. 431-432.   E176.J68

125. **King, Winnifred B.** First American satirists. Connecticut magazine (Hartford) July-Sept. 1906, v. 10: 403-411.
    The Hartford wits: Joel Barlow, Lemuel Hopkins, David Humphreys; John Trumble.   F91.C8, v.10

126. **Knight, Grant C.** American literature and culture. New York, R. Long & R. R. Smith, inc., 1932. 523 p.
    Joel Barlow: p. 81, 83-84, 232.   PS88.K6

127. **Lanman, Charles.** Biographical annals of the civil government of the United States, during its first century. Washington, J. Anglim, 1876. 676 p.
    Joel Barlow: p. 20-21.   E176.L291

128. **Leisy, Ernest E.** American literature; an interpretative survey. New York, Thomas Y. Crowell co. [1929] 299 p.
    Joel Barlow: p. 19, 39, 41-42.   PS88.L4

129. **Long, Harry A.** Personal and family names; . . . London, Hamilton, Adams & co., 1883. 362 p.
    Barlow: p. 199.   CS2305.L6

130. **Lossing, Benson J.** Eminent Americans: comprising brief biographies of three hundred and thirty distinguished persons. New York, John B. Alden, 1886. 509 p.
    Joel Barlow: p. 117.   E176.L855

131. ——— The pictorial field-book of the revolution; or, Illustrations by pen and pencil, of the history, biography, scenery, relics, and traditions of the war of independence. New York, Harper & brothers [1860] 2 v.
    Joel Barlow: v. 1, p. 404-405; Anecdote of him and Oliver Arnold: p. 606-607.   E208.L883

132. **McCabe, Joseph.** A biographical dictionary of modern rationalists. London, Watts & co., 1920. 934 numb. col.
    Joel Barlow: col. 47-48.   BL2785.M25

133. **McMaster, John Bach.** A history of the people of the United States, from the Revolution to the civil war. New York, D. Appleton and co., 1927-29. 8 v.   E301.M165
    Joel Barlow and Scioto company: v. 2, p. 146-148; letter to Baldwin; p. 399; Appointed Minister to France: v. 3, p. 184; ordered to depart: p. 411, v. 5, p. 284.

134. **Madison, James.** The writings of James Madison, comprising his public papers and his private correspondence, . . . Ed. by Gaillard Hunt. New York, G. P. Putnam's sons, 1900-10. 9 v.   E302.M22

Letters to Joel Barlow: v. 8, p. 168-172, 177-182, 208-210; blunders of: v. 8, p. 189; death of: p. 247.

135. **Marble,** *Mrs.* **Annie (Russell)** Heralds of American literature; a group of patriot writers of the revolutionary and national periods. Chicago, The University of Chicago press, 1907. 383 p.   PS186.M3

A group of Hartford wits: p. 149-189.

136. **Massachusetts historical society.** Historical index to the Pickering papers [Timothy Pickering, 1745-1829]. (*Its* Collections. 6th ser. v. 8. Boston, 1896. 580 p.)

Joel Barlow: p. 35-36.   F61.M41,6th s.v.8

137. **Miller, Victor C.** Joel Barlow: revolutionist, London, 1791-92. Hamburg, Friederichsen, de Gruyter & co., m.b.h., 1932. 3 p.l., v, 99 p. 7 l. (Britannica. . .hrsg. von

Contents.—Introduction.—Conclusions.—Chronology. —Political activities of Barlow.—Political writings of Barlow. —An evaluation.—Bibliography.—Appendix: The conspiracy of kings, by Joel Barlow.   JC211.M5

138. **Mitchell, Donald G.** American lands and letters. New York, C. Scribner's sons, 1897-99. 2 v.   P88S.M5

Joel Barlow: v. 1, p. 168-178. Port. opp. p. 168.

139. **Moulton, Charles W.** *ed.* The library of literary criticism of English and American authors. Buffalo, N.Y., Moulton publ co., 1901-05. 8 v.   PR83.M73

Joel Barlow, 1754-1812: v. 4, p. 573-577.

140. **Nathaniel Baldwin and one line of his descendants—Baldwin, Byron A.** New England historical and genealogical register, Apr. 1871, v. 25: 153-156.   F1.N56,v.25
   Family of Ruth Baldwin, wife of Joel Barlow.

141. New England historical and genealogical register.
   F1.N56
   Joel Barlow mentioned in v. 18: 295; v. 20: 278, 310; v. 21: 255; v. 23: 225; v. 25: 154; v. 37: 340; v. 42: 86; v. 65: 53, 61, 83.

142. [**Oelsner, Konrad E.**] Notice sur la vie et les ecrits de m. Joel Barlow, ministre plenipotentiaire des Etats-Unis d'Amerique aupres de S. M. l'empereur des Francais. Paris, De l'impr. de Smith. 1813. 31 p.
   The beginning of the Columbiad with French translation: p. 20-31.   PS705.O4

143. **Otis, William Bradley.** American verse, 1625-1807; a history. New York, Moffat, Yard and co., 1909. 303 p.
   Joel Barlow: p. 29-30, 106, 114, 118-119, 154, 162-171, 175, 206, 209.   PS312.O7

144. **Paine, Thomas.** The life and works of Thomas Paine. Patriots' ed. New Rochelle, N.Y., Thomas Paine national historical association, 1925. 10 v.   JC177.A3 1925
   Joel Barlow: v. 1, p. 185, 325, 358, v. 8, p. 105.

145. ——— The writings of Thomas Paine; collected and ed. by Moncure Daniel Conway. New York, G. P. Putnam's sons, 1894-96. 4 v.
   Joel Barlow: v. 3, introd., p. 376, 395, 421; v. 4, p. 12, 15, 86.   JC177.A3 1894

146. **Parrington, Vernon Louis**. Main currents in American thought; an interpretation of American literature from the beginnings to 1920. [New York, Harcourt, Brace and co., 1927-30] 3 v.

    Joel Barlow, Jacobin: v. 1, p. 382-389.

                                                         PS88.P3,v.1

147. ——— *ed.* The Connecticut wits. New York, Harcourt, Brace and co., [1926] 514 p. (American authors series, general editor, S. T. Williams)

    Introduction: p. ix-xlviii. Joel Barlow: p. lii-liii, 288-382.   PS548.C8P3

148. **Pattee, Fred Lewis**. A history of American literature, with a view to the fundamental principles underlying its development; a text-book for schools and colleges. New ed., rev. and enl. New York, Boston, Silver, Burdett and co. [1909] 475 p.

    Joel Barlow: p. 96-97, 154.   PS92.P4 1909

149. **Patterson, Samuel White**. The spirit of the American revolution, as revealed in the poetry of the period; a study of American patriotic verse from 1760 to 1783. Boston, R. G. Badger, [1915] 235 p. (Studies in English literature)

    See p. 66-68, 79-80, 128-130, 154, 195-197. Port. opp. p. 66.   PS314.P3 1915

150. **Pearson, Charles William**. Literary and biographical essays; a volume of papers by the way. Boston, Sherman, French & co., 1908. 260 p.   PN511.P35
Early American poetry [Joel Barlow] :p. 36-43.

151. **Pease, John C.** and **John M. Niles.** A gazetteer of the states of Connecticut and Rhode-Island. Hartford: Printed and published by William S. Marsh, 1819. 389 p.   F77.P36
    Joel Barlow: p. 187-191.   F92.P36

152. **Pickering, Octavius.** The life of Timothy Pickering. By his son. Boston, Little, Brown, and co., 1867-73. 4 v.
    Joel Barlow: v. 3, p. 270, 273.   E302.6.P5P5

153. **Prescott, Frederick C.** *and* **John H. Nelson,** *eds.* Prose and poetry of the revolution. The establishment of the nation, 1765-1789. New York, Thomas Y. Crowell co. [1925] 266 p.
    Joel Barlow: p. 170-172. Extracts from his writings: p. 173-190.   PS533.P7

154. **Richardson, Charles F.** American literature 1607-1885. New York, G. P. Putnam's sons, 1887-89. 2 v.
    Joel Barlow: v. 2, p. 12, 13, 23, 35.   PS83.R5

155. **Rosenthal, Lewis.** America and France; the influence of the United States on France in the XVIIIth century. New York, H. Holt and co., 1882. 302 p.
    Joel Barlow: p. 264-265.   DC158.8.R7

156. **[Ryan, Daniel J.]** The Scioto company and its purchase. Ohio archaeological and historical quarterly, 1891, v. 3: 107-136.
    Port. opp. p. 113.   F486.051,v.3

157. **Schenck,** *Mrs.* **Elizabeth Hubbell (Godfrey)** The history of Fairfield, Fairfield County, Connecticut, from

the settlement of the town in 1639 to 1818. New York, The author, 1889-1905. 2 v.
    Joel Barlow: v. 1, p. 352-353.   F104.F2S3

158. **Sears, Lorenzo.** American literature in the colonial and national periods. Boston, Little, Brown, and co., 1902. 480 p.
    Joel Barlow: p. 155, 158-162.   PS92.S3 1902

159. [**Seaton, Josephine**] William Winston Seaton of the "National intelligencer". A biographical sketch. With passing notices of his associates and friends. Boston, J. R. Osgood and co., 1871. 385 p.
    Joel Barlow: p. 69-70, 100-108.   PN4874.84S4

160. **Sheldon, F.** The Pleiadas of Connecticut. Atlantic monthly (Boston) Feb. 1865, v. 15: 187-201.
    Joel Barlow: p. 193-195.   AP2.A8,v.15

161. Sketch of the life and writings of Joel Barlow. Analectic magazine (Philadelphia) Aug. 1814, v. 4: 130-138.   AP2.A48,v.4*

162. [**Smith, W. P.**] Account of Mr. Joel Barlow, an American poet. Monthly magazine, and British register (London) Oct. 1798, v. 6: 250-251.   AP4.M8,v.6

163. **Squires, Vernon P.** Joel Barlow—patriot, democrat, and man of letters. Quarterly journal of the University of North Dakota, July, 1919, v. 9: 299-308.   AS36.N6,v.9

164. **Stodman, Edmund C.** *and* **Ellen M. Hutchinson,** *eds.* A library of American literature from earliest settlement to the present time. New ed. New York, W. E. Benjamin [1894] 11 v.

    Joel Barlow: Biographical sketch, v. 11, p. 473-474. The Hasty pudding and A judicial estimate of the character and genius of Thomas Paine: v. 4, p. 46-57. See also Connecticut wits: v. 3, p. 422-429.   PS504.S7 1894

165. **Stephens, Alexander.** Memoirs of John Horne Tooke, interspersed with original documents. London, Printed for J. Johnson and co., 1813. 2 v.

    Mr. Joel Barlow: v. 2, p. 330-331.   DA506.T6S8

166. **Stiles, Ezra.** The literary diary of Ezra Stiles... ed. ... by Franklin Bowditch Dexter. New York, C. Scribner's sons, 1901. 3 v.

    See v. 2, p. 288, 456, 458, 556-557; v. 3, p. 155-156.   BX7260.S8A3

167. **Stokes, Ansen Phelps.** Memorials of eminent Yale men; a biographical study of student life and university influences during the eighteenth and nineteenth centuries. New Haven, Yale university press, 1914. 2 v.   LD6323.88

    Joel Barlow, Class of 1778: v. 1, p. 126-135.

168. **Swift, Lindsay.** Our literary diplomats. Part I. From the period of the Revolution to the "era of good feeling", 1776-1820. [David Humphreys and Joel Barlow] Ports. Book buyer, June, 1900, n.c.v.20: 369-375.

    Z1219.B72,n.s.v.20

169. **Todd, Charles Burr.** A forgotten American worthy. Lippincott's magazine (Philadelphia) July, 1880, v. 26: 68-83. AP2.L55,v.26

170. ———— The history of Redding, Connecticut, from its first settlement to the present time, with notes on the Adams, Banks, Barlow ... and Strong families [2d ed.] New York, The Grafton press, [1906] 303 p. F104.R3T7
    Joel Barlow: p. 55, 64, 89, 146-149, 158.
    L.C. has also the 1st ed., 1880.

171. **Todd, Charles Burr.** Life and letters of Joel Barlow, LL.D., poet, statesman, philosopher, with extracts from his works and hitherto unpublished poems. New York, G. P. Putnam's sons, 1886. iv, 306 p. port. PS705.T6
    Reviews:
    Nation (New York) May 13, 1886, v. 42: 406-407.
AP2.N2,v.42
    Albert H. Hoyt, New England historical and genealogical register, July, 1886, v. 40: 335-336.
F1.N56,v.40
    L.,J.P., The American (Philadelphia) July 10, 1886, v. 12: 184-185. AP2.A317,v.12
    Athenasum (London) July 24, 1886, p. 112-113.
AP4.A8 1886(July-Dec.)
    F. Sheldon, Atlantic monthly (Boston) Aug. 1886, v. 58: 275-279. AP2.A8,v.58
    Ernest Whitney, New Englander (New Haven) Oct. 1886, v. 45: 825-835. AP2.N5, v.45

172. **Trent, William P.** A history of American literature, 1607-1865. New York, D. Appleton and co., 1929. 608 p.

(Short histories of the literatures of the world, edited by Edmund Gosse)

    Joel Barlow: p. 164, 167, 168, 173-178, 197, 215, 221, 585.   PS92.T7 1929

173. **Tyler, Moses Coit**. Three men of letters. New York, G. P. Putnam's sons, 1895. 200 p.   PS185.T85

    The literary strivings of Mr. Joel Barlow: p. 131-180.

174. **Warner library**. The world's best literature. University ed. v. 3. New York, the Knickerbocker press, 1917.

    Joel Barlow, critical essay: p. 1557-1559. A feast, from 'Hasty pudding': p. 1559-1562.   PN6013.W3,v.3

175. **Washington, George**. The writings of George Washington. By Jared Sparks. New York, Harper & brothers, 1847. 12 v.

    Barlow goes to Europe: v. 9, p. 381, 386; Consul at Algiers: v. 11, p. 158; A letter of Barlow's, Oct. 2, 1798, forwarded to Pres. Adams: p. 398, 404, 560-563.

    E312.7. 1847

176. ——— The writings of George Washington; collected and ed. by Worthington Chauncey Ford. New York, G. P. Putnam's sons, 1889-93. 14 v.

    Joel Barlow, recommended to Lafayette: v. 11, p. 265; Consul to Algiers: v. 13, p. 460.   E312.7 1889

177. **Wendell, Barrett**. A literary history of America. New York, C. Scribner's sons, 1900. 574 p. (The library of literary history)

Joel Barlow: p. 123, 126-128, 129, 165.
PS88.W4 1900

178. **Whitcomb, Selden L.** Chronological outlines of American literature. New York, Macmillan and co., 1894. 286 p.
Joel Barlow: p. 83, 125, 230.   PS94.W4

179. **Willson, Beckles.** America's ambassadors to France (1777-1927) A narrative of Franco-American diplomatic relations. New York, Frederick A. Stokes co., 1928. 433 p.
Joel Barlow: p. 102-117.   E183.8.F8W72
Same. English ed. London, J. Murray, [1928] 433 p.
E183.8.F8W7

180. **Winsor, Justin,** *ed.* Narrative and critical history of America. Boston and New York, Houghton, Mifflin and co., 1884-89. 8 v.
Joel Barlow: v. 7, p. 300, 525; in France, p. 514, port. p. 531; his map, Plan des achats des Compagnies de l'Ohio et du Scioto, p. 532; agent in Europe, p. 535; had the Gates papers: v. 8, p. 435; Memoir: p. 494-495.
F18.W765

181. ——— The westward movement . . . The colonies and the republic west of the Alleganies, 1763-1798. With full cartographical illustrations from contemporary sources. Boston and New York, Houghton, Mifflin and co., 1897. 595 p.
Joel Barlow, agent for the Scioto company: p. 311, his map, p. 311-313; and the Scioto company: p. 402-407.   F352.W78

182. **Yarborough, Minnie Clare.** John Horne Tooke. New York, Columbia university press, 1926. 252 p. (Columbia university studies in English and comparative literature)
    Joel Barlow: p. 92.   DA506.T6Y4 1926

183. **Zunder, Theodore Albert.** The early days of Joel Barlow, a Connecticut wit. Yale graduate, editor, lawyer and poet, chaplain during the revolutionary war; his life and works from 1754 to 1787. New Haven, Yale university press; London, H. Milford, Oxford university press, 1934. 320 p. port. (Yale studies in English, vol. LXXXIV)
    Contents.–Preface; Chap. I. Redding days; II. Vox clamantis in deserto; III. Undergraduate years at Yale; IV. The beginning of Barlow's career; V. Chaplain; VI. The Commencement poem; VII. The first trip to Philadelphia; VIII. Literary ventures; IX. *The Anarchiad*; X. *The Vision of Columbus.* Appendix A. Footnotes; Appendix B. Bibliography of books and articles on the life and works of Joel Barlow; Index.   PR13.Y3, v.84

184. ——— Joel Barlow and George Washington. Modern language notes (Baltimore, Md.) Apr. 1929, v. 44: 254-256.
    PB1.M6,v.44

185. ——— Joel Barlow and seasickness. Yale journal of biology and medicine (New Haven) July 1, 1929, v. 1: 385-390.

186. **Zunder. Theodore A.** *and* **Stanley A. Williams.** Joel Barlow (Mar. 24, 1754–Dec. 24, 1812) (*In* Dictionary of American biography, ed. by Allen Johnson. v. 1. New York, C. Scribner's sons, 1928. p. 609-613.)   E176.D56,v.1

PORTRAITS:

In addition to the portraits noted above others may be found in the following publications:

Century magazine (New York) Oct. 1908, v. 76: 932.　　　　　　　　　　　　　　AP2.C4,v.76
Century magazine (New York) Sept. 1909, v. 78: 758.　　　　　　　　　　　　　　AP2.C4,v.78
Critic (New York) Oct. 1902, v. 41: 336.
　　　　　　　　　　　　　　　AP2.C92,v.41
Harper's weekly (New York) Jan. 26, 1895, v. 39: 87.　　　　　　　　　　　　　　AP2.H32,v.39
McClure's magazine (New York) June, 1895, v. 5: 37.　　　　　　　　　　　　　　AP2.M2,v.37
Magazine of American history (New York) Aug. 1890, v. 24: 103.　　　　　　E171.M18,v.24
New England magazine (Boston) Feb. 1904, n.s.v.29:697.　　　　　　　AP2.N4,n.s.v.29
Palette and bench (Syracuse, N.Y.) Jan. 1910, v. 2: 78.　　　　　　　　　　　　　　N1.P3,v.2
Revue de l'art ancien et moderne (Paris) Sept.-Oct. 1929, v. 56: 169.　　　　　　　　N2.R4,v.56

THE
POLITICAL WRITINGS
OF
JOEL BARLOW

—CONTAINING—

ADVICE TO THE PRIVILEGED ORDERS.
LETTER TO THE NATIONAL CONVENTION.
LETTER TO THE PEOPLE OF PIEDMONT.
THE CONSPIRACY OF KINGS.

ADVICE

TO THE

PRIVILEGED ORDERS.

INTRODUCTION.

THE French Revolution is at laſt not only accompliſhed, but its accompliſhment univerſally acknowledged, beyond contradiction abroad, or the power of retraction at home.* It has finiſhed its work, by organizing a government, on principles approved by reaſon; an object long contemplated by different writers, but never before exhibited, in this quarter of the globe. The experiment now

---

* The reader will bear in mind that this was written in the latter end of the year 1791, juſt as the French had eſtabliſhed their firſt conſtitution, and were determined to try the experiment of a limited monarchy. It is in this ſenſe that the author conſidered the revolution as finiſhed; though he did not believe, as will appear in this introduction, that a government ſo conſtructed, and ſo little congenial to the ſpirit of the times, would be of long duration.

He did not believe in the neceſſity of a war to introduce and eſtabliſh the republic. For though the treaty of Pilnitz had then been publiſhed, and though it bore the marks of that folly whicn is

in operation will solve a question of the first magnitude in human affairs: Whether *Theory* and *Practice*, which always agree together in things of slighter moment, are really to remain eternal enemies in the highest concerns of men?

The change of government in France is, properly speaking, a renovation of society; an object peculiarly fitted to hurry the mind into a field of thought, which can scarcely be limited by the concerns of a nation, or the improvements of an age. As there is a tendency in human nature to imitation; and as all the apparent causes exist in most of the governments of the world, to induce the people to wish for a similar change; it becomes interesting to the cause of humanity, to take a deliberate view of the real nature and extent of this change, and find what are the advantages and disadvantages to be expected from it.

There is not that necromancy in politics, which prevents our foreseeing, with tolerable certainty, what is to be the result of operations so universal, in which all the people concur. Many truths are as perceptible when first presented to the mind, as an age or a world of experience could make them; others require only an indirect and collateral experience; some demand an experience direct and positive.

---

common to the enemies of reform in all ages, still it does not appear from any subsequent events, that the parties to that treaty had any intention of pushing their opposition to open hostilities. This opinion is more fully developed in the preface to *The Conspiracy of Kings*, and in the note on Mr. Burke, at the end of the volume.

INTRODUCTION.

It is happy for human nature, that in morals we have much to do with this firſt claſs of truths, leſs with the ſecond, and very little with the third; while in phyſics we are perpetually driven to the ſlow proceſs of patient and poſitive experience.

The Revolution in France certainly comes recommended to us under one aſpect which renders it at firſt view extremely inviting: it is the work of argument and rational conviction, not of the ſword. The *ultima ratio regum* had nothing to do with it. It was an operation deſigned for the benefit of the people; it originated in the people, and was conducted by the people. It had therefore a legitimate origin; and this circumſtance entitles it to our ſerious contemplation, on two accounts: becauſe there is ſomething venerable in the idea, and becauſe other nations, in ſimilar circumſtances, will certainly be diſpoſed to imitate it.

I ſhall therefore examine the nature and conſequences of a ſimilar revolution in government, as it will affect the following principal objects, which make up the affairs of nations in the preſent ſtate of Europe:

I. The Feudal Syſtem,
II. The Church,
III. The Military,
IV. The Adminiſtration of Juſtice,
V. Revenue and public expenditure.

It muſt be of vaſt importance to all the claſſes of ſociety, as it now ſtands claſſed in Europe, to calculate before-hand what they are to gain or to looſe by the approaching change; that, like prudent ſtock-jobbers, they may buy in or ſell out, according as this great event ſhall affect them.

Philoſophers and contemplative men, who may think themſelves diſintereſted ſpectators of ſo great a political drama, will do well to confider how far the cataftrophe is to be beneficial or detrimental to the human race; in order to determine whether in confcience they ought to promote or difcourage, accelerate or retard it, by the publication of their opinions. It is true, the work was fet on foot by this fort of men; but they have not all been of the fame opinion relative to the beft organization of the governing power, or how far the reform of abufes ought to extend. Montefquieu, Voltaire, and many other refpectable authorities, have accredited the principle, that republicanifm is not convenient for a great ftate. Others take no notice of the diftinction between great and fmall ftates, in deciding, that this is the only government proper to enfure the happinefs, and fupport the dignity of man. Of the former opinion was a great majority of the conftituant national affembly of France. Probably not many years will pafs, before a third opinion will be univerfally adopted, never to be laid afide: That the republican principle is not only proper and fafe for the government of any people; but that its propriety and fafety are in proportion to the magnitude of the fociety and extent of the territory.

Among fincere enquirers after truth, all general queftions on this fubject reduce themfelves to this: Whether men are to perform their duties by an eafy choice or an expenfive cheat; or, whether our reafon be given us to be improved or ftifled, to render us greater or lefs than brutes, to increafe our happinefs or aggravate our mifery.

Among thofe whofe anxieties arife only from intereft, the inquiry is, how their privileges or their profeffions are to be affected by the new order of things. Thefe form a clafs of men refpectable both for their numbers and sensibility; it is our duty to attend to their case. I sincerely hope to administer some consolation to them in the course of this essay. And though I have a better opinion of their philanthrophy, than political opponents generally entertain of each other, yet I do not altogether rely upon their presumed sympathy with their fellow-citizens, and their supposed willingness to sacrifice to the public good ; but I hope to convince them, that the establishment of general liberty will be less injurious to those who now live by abuses, than is commonly imagined ; that protected industry will produce effects far more astonishing than have ever been calculated ; that the increase of enjoyments will be such, as to ameliorate the condition of every human creature.

To persuade this class of mankind, that it is neither their duty nor their interest to endeavour to perpetuate the ancient forms of government, would be an high and holy office ; it would be the greatest act of charity to them, as it might teach them to avoid a danger that is otherwise unavoidable ; it would preclude the occasion of the people's indulging what is sometimes called a ferocious disposition, which is apt to grow upon the revenge of injuries, and render them less harmonious in their new station of citizens ; it would prevent the civil wars, which might attend the insurrections of the people, where there should be a great want of unanimity,—for we are not to expect in every country that mildness and dignity which have uniformly characterized the French, even in their most tumultuous movements* ; it would remove every

---

Whatever reason may be given for the fact, I believe all those who have been witnesses of what

obstacle and every danger that may seem to attend that rational system of public felicity to which the nations of Europe are moving with rapid strides, and which in prospect is so consoling to the enlightened friends of humanity.

To induce the men who now govern the world to adopt these ideas, is the duty of those who now

---

are called *mobs* in France (during the revolution) will join with me in opinion, that they are by no means to be compared with English mobs, in point of indiscriminate ferocity and private plunder. A popular commotion in Paris was uniformly directed to a certain well-explained object; from which it never was known to deviate. Whether this object were to hang a man, to arrest the king, to intimidate the court, or to break the furniture of a hotel, all other persons and all other property, that fell in the way of the mob, were perfectly safe.

The truth is, those collections were composed of honest and industrious people, who had nothing in view but the public good. They believed that the cause of their country required an execution of justice more prompt than could be expected from any established tribunal. Besides, they were in the crisis of a revolution, when they were sensible, that the crimes of their enemies would remain unpunished, for want of a known rule by which they could be judged. Though a violation of *right*, is not always a violation of *law*; yet, in their opinion, occasions might exist, when it would be dangerous to let it pass with impunity.

It is indeed to be hoped, that whenever mobs in other countries shall be animated by the same cause, they will conduct themselves with the same dignity; and that this singular phenomenon will be found not altogether attributable to national character.

INTRODUCTION.

possess them. I confess the task, at first view, appears more than Herculean; it will be thought an object from which the eloquence of the closet must shrink in despair, and which prudence would leave to the more powerful arguments of events. But I believe at the same time that some success may be expected; that though the harvest be great, the labourers may not be few; that prejudice and interest cannot always be relied on to garrison the mind against the assaults of truth. This belief, ill-grounded as it may appear, is sufficient to animate me in the cause; and to the venerable host of republican writers, who have preceeded me in the discussions occasioned by the French revolution, this belief is my only apology for offering to join the fraternity, and for thus practically declaring my opinion, that they have not exhausted the subject.

Two very powerful weapons, the force of reason and the force of numbers, are in the hands of the political reformers. While the use of the first brings into action the second, and ensures its co-operation, it remains a sacred duty, imposed on them by the God of reason to wield with dexterity this mild and beneficent weapon, before recurring to the use of the other; which, though legitimate, may be less harmless; though infallible in operation, may be less glorious in victory.

The tyrannies of the world, whatever be the appellation of the government under which they are exercised, are all aristocratical tyrannies. An ordinance to plunder and murder, whether it fulminate from the Vatican, or steal silently forth from the Harem; whether it come clothed in the *certain science* of a Bed of Justice, or in the legal solemnities of a bench of lawyers; whether it be purchafed by the careffes of a woman, or the treafures of a nation;—never confines its effects to the benefit of a fingle individual; it goes to enrich the whole combination of confpirators, whofe bufinefs it is to dupe and to govern the nation. It carries its own bribery with itfelf through all its progrefs and connexions,—in its origination, in its enaction, in its vindication, in its execution; it is a fertilizing ftream, that waters and vivifies its happy plants in the numerous channels of its communication. Minifters and fecretaries, commanders of armies, contractors, collectors and tide-waiters, intendants, judges and lawyers,—whoever is permitted to drink of the falutary ftream,—are all interefted in removing the obftructions and in praifing the fountain from which it flows.

The ftate of human nature requires that this fhould be the cafe. Among beings fo nearly equal in power and capacity as men of the fame community are, it is impoffible that a folitary tyrant fhould exift. Laws that are defigned to operate unequally on fociety, muft offer an exclufive intereft to a confiderable portion of its members, to enfure their execution upon the reft. Hence has arifen the neceffity of that ftrange complication in the governing power, which has made of politics an inexpliclable fcience; hence the reafon for arming one clafs of our fellow creatures with the weapons of bodily deftruction, and another with the myfterious artillery of the vengeance of heaven; hence the caufe of what in England is called the independence of the judges, and what on the continent has created a judiciary nobility, a fet of men who purchafe the privilege of being the profeffional enemies of the people, of felling their decifions to the rich, and of diftributing individual oppreffion;

INTRODUCTION. xi

hence the fource of thofe Draconian codes of criminal jurifprudence which enfhrine the idol property in a bloody fanctuary, and teach the modern European, that his life is of lefs value than the fhoes on his feet; hence the pofitive difcouragements laid upon agriculture, manufacture, commerce, and every method of improving the condition of men; for it is to be obferved, that in every country the fhackles impofed upon induftry are in proportion to the degree of general defpotifm that reigns in the government. This arifes not only from the greater debility and want of enterprife in the people, but from the fuperior neceffity that fuch governments are under, to prevent their fubjects from acquiring that eafe and information, by which they could difcern the evil and apply the remedy.

To the fame fruitful fource of calamities we are to trace that perverfity of reafon, which, in governments where men are permitted to difcufs political fubjects, has given rife to thofe perpetual fhifts of fophiftry, by which they vindicate the prerogative of kings. In one age it is the *right of conqueft*, in another *the divine right*, then it comes to be a *compact between king and people*, and laft of all, it is faid to be founded on general convenience, *the good of the whole community*. In England thefe feveral arguments have all had their day; though it is aftonifhing that the two former could ever have been the fubjects of rational debate: the firft is the logic of the mufquet, and the fecond of the chalice; the one was buried at Rennimede on the fignature of Magna Charta, the other took its flight to the continent with James the Second. The compact of king and people has lain dormant the greater part of the prefent century; till it was roufed from flumber by the French revolution, and came into the fervice of Mr. Burke.

Hafty men difcover their errors when it is too late. It had certainly been much more confiftent with the temperament of that writer's mind, and quite as ferviceable to his caufe, to have recalled the fugitive claim of the divine right of kings. It would have given a myftic force to his declamation, afforded him many new epithets, and furnifhed fubjects perfectly accordant with the copious charges of *facrilege, atheifm, murders, affaffinations, rapes* and *plunders* with which his three volumes abound.* He then could not have difappointed his friends by his total want of argument, as he now does in his two firft effays; for on fuch a fubject no argument could be expected; and in his third, where it is patiently attempted, he would have avoided the neceffity of fhowing that he has none, by giving a different title to his book; for the " Appeal," inftead of being "' from the New to the Old Whigs," would have been *from the new whigs to the old tories*; and he might as well have appealed to Cæfar; he could have found at this day no court to take cognizance of his caufe.

But the great advantage of this mode of handling the fubject would have been, that it could have provoked no anfwers; the gauntlet might have been thrown, without a champion to have taken it up; and the laft folitary admirer of chivalry have retired in negative triumph from the field.

---

* Thefe three works are, his *Reflections on the Revolution in France*, his *Letter to a Member of the National Affembly*, and his *Appeal from the New to the Old Whigs*.

Mr. Burke, however, in his defence of royalty, does not rely on this argument of the compact. Whether it be, that he is confcious of its futility, or that in his rage he forgets that he has ufed it, he is perpetually recurring to the laft ground that has yet been heard of, on which we are called upon to confider kings even as a tolerable nuifance, and to fupport the exifting forms of government: this ground is *the general good of the community*. It is faid to be dangerous to pull down fyftems that are already formed, or even to attempt to improve them; and it is likewife faid, that, were they peaceably deftroyed, and we had fociety to build up anew, it would be beft to create hereditary kings, hereditary orders, and exclufive privileges.

Thefe are fober opinions, uniting a clafs of reafoners too numerous and too refpectable to be treated with contempt. I believe, however, that their number is every day diminifhing, and I believe the example which France will foon be obliged to exhibit to the world on this fubject, will induce every man to reject them, who is not perfonally and exclufively interefted in their fupport.

The inconfiftency of the the conftituent affembly, in retaining an hereditary king, armed with an enormous civil lift, to wage war with a popular government, has induced fome perfons to predict the downfall of their conftitution. But this meafure had a different origin from what is commonly affigned to it, and will probably have a different iffue. It was the refult rather of local and temporary circumftances, than of any general belief in the utility of kings, under any modifications or limitations that could be attached to the office.

It is to be observed, *first*, that the French had a king upon their hands. This king had always been confidered as a well-difpofed man; fo that, by a fatality fomewhat fingular, though not unexampled in *regal hiftory*, he gained the love of the people, almoſt in proportion to the mifchief which he did them. *Secondly*, their king had very powerful family connexions, in the fovereigns of Spain, Auſtria, Naples and Sardinia; befides his relations within the kingdom, whom it was neceſſary to attach, if poſſible, to the intereſts of the community. *Thirdly*, the revolution was confidered by all Europe as a high and dangerous experiment. It was neceſſary to hide as much as poſſible the appearance of its magnitude from the eye of the diſtant obferver. The reformers confidered it as their duty to produce an internal regeneration of fociety, rather than an external change in the appearance of the court; to fet in order the counting-houfe and the kitchen, before arranging the drawing-room. This would leave the fovereigns of Europe totally without a pretext for interfering; while it would be confoling to that clafs of philofophers, who ſtill believed in the compatibility of royalty and liberty. *Fourthly*, this decree, That *France ſhould have a king*, and that he *could do no wrong*, was paſſed at an early period of their operations; when the above reafons were apparently more urgent than they were afterwards, or probably will ever be again.

From thefe confiderations we may conclude, that royalty is preferved in France for reafons which are fugitive; that a majory of the conſtituent aſſembly did not believe in it, as an abſtract principle; that a majority of the people will learn to be difgüefted with fo unnatural and ponderous a deformity in their new edifice, and will foon hew it off.

After this improvement fhall have been made, a few years experience in the face of Europe, and on fo great a theatre as that of France, will probably leave but one opinion in the minds of honeft men, relative to the republican principle, or the great fimplicity of nature applied to the organization of fociety.

The example of America would have had great weight in producing this conviction; but it is too little known to the European reafoner, to be a fubject of accurate inveftigation. Befides the difference of circumftances between that country and the ftates of Europe has given occafion for imagining many diftinctions which exift not in fact, and has prevented the application of principles which are permanently founded in nature, and follow not the trifling variations in the ftate of fociety.

But I have not prefcribed to myfelf the tafk of entering into arguments on the utility of kings, or of inveftigating the meaning of Mr. Burke, in order to compliment him with an additional refutation. My fubject furnifhes a more extenfive fcope. It depends not on me, or Mr. Burke, or any other writer, or defcription of writers, to determine the queftion, whether a change of government fhall take place, and extend through Europe. It depends on a much more important clafs of men, the clafs that cannot write; and in a great meafure, on thofe who cannnot read. It is to be decided by men who reafon better without books, than we do with all the books in the world. Taking it for granted, therefore, that a general revolution is at hand, whofe progrefs is *irrefiftable*, my object is to contemplate its probable effects, and to comfort thofe who are afflicted at the profpect.

Note,—A miftake has been committed in heading the firft part of this work, page 3; it fhould read thus:—*Advice to the Privileged Orders in the feveral States of Europe, refulting from the neceffity and propriety of a general revolution in the principles of government.* Editor.

CHAP. I.

FEUDAL SYSTEM.

THE most prominent feature in the moral face of Europe, was imprinted upon it by conquest. It is the result of the subordination necessary among military savages, on their becoming cultivators of the soil which they had desolated, and making an advantageous use of such of the inhabitants as they did not choose to massacre, and could not sell to foreigners for slaves.

The relation thus established between the officers and the soldiers, between the victors and the vanquished, and between them all and the lands which they were to cultivate, modified by the experience of unlettered ages, has obtained the name of the Feudal System, and may be considered as the foundation of all the political institutions in this quarter of the world. The claims resulting to particular classes of men, under this modification of society, are called Feudal Rights; and to the individual possessors they are either nominal or real, conveying an empty title or a substantial profit.

My intention is not to enter on the details of this system, as a lawyer, or to trace its progress with the accuracy of an historian, and show its peculiar fitness to the rude ages of society which gave it birth. But, viewing it as an ancient edifice, whofe foundation, worn away by the current of events, can no longer fupport its weight, I would fketch a few drawings to fhow the ftile of its architecture, and compare it with the model of the new building to be erected in its place.

The *philofophy* of the Feudal Syftem, is all that remains of it worthy of our contemplation. This I will attempt to trace in fome of its leading points, leaving the practical part to fall, with its ancient founders and its modern admirers, into the peaceful gulph of oblivion; to which I wifh it a fpeedy and an unobftructed paffage.

The original object of this inftitution was undoubtedly, what it was alleged to be, the prefervation of turbulent focieties, in which men are held together but by feeble ties; and it effected its purpofe by uniting the perfonal intereft of the head of each family, with the perpetual fafety of the ftate. Thus far the purpofe was laudable, and the means extremely well calculated for the end. But it was the fortune of this fyftem to attach itfelf to thofe paffions of human nature which vary not with the change of circumftances. While national motives ceafed by degrees to require its continuance, family motives forbade to lay it afide. The fame progreffive improvements in fociety, which rendered military tenures and military titles firft unneceffary and then injurious to the general intereft, at the fame time fharpened the avarice, and piqued the honour of thofe who poffeffed them, to preferve the exclufive privileges which rendered them thus diftinguifhed. And thefe privileges, united with the operations of the church, have founded and fupported the despotisms of Europe in all their divisions, combinations, and refinements.

Feudal Rights are either *territorial* or *personal*. I shall divide them into these two classes, for the sake of bestowing a few observations upon each.

The pernicious effects of the system on territorial tenures are inconceivable, various and great. In a legal view, it has led to those intricacies and vexations, which we find attached to every circumstance of real property, which have perplexed the science of civil jurisprudence, which have perpetuated the ignorance of the people relative to the administration of justice, rendered necessary the intervention of lawyers, and multiplied, the means of oppression. But, in a political view, its consequences are still more serious, and demand a particular consideration.

The first quality of the feudal tenure is to confine the descendible property to the *eldest male issue*. To say that this is contrary to nature, is but a feeble expression. So abominable is its operation, that it has seduced and perverted nature ; her voice is stifled, interest itself is laid asleep, and nothing but the eloquence of an incomprehensible pride is heard on the occasion. You will hear father and mother, younger brothers and sisters, rejoice in this provision of the law ; the former consigning their daughters to the gloomy prison of a convent, and their younger sons to the church or the army, to ensure their celibacy ; that no remnant of the family may remain but the heir of the estate entire ; the latter congratulating each other, that the elder brother will transmit unimpaired the title and the property, while they themselves are content to perish in the obscurity of their several destinations. It is probable that, in another age, a tale of this kind will scarcely gain credit, and that the tear of sensibility may be spared by a disbelief of the fact. It is, however, no creature of the imagination; it happened every day in France previous to the revolution; I have seen it with my own eyes, and heard it with my own ears; it is now to be seen and heard in most other Catholic countries.

But other points of view show this disposition of the law to be still more reprehensible in the eye of political philosophy. It swells the inequality of wealth, which, even in the best regulated society, is but too considerable; it habituates the people to believe in an unnatural inequality in the rights of men, and by these means prepares them for servility and oppression; it prevents the improvement of lands, and impedes the progress of industry and cultivation, which are best promoted on small estates, where proprietors cultivate for themselves; it discourages population, by inducing to a life of celibacy.—But I shall speak of celibacy when I speak of the church.

Whether men are born to govern, or to obey, or to enjoy equal liberty, depends not on the original capacity of the mind, but on the *instinct of analogy*, or the *habit of thinking*. When children of the same family are taught to believe in the unconquerable distinctions of birth among themselves, they are completely fitted for a feudal government; because their minds are familiarised with all the gradations and degradations that such a government requires. The birth-right of domineering is not more readily claimed on the one hand, than it is acknowledged on the other; and the Jamaica planter is not more habitually convinced that an European is superior to an African, than he is that a Lord is better than himself.

This subject deserves to be placed in a light, in which no writer, as far as I know, has yet considered it. When a person was repeating to Fontenelle the common adage *habit is the second nature*, the philosopher replied, *and do me the favour to tell me which is the first*. When we assert that nature has established *inequalities* among men, and has thus given to some the right of governing others, or when we maintain the *contrary* of this position, we should be careful to define what sort of nature we mean, whether the *first* or *second nature*; or whether we mean that there is but one. A mere savage, Colocolo* for instance, would decide the question of equality by a trial of bodily strength, designating the man that could lift the heaviest beam to be the legislator; and unless all men could lift the same beam, they could not be equal in their rights. Aristotle would give the preference to him that excelled in mental capacity. Ulysses would make the decision upon a compound ratio of both. But there appears to me another step in this ladder, and that the *habit of thinking* is the only safe and universal criterion to which, in practice, the question can be referred. Indeed, when interest is laid aside, it is the only one to which, in civilized ages, it ever is referred. We never submit to a King, because he is stronger than we in bodily force, nor because he is superior in understanding or in information; but because we believe him born to govern, or at least, because a majority of the society believes it.

---

* See the Araucana of Ercilla.

This *habit of thinking* has so much of nature in it, it is so undistinguishable from the indelible marks of the man, that it is a perfectly safe foundation for any system that we may choose to build upon it; indeed it is the *only* foundation, for it is the only point of contact by which men communicate as moral associates. As a practical position therefore, and as relating to almost all places and almost all times, in which the experiment has yet been made, Aristotle was as right in teaching, *That some are born to command, and others to be commanded*, as the National Assembly was in declaring, *That men are born and always continue free and equal in respect to their rights*. The latter is as apparently false in the diet of Ratisbon, as the former is in the hall of the Jacobins.

Abstractly considered, there can be no doubt of the unchangeable truth of the assembly's declaration; and they have taken the right method to make it a *practical* truth, by publishing it to the world for discussion. A general belief *that it is a truth*, makes it at once practical, confirms it in one nation, and extends it to others.

A due attention to the astonishing effects that are wrought in the world by *the habit of thinking*, will serve many valuable purposes. I cannot therefore dismiss the subject so soon as I intended; but will mention one or two instances of these effects, and leave the reflection of the reader to make the application to a thousand others.

First, It is evident that all the arbitrary systems in the world are founded and supported on this *second nature* of man, in counteraction of the *first*. Systems which distort and crush and subjugate every thing that we can suppose original and characteristic in man, as an undistorted being. It sustains the most absurd and abominable theories of religion, and honours them with as many martyrs as it does those that are the most peaceful and beneficent.

But *secondly*, we find for our consolation, that it will likewise support systems of equal liberty and national happiness. In the United States of America, the science of liberty is universally understood, felt, and practised, as much by the simple as the wise, the weak as the strong. Their deep-rooted and inveterate habit of thinking is, that *all men are equal in their rights*, that *it is impossible to make them otherwise*; and this being their undisturbed belief, they have no conception how any man in his senses can entertain any other. This point once settled, every thing is settled. Many operations, which in Europe have been considered as incredible tales or dangerous experiments, are but the infallible consequences of this great principle. The first of these operations is *the business of election*, which, with that people, is carried on with as much gravity as their daily labour. There is no jealousy on the occasion, nothing lucrative in office; any man in society may attain to any place in the government, and may exercise its functions. They believe that there is nothing more difficult in the management of the affairs of a nation, than the affairs of a family; that it only requires more hands. They believe that it is the juggle of keeping up impositions to blind the eyes of the vulgar, that constitutes the intricacy of state. Banish the mysticism of inequality, and you banish almost all the evils attendant on human nature.

The people, being habituated to the election of all kinds of officers, the *magnitude* of the office makes no difficulty in the case. The president of the United States, who has more power while in office than some of the kings of Europe, is chosen with as little commotion as a churchwarden. There is a public service to be performed, and the people say who shall do it. The servant feels honoured with the confidence reposed in him, and generally expresses his gratitude by a faithful performance.

Another of these operations is making every citizen a soldier, and every soldier a citizen; not only *permitting* every man to arm, but *obliging* him to arm. This fact, told in Europe, previous to the French revolution, would have gained little credit; or at least it would have been regarded as a mark of an uncivilized people, extremely dangerous to a well ordered society. Men who build systems on an inversion of nature, are obliged to invert every thing that is to make part of that system. It is *because the people are civilized, that they are with safety armed.* It is an effect of their conscious dignity, as citizens enjoying equal rights, that they wish not to invade the rights of others. The danger (where there is any) from armed citizens, is only to the *government*, not to the *society*; and as long as they have nothing to revenge in the government (which they cannot have while it is in their own hands) there are many advantages in their being accustomed to the use of arms, and no possible disadvantage.

Power, habitually in the hands of a whole community, loses all the ordinary associated ideas of power. The exercise of power is a relative term; it supposes an opposition,—something to operate upon. We perceive no exertion of power in the motion of the planetary system, but a very strong one in the movement of a whirlwind, it is because we see obstructions to the latter, but none to the former. Where the government is *not* in the hands of the people, there you find opposition, you perceive two contending interests, and get an idea of the exercise of power; and whether this power be in the hands of the government or of the people, or whether it change from side to side, it is always to be dreaded. But the word *people*, in America, has a different meaning from what it has in Europe. It there means the whole community, and comprehends every human creature; here it means something else, more difficult to define.

Another consequence of the habitual idea of equality, is the *facility of changing the structure of their government*, whenever, and as often as the society shall think there is any thing in it to amend. As Mr. Burke has written no " reflections on the " revolution" in America, the people there have never yet been told that they have no *right* " to " frame a government for themselves;" they have therefore done much in this business, without ever affixing to it the idea of " sacrilege" or " usurpation," or any other term of rant, to be found in that gentleman's vocabulary.

Within a few years the fifteen states have not only framed each its own state constitution, and two successive federal constitutions; but since the settlement of the present general government in the year 1789, three of the states, Pennsylvania, South-Carolina, and Georgia, have totally new modelled their own. And all this is done without the least confusion; the operation being scarcely known beyond the limits of the state where it is performed. Thus they are in the habit of " choos-

"ing their own governors," of "cashiering them for misconduct," of "framing a government for themselves," and all those abominable things, the mere naming of which, in Mr. Burke's opinion, has polluted the pulpit in the Old Jewry.*

But it is said, These things will do very well for America, where the people are less numerous, less indigent, and better instructed; but they will not apply to Europe. This objection deserves a reply, not because it is solid, but because it is fashionable. It may be answered, that some parts of Spain, much of Poland, and almost the whole of Russia, are less peopled than the settled country in the United States; that poverty and ignorance are *effects* of slavery rather than its *causes*; but the best answer to be given, is the example of France. To the event of that revolution I will trust the argument. Let the people have time to become thoroughly and soberly grounded in the doctrine of *equality*, and there is no danger of oppression either from government or from anarchy. Very little instruction is necessary to teach a man his rights; and there is no person of common intellects, in the most ignorant corner of Europe, but receives lessons enough, if they were of the proper kind. For writing and reading are not indispensable to the object; it is *thinking* right which makes them act right. Every child is taught to repeat about fifty Latin prayers, which set up the Pope, the Bishop, and the King, as the trinity of his adoration; he is taught that *the powers that*

---

* See Dr. Price's Sermon preached in the Old Jewry before the Revolutionary Society, and Mr. Burke's abusive strictures on the above expressions used by the Doctor.

be, are ordained of God, and therefore the foldier quartered in the parifh has a right to cut his throat. Half this inftruction, upon oppofite principles, would go a great way; in that cafe nature would be affifted, while here fhe is counteracted. Engrave it on the heart of a man, *that all men are equal in rights,* and that the *government is their own,* and then perfuade him to fell his crucifix and buy a mufquet,—and you have made him a good citizen.

Another confequence of a fettled belief in the equality of rights is, that under this belief *there is no danger from anarchy.* This word has likewife acquired a different meaning in America from what we read of it in books. In Europe it means confufion, attended with mobs and carnage, where the innocent perifh with the guilty. But it is very different where a country is *ufed* to a reprefentative government, though it fhould have an interval of no government at all. Where the people at large feel and know that they *can do every thing* by themfelves perfonally, they really *do nothing* by themfelves perfonally. In the heat of the American revolution, when the people in fome ftates were for a long time without the leaft fhadow of law or government, they always acted by committees and reprefentation. This they muft call anarchy, for they know no other.

Thefe are materials for the formation of governments, which need not be dreaded, though disjointed and laid afunder to make fome repairs. They are deep-rooted habits of thinking, which almoft change the moral nature of man; they are principles as much unknown to the ancient republics as to the modern monarchies of Europe.

We muſt not therefore rely upon ſyſtems drawn from the experimental reaſonings of Ariſtotle, when we find them contradicted by what we feel to be the eternal truth of nature, and ſee them brought to the teſt of our own experience. Ariſtotle was certainly a great politician; and Claudius Ptolemy was a great geographer; but the latter has ſaid not a word of America, the largeſt quarter of the globe; nor the former, of repreſentative republics, the reſource of afflicted humanity.

Since I have brought theſe two great luminaries of ſcience ſo near together, I will keep them in company a moment longer, to ſhow the ſtrange partiality that we may retain for one ſuperſtition after having laid aſide another, though they are built on ſimilar foundations. Ptolemy wrote a ſyſtem of Aſtronomy; in which he taught among other things, that the earth was the centre of the univerſe, and that the heavenly bodies moved round it. This ſyſtem is now taught (to the excluſion by an anathema of all others) in Turkey, Arabia, Perſia, Paleſtine, Egypt, and where ever the doctrines of Mahomet are taught; while at the ſame time, and with the ſame reverence, the politics of Ariſtotle are taught at the univerſity of Oxford. The ground which ſupports the one is, that the ſun ſtopt its courſe at the command of Joſhua, which it could not have done, had it not been in motion; and the other, that *the powers that be, are ordained of God.* Mention to a Muſſelman the Copernican ſyſtem, and you might as well ſpeak to Mr. Burke about the rights of man; they both call you an atheiſt.—But I will proceed with the feudal ſyſtem.

The next quality of a feudal tenure is what is

commonly called on the Continent the right of *substitution*, in the English law, known by the name of *entail*. Of all the methods that have yet been discovered to prevent men from enjoying the advantages that nature has laid before them, this is the most extraordinary, and in many respects the most effectual. There have been superstitions entertained by many nations relative to property in lands; rendering them more difficult of alienation than any other possessions, and consequently less productive. Such were the *jus retractus* of the Romans, the family-right of redemption, and the absolute restoration once in fifty years among the Jews, similar regulations among the ancient Egyptians, and laws to the same purpose under the government of the Incas in Peru.

These were all calculated to perpetuate family distinctions, and to temper the minds of men to an aristocratical subordination. But none of them were attended with the barbarous exclusion of younger brothers; nor had they the presumption to put it into the power of a dying man, who could not regulate the disposition of his sandals for one hour after his death, to say to all mankind thenceforward to the end of time, " Touch not my inheritance! I will that this tract of country, on which I have taken my pleasure, shall remain to the wild beasts and to the fowls of heaven; that one man only of each generation shall exist upon it; that all the rest, even of my own posterity, shall be driven out hence, as soon as born; and that the inheritor himself shall not increase his enjoyments by alienating a part to ameliorate the rest."

There might have been individual madmen, in all ages, capable of *expressing* a desire of this kind; but for whole nations, for many centuries together, to agree to *reverence* and *execute* such hostile testaments as these, comported not with the wisdom of the ancients; it is a suicide of society, reserved for the days of chivalry,—to support the governments of modern Europe.

Sir Edward Coke should have spared his panegyric on the parliament of Edward the first, as the fathers of the laws of entailments. He quotes with singular pleasure the words of Sir William Herle, who informs us, that " King " Edward I. was the wisest King that ever was, " and they were sage men, who made this statute." Whatever wisdom there is in the statute, is of an elder growth. It is a plant of genuine feudal extraction, brought into England by the Normans or Saxons, or some other conquerors; and though settled as common law, it began to be disregarded and despised by the judicial tribunals, as a sense of good policy prevailed. But the progress of liberality was arrested by that parliament, and the law of entailments passed into the statute of Westminster the second.

This was considered as law in America, previous to the revolution. But that epoch of light and liberty has freed one quarter of the world from this miserable appendage of Gothicism; and France has now begun to break the shackles from another quarter, where they were more strongly rivetted. The simple destruction of these two laws, of *entailment* and *primogeniture*, if you add to it the *freedom of the press*, will ensure the continuance of liberty in any country where it is once established.

Other territorial rights, peculiar to the feudal tenure, are lefs general in their operation, though almoft infinite in their number and variety. Not a current of water, nor a mill-feat, nor a fifh-pond, nor a foreft, nor the dividing line of a village or a farm, but gives name to and fupports fome feigneurial impofition; befides the number-lefs claims predicated upon all the poffible actions and ceremonies that pafs, or are fuppofed to pafs, between the great Lord and the little Lord, and between the little Lord and the lefs Lord, and between him and the Lord knows whom. The National Affembly, in one decree, fuppreffed about one hundred and fifty of thefe taxes by name, befides a general fweeping claufe in the act, which perhaps deftroyed as many more, the names of which no man could report.

One general character will apply to all thefe impofitions: they are a difcouragement to agriculture, an embarraffment to commerce,—they humiliate one part of the community, fwell the pride of the other, and are a real pecuniary difadvantage to both.

But it is time to pay our refpects to thofe feudal claims that we call *perfonal*. The firft of thefe is *allegiance*,—in its genuine Gothic fenfe, called *perpetual allegiance*. It is difficult to exprefs a fuitable contempt for this idea, without defcending to language below the dignity of philofophy. On the firft inveftiture of a fief, the fuperior Lord (fuppofing he had any right to it himfelf) has doubtlefs the power of granting it on whatever terms the vaffal will agree to. It is an even bargain between the parties; and an unchangeable allegiance during the lives of thefe parties may be a condition of it. But for a man to be *born* to such an allegiance to another man, is to have an evil ftar indeed ; it is to be born to unchangeable flavery.

A nobleman of Venice, at this moment, cannot ftep his foot over the limits of the republic without leave from the Senate, on pain of forfeiting his eftate. Similar laws prevail in all feudal countries, where revolutions have not yet prevailed. They flee before the fearching eye of liberty, and will foon flee from Europe.

Hitherto we have treated of claims, whether perfonal or territorial, that are confined to the eldeft fons of families; but there is one genuine feudal claim, which " fpreads undivided" to all the children, runs in all collateral directions, and extends to every drop of noble blood, wherever found, however mixt or adulterated,—it is the claim of *idlenefs*. In general it is fuppofed, that all indigent noble children are to be provided for by the government. But alas ! the fwarm is too great to be eafily hived. Though the army, the navy, and the church, with all their poffible multiplication of places, are occupied only by them, yet their number becomes fo confiderable, that many remain out of employment and deftitute of the means of fupport.

In contemplating the peculiar deftiny of this defcription of men, we cannot but feel a mixture of emotions, in which compaffion gets the better of contempt. In addition to the misfortunes incident to other claffes of fociety, their noble birth has entailed upon them a fingular curfe ; it has interdicted them every kind of bufinefs or occupation, even for procuring the neceffaries of life. Other men may be found who have been deprived of their juft inheritance by the barbarous laws of descent, who may have been neglected in youth and not educated to business, or who by aversion to industry are rendered incapable of any useful employment ; but none but the offspring of a noble family can experience the superadded fatality of being told, that to put his hand to the plough, or his foot into a counting-house, would disgrace an illustrious line of ancestors, and wither a tree of genealogy, which takes its root in a groom of some fortunate robber, who perhaps was an archer of Charlemagne.

Every capital in Europe, if you except London, throngs with this miserable class of noblesse, who are really and literally tormented between their pride and their poverty. Indeed, such is the preposterous tyranny of custom, that those who are rich, and take the lead in society, have the cruelty to make *idleness* a *criterion of noblesse*. A proof of inoccupation is a ticket of admission into their houses, and an indispensible badge of welcome to their parties.

But in France their hands are at last untied ; the charm is broken, and the feudal system, with all its infamous idolatries, has fallen to the ground. Honour is restored to the heart of man, instead of being suspended from his button-hole ; and useful industry gives a title to respect. The men who were formerly Dukes and Marquisses, are now exalted to farmers, manufacturers and merchants ; the rising generation among all classes of people are forming their maxims on a just estimate of things ; and society is extracting the poisoned dagger which conquest had planted in her vitals.

CHAP. II.

THE CHURCH.

BUT it would have been impossible for the feudal system, with all its powers of inversion, to have held human nature so long debased, without the aid of an agent more powerful than an arm of flesh, and without assailing the mind with other weapons than those which are furnished from its temporal concerns. Mankind are by nature religious; the governors of nations, or those persons, who contrive to live upon the labours of their fellow-creatures must necessarily be few, in comparison to those who bear the burthens of the whole; their object therefore is to dupe the community at large, to conceal the strength of the many, and magnify that of the few. An open arrangement of forces, whether physical or moral, must be artfully avoided; for men, however ignorant, are as naturally disposed to calculation, as they are to religion; they perceive as readily that an hundred soldiers can destroy the captain they have made, as that thunder and lightning can destroy a man. Recourse must therefore be had to mysteries and invisibilities; an engine must be forged out of the *religion* of human nature, and erected on its *credulity*, to play upon and extinguish the light of reason, which was placed in the mind as a caution to the one, and a kind companion to the other.

This engine, in all ages of the world, has been the Church*. It has varied in its appellation, at different periods and in different countries, according to the circumstances of nations; but has never changed its character; and it is difficult to say, under which of its names it has done the most mischief, and exterminated the greatest number of the human race. Were it not for the danger of being misled by the want of information, we should readily determine, that under the assumption of christianity it has committed greater ravages than under any other of its dreadful denominations.

But we must not be hasty in deciding this question; as, during the last fifteen centuries, in which we are able to trace with compassionate

---

* From that association of ideas, which usually connects the *church* with *religion*, I may run the risque of being misunderstood by some readers, unless I advertise them, that I consider no connection as existing between these two subjects; and that where I speak of church *indefinitely*, I mean the government of a state, assuming the name of God, to govern by divine authority; or in other words, *darkening the consciences of men, in order to oppress them*.

In the United States of America, there is strictly speaking, no such thing as a Church; and yet in no country are the people more religious. All sorts of religious opinions are entertained there, and yet no *heresy* among them all; all modes of worship are practised, and yet there is no *schism*; men frequently change their creed and their worship, and yet there is no *apostacy*; they have ministers of religion, but no *priests*. In short, religion is there a *personal* and not a *corporate* concern.

indignation the frenzy of our anceſtors, and contemplate the wandering demon of carnage, conducted by the *croſs* of the Weſt, the lights of hiſtory fail us with regard to the reſt of the world,—we cannot travel with the *creſcent* of the Eaſt, in its unmeaſurable devaſtations from the Euxine to the Ganges; nor tell by what other incantations mankind have been inflamed with the luſt of ſlaughter, from thence to the north of Siberia or to the ſouth of Africa.

Could we form an eſtimate of the lives loſt in the wars and perſecutions of the Chriſtian Church alone, we ſhould find it nearly equal to the number of ſouls now exiſting in Europe. But it is perhaps a mercy to mankind, that we are not able to calculate, with any accuracy, even this portion of human calamities. When Conſtantine ordered that the *hierarchy* ſhould aſſume the name of Chriſt, we are not to conſider him as forming a new weapon of deſtruction; he only changed a name, which had grown into diſrepute, and would ſerve the purpoſe no longer, for one that was gaining an extenſive reputation; it being built on a faith that was likely to meet the aſſent of a conſiderable portion of mankind. The coldhearted* cruelty of that monarch's character, and

---

* The report of Zoſimus, reſpecting the motives which induced Conſtantine to embrace Chriſtianity, has not been generally credited, though the circumſtance is probable in itſelf, and the author is conſidered in other reſpects an hiſtorian of undoubted veracity; having written the hiſtory of all the Emperors, down to his own time, which was the beginning of the fifth century. His account is, that Conſtantine could not be admitted into the *old eſtabliſhed church of Ceres* at Eleuſis, on account of the

his embracing the new doctrines with a temper hardened in the slaughter of his relations, were omens unfavourable to the future complexion of the hierarchy; though he had thus coupled it with a name that had hitherto been remarkable for its meeknefs and humlity. This tranfaction has therefore given colour to a fcene of enormities, which may be regarded as nothing more than the genuine offspring of the *alliance of church and ftate*.

This fatal deviation from the principles of the firft founder of the faith, who declared that his

---

enormity of his crimes, in the murder of many of his own family. But on his demanding admiffion, the hierophant cried out with horror, " Be gone, thou parricide, whom the Gods will not pardon." The Chriftian doctors feized this occafion to adminifter to the wants of the Emperor, on condition that he would adminifter to theirs; the bargain was advantageous on both fides; he declared himfelf a Chriftian, and took the church under his protection, and they pronounced his pardon.

The fawning fervility of the new church and the blunt feverity of the old, on that occafion, mark the precife character of the ecclefiaftical policy of all ages; and both examples have been followed in numerous inftances. The manœuvres of the Pope on the converfion of Clovis, on fanctioning the ufurpation of Pepin, and on the coronation of Charlemagne, are among the imitations of the former; the ridiculous chaftifment of Henry the fecond of England, and the numerous anathemas fulminated againft whole kingdoms, are proofs of the latter. We may likewife remark, that the conduct of Conftantine has been copied in all its effential points by Henry the eighth.

D

kingdom was not of this world, has deluged Europe in blood for a long fucceffion of ages, and carried occafional ravages into all the other quarters of the globe. The pretence of extirpating the idolatries of ancient eftablifhments, and the innumerable herefies of the new, has been the never-failing argument of princes as well as pontiffs, from the wars of Conftantine, down to the pitiful, ftillborn rebellion of Calonne and the Count d'Artois*.

From the time of the converfion of Clovis, through all the Merovingian race, France and Germany groaned under the fury of ecclefiaftical monfters, hunting down the Druids, overturning the temples of the Roman Polytheifts, and drenching the plains with the blood of Arians†. The

---

* See *Expofition des motifs* des Princes, freres du Roi,—*A declaration of the motives of the King's brothers, for raifing an army to chaftife the French nation,* publifhed at Coblentz in January 1792. The firft article mentioned in reciting the objects of this expedition is, "*pour retablir le refpect du à la religion Catholique, et à fes miniftres.*"

What Chriftian emperor ever had a better right to eftablifh religion than the count d'Artois? His name, to be fure, is a burlefque upon every poffible virtue, and a fatire upon human nature. But why fhould this hinder him from being an excellent advocate for *la Religion Catholique ?*

† Exterminating heretics was a principal object of national ambition. Childebert I. who died in 558, has the following epitaph on his tomb in the Abbey of *St. Germaine des, Prés,* at Paris.

Le fang des Arriens dont rougirent les plaines,
De montagnes de corps leur pays tout couvert,
Et leurs chefs mis à mort, font des preuves certaines
De ce que les François firent fous Childebert.

wars of Charlemagne againſt the Saxons, the Huns, the Lombards and the Moors, which deſolated Europe for forty years, had for their principal object the extending and purifying of the Chriſtian faith. The cruſades, which drained Europe of its young men at eight ſucceſſive periods, muſt have ſacrificed, including Aſiatics and Africans, at leaſt four millions of lives. The wars of the Guelfs, and Gibelins, or Pope and Anti-pope, ravaged Italy, and involved half Europe in factions for two centuries together. The expulſion of the Moors from Spain depopulated that kingdom, by a war of ſeven hundred years, and eſtabliſhed the inquiſition to interdict the reſurrection of ſociety; while millions of the natives of South America have been deſtroyed by attempting to convert them.

In this enumeration, we have taken no notice of that train of calamities, which attended the reconverſion of the eaſtern empire, and attaching it to the faith of Mahomet; nor of the various havoc, which followed the diſmemberment of the catholic church, by that fortunate ſchiſm, which, by ſome, is denominated the Lutheran hereſy, and by others, the Proteſtant reformation.

But theſe, it will be ſaid, are only general traits of uncivilized character, which we all contemplate with equal horror, and which, among enlightened nations, there can be no danger of ſeeing renewed. It is true, that, in ſeveral countries, the glooms of intolerance ſeem to be pierced by the rays of philoſophy; and we may ſoon expect to ſee Europe univerſally diſclaiming the right of one man to interfere in the religion of another. We may remark, however, *firſt*, that this is far from being the case at this moment; and *secondly*, that it is a blessing which never can originate from any state-establishment of religion. For proofs of the former, we need not penetrate into Spain or Italy, nor recal the history of the late fanatical management of the war in Brabant,—but look to the two most enlightened countries in Europe; see the riots at Birmingham, and the conduct of the refractory priests in France.

With regard to the second remark,—we may as well own the truth at first as at last, and have sense this year as the next: *The existence of any kind of liberty is incompatible with the existence of any kind of church.* By *liberty*, I mean the enjoyment of equal rights, and by *church* I mean any mode of worship declared to be national, or declared to have any preference in the eye of the law.

To render this truth a little more familiar to the mind of any reader who shall find himself startled with it, we will take a view of the church in a different light from what we have yet considered it. We have hitherto noticed only its most striking characteristics, in which it appears like a giant, stalking over society, and wielding the sword of slaughter; but it likewise performs the office of silent disease, and of unperceived decay; where we may contemplate it as a canker, corroding the vitals of the moral world, and debasing all that is noble in man.

If I mention some traits which are rather peculiar to the Roman Catholic constitution, it is because that is the predominant church in those parts of Europe, where revolutions are soonest expected; and not because it is any worse, or any better, than any other that ever has or ever can exist. I hinted before, and it may not be amiss to repeat, that the hierarchy is every where the same, so far as the circumstances of society will permit; for it borrows and lends, and interchanges its features, in some measure, with the age and nation, with which it has to deal, without ever losing sight of its object. It is every where the same engine of state; and whether it be guided by a Lama or a Mufti, by a Pontifex or a Pope, by a Bramin, a Bishop or a Druid, it is entitled to an equal share of respect.

The first great object of the priest is to establish a belief in the minds of the people, that *he himself is possessed of supernatural powers*; and the church at all times has made its way in the world, in proportion as the priest has succeeded in this particular. This is the foundation of every thing,—the life and soul of all that is subversive and unaccountable in human affairs; it is introducing a new element into society; it is the rudder under the water, steering the ship almost directly contrary to the wind that gives it motion.

A belief in the supernatural powers of the priest, has been inspired by means, which, in different nations, have been known by different names,—such as astrologies auguries, oracles, or incantations. This article once established, its continuation is not a difficult task. For, as the church acquires wealth, it furnishes itself with the necessary apparatus, and the trade is carried on to advantage. The imposition too becomes more easy from the authority of precedent, by which the inquisitive faculties of the mind are benumbed; men believe by prescription, and orthodoxy is heriditary.

In this manner every nation of antiquity received the poison in its infancy, and was rendered incapable of acquiring a vigorous manhood, of speaking a national will, or of acting with that dignity and generosity, which are natural to man in society. The moment that Romulus consulted the oracles for the building of his city, that moment he interdicted its future citizens the enjoyment of liberty among themselves, as well as all ideas of justice towards their neighbours. Men never act their own opinions, in company with those who can give them the opinions of Gods; and as long as governors have an established mode of consulting the auspices, there is no necessity to establish any mode of consulting the people. *Nihil publice sine auspiciis nec domi nec militiæ gerebatur**, was the Roman *Magna Charta*; and it stood in place of a declaration of the rights of man. There is something extremely imposing in a maxim of this kind. Nothing is more pious, peaceful, and moderate in appearance; and nothing more savage and abominable in its operation. But it is a genuine *church-maxim*, and, as such, deserves a further consideration.

One obvious tendency of this maxim is, like the feudal rights, to inculcate radical ideas of inequalities among men; and it does this in a much greater degree. The feudal distance between man and man, is perceptible and definite; but the moment you give one member of society a familiar intercourse with God, you launch him into the region of infinities and invisibilities; you unfit him, and his brethren, to live together, on any terms but those of stupid reverence and of insolent abuse.

---

* *Cicero de divinatione.* Lib. I.

Another tendency is to make men cruel and favage in a preternatural degree. When a perfon believes that he is doing the immediate work of God, he divefts himfelf of the feelings of a man. And an ambitious general, who wifhes to extirpate or to plunder a neighbouring nation, has only to order the prieft to do his duty, and fet the people at work by an oracle; they then know no other bounds to their frenzy than the will of their leader, pronounced by the prieft; whofe voice to them is the voice of God. In this cafe the leaft attention to mercy or juftice would be abhorred as a difobedience to the divine command. This circumftance alone, is fufficient to account for two-thirds of the cruelty of all wars,—perhaps in a great meafure for their exiftence,—and has given rife to an opinion, that nations are cruel in proportion as they are religious. But the obfervation ought to ftand thus, *That nations are cruel in proportion as they are guided by priefts;* than which there is no axiom more undeniably without exception.

Another tendency of governing men by oracles, is to make them factious and turbulent in the ufe of liberty, when they feel themfelves in poffeffion of it. In all ancient democracies, the great body of the people enjoyed no liberty at all; and thofe who were called freemen, exercifed it only by ftarts, for the purpofe of *revenging* injuries,—not in a regular conftituted mode of *preventing* them: the body politic ufed liberty as a medicine, and not as daily bread. Hence it has happened, that the hiftories of ancient democracies, and of modern infurrections, are quoted upon us, to the infult of common fenfe, to prove that a whole people is not capable of governing itfelf. The whole of the reasoning on this subject, from the profound disquisitions of Aristotle, down to the puny whinings of Dr. Tatham,* are founded on a direct inversion of historical fact. It is the *want* of liberty, not the *enjoyment* of it, which has occasioned all the factions in society from the beginning of time, and will do so to the end; it is because the people are *not* habitually free from civil and ecclesiastical tyrants, that they are disposed to exercise tyranny themselves. Habitual freedom produces effects directly the reverse in every particular. For a proof of this, look into America, or, if that be too much trouble, look into human nature, with the eyes of common sense.

When the Christian religion was perverted, and pressed into the service of government, under the name of the *christian church*, it became necessary that its priests should set up for supernatural powers, and invest themselves in the same cloak of infallibility, of which they had stripped their predecessors, the druids and the augurs. This they effected by miracles; for which they gained so great a reputation, that they were canonized after death, and have furnished modern Europe with a much greater catalogue of saints, than could be found in any breviary of the ancients. The polytheism of the catholic church, is more splendid for the number of its divinities, than that of the

---

* It may be necessary to inform the reader, that Dr. Tatham of Oxford has written a book in defence of royalty and Mr. Burke. As this is the last as well as the weakest thing against liberty that I have met with, it is mentioned in the text for the sake of widening the grasp of my assertion, as well as for heightening the contrast among all possible authors.

Eleusinian; and they are not inferior in point of attributes. The Denis of France is at least equal to the Jupiter of Greece or the Apis of Egypt. As to supernatural powers, the case is precisely the same in both; and the portions of infallibility are dealt out from the pope to the subordinate priests, according to their rank, in such a manner as to complete the harmony of the system.

Cicero has written with as much judgment and erudition on the "corruptions" of the old Roman Church, as Dr. Priestly has on those of the new. But the difficulty is not that the *church* is corrupted by men; it is, that *men* are corrupted by the church; for the very existence of a church, as I have before defined it, is founded on a lie; it sets out with the blasphemy of giving to one class of men the attributes of God; and the practising of these sorceries by that class, and the believing of them by another, corrupt and vitiate the whole.

One of the most admirable contrivances of the Christian church, is the business of *confessions*. It requires great reflection to give us an idea of the effects wrought on society by this part of the machinary. It is a solemn recognition of the supernatural powers of the priest, repeated every day in the year, by every human creature above the age of twelve years. Nothing is more natural than for men to judge of every thing around them, and even of themselves, by *comparison*; and in this case, what opinion are the laity to form of their own dignity? When a poor, ignorant, vitious mortal is set up for the *God*, what must be the *man*? I cannot conceive of any person going seriously to a confessional and believing in the equality of rights, or possessing one moral sentiment, that is worthy of a rational being*.

Another contrivance of the same sort, and little inferior in efficacy, is the law of *celibacy*, imposed on the priesthood, both male and female, in almost all church-establishments, that have hitherto existed. The priest is in the first place armed with the weapons of moral destruction, by which he is made the professional enemy of his fellow men ; and then, for fear he should neglect to use those weapons,—for fear he should contract the feelings and friendships of rational beings, by mingling with society and becoming one of its members,—for fear his impositions should be discovered by the intimacy of family connexions,—he is interdicted the most cordial endearments of life ; he is severed from the sympathies of his fellow-creatures, and yet compelled to be with them ; his affections are held in the *mortmain* of perpetual inactivity ; and, like the

---

* The following tariff of the prices of absolution will show what ideas these holy fathers have inculcated relative to the proportional degree of moral turpitude in different crimes. It was reprinted at Rome no longer ago than the last century.

	£.	s.	d.
For a layman who shall strike a priest without effusion of blood		5	0
For one layman who shall kill another	0	3	3
For murdering a father, mother, wife, or sister	0	5	0
For eating meat in Lent	0	5	5
For him who lies with his mother or sister	0	3	8
For marrying on those days when the church forbids matrimony	2	0	0
For the absolution of all crimes	2	16	0

dead men of Mezentius, he is lafhed to fociety for tyranny and contamination.

The whole of this management, in felecting, preparing, and organizing the members of the ecclefiaftical body, is purfued with the fame uniform, cold-blooded hoftility, againft the focial harmonies of life. The fubjects are taken from the younger fons of noble families, who, from their birth, are confidered as a nuifance to the houfe, and an outcaft from parental attachment. They are then cut off from all opportunities of forming fraternal affections, and educated in a cloifter; till they enter upon their public functions, as difconnected from the feelings of the community, as it is defigned they fhall ever remain from its interefts.

I will not mention the corruption of morals, which muft refult from the combined caufes of the ardent paffions of conftrained celibacy, and the fecret interviews of the prieft with the women of his charge, for the purpofe of confeffions : I will draw no arguments from the diffenfions fown in families ; the jealoufies and confequent aberrations of both hufband and wife, occafioned by an intriguing ftranger being in the fecrets of both ; the difcouragements laid upon matrimony by a general dread of thefe confequences, in the minds of men of reflection,—effects which are remarkable in all catholic countries ; but I will conclude this article by obferving the direct influence that ecclefiaftical celibacy alone, has had on the population of Europe.

This policy of the church muft have produced, at leaft, as great an effect, in thining fociety, as the whole of her wars and perfecutions. In catholic Europe, there muft be near a million of ecclefiaftics.* This proportion of mankind continuing deducted from the agents of population, for fifteen centuries, muft have precluded the exiftence of more than one hundred millions of the human fpecies.

Should the reader be difpofed, on this remark, to liften to the reply, which is fometimes made, that Europe is fufficiently populous; I beg he would fufpend his decifion, till he fhall fee what may be faid, in the courfe of this work, on protected induftry; and until he fhall well confider the effects of liberty on the means of fubfiftence. That reply is certainly one of the axioms of tyranny, and is of kin to the famous wifh of Caligula, that the whole Roman people had but one neck.

The French have gone as far in the deftruction of the hierarchy as could have been expected, confidering the habits of the people, and the prefent circumftances of Europe. The church in that country was like royalty,—the prejudices in its favour were too ftrong to be vanquifhed all at once. The moft that could be done, was to tear the bandage from the eyes of mankind, break the

---

* Boulanger, (vol. 7. page 294) computes the ecclefiaftics in Spain alone, at half a million. I am inclined to think this account exaggerated. If it were exact, and the other catholic countries of Europe poffeffed them in as great numbers, in proportion to their population, there muft be at leaft three millions and a half. It is true, that in France, the Auftrian Netherlands, Poland, Sweden, Ireland, and fome parts of Germany, the proportion is not fo great; but in Italy, Portugal, and in parts of Germany, it is full equal to what it is in Spain.

charm of inequality, demolifh ranks and infalli-
billities, and teach the people that mitres and
crowns did not confer fupernatural powers. As
long as public teachers are chofen by the people,
are falaried and removeable by the people, are
born and married among the people, have families to be educated and protected from oppreffion
and from vice,—as long as they have all the common fympathies of fociety, to bind them to the
public intereft, there is very little danger of their
becoming tyrants by force ; and the liberty of the
prefs will prevent their being fo by craft.

In the United States of America there is no
church ; and this is one of the principal circumftances which diftinguifh that government from
all others, that ever exifted ; it enfures the unem-
barraffed exercife of religion, the continuation of
public inftruction, in the fcience of liberty and
happinefs, and promifes a long duration to a reprefentative government.

CHAP. III.

THE MILITARY SYSTEM.

Il importoit au maintien de l'autorité du roi, d'entre-
tenir la guerre.
HISTOIRE DE CHARLEMAGNE.

THE church, in all modern Europe, may be considered as a kind of standing army; as the members of that community have been, in every nation, the surest supporters of arbitrary power, both for internal oppression and for external violence. But this not being sufficient of itself, an additional instrument, to be known by the name of the *military system*, became necessary; and it seems to have been expedient to call up another element of human nature, out of which this new instrument might be created and maintained. The church was in possession of the strongest ground that could be taken in the human mind, the *principle of religion*; a principle dealing with things invisible; and consequently the most capable of being itself perverted, and then of perverting the whole mind, and subjecting it to any unreasonable pursuit.

Next to that of religion, and similar to it in most of its characteristics, is the principle of *honour*. Honour, like religion, is an original, indelible sentiment of the mind, an indispensable ingredient in our nature. But its object is incapable of precise definition; and consequently, though given us in aid of the more definable feelings of morality, it is capable of total perversion, of losing sight of its own original nature, and still retaining its name; of pursuing the destruction of moral sentiments, instead of being their ornament; of debasing, instead of supporting, the dignity of man.

This camelion principle was, therefore, a proper element of imposition, and was destined to make an immense figure in the world, as the foundation and support of the military system of all unequal governments. We must look pretty far into human nature, before we shall discover the cause, why killing men in battle should be deemed, *in itself*, an honourable employment. A hangman is universally despised; he exercises an office, which not only the feelings, but the policy of all nations, have agreed to regard as infamous. What is it that should make the difference of these two occupations, in favour of the former? Surely it is not because the victims in the former case are *innocent*, and the latter *guilty*. To assert this, would be a greater libel upon human society, than I can bring myself to utter; it would make the tyranny of opinion the most *detestable*, as well as the most sovereign of all possible tyrannies. But what can it be? It is not, what is sometimes alleged, that *courage* is the foundation of the business; that fighting is honourable because it is dangerous; there is often as much courage displayed in highway-robbery, as in the warmest conflict of armies; and yet it does no honour to the party; a Robin Hood is as dishonourable a character as a Jack Ketch. It is not because there is any idea of *justice* or *honesty* in the case; for, to say the best that can be said of war, it is impossible that more than one side can be just or honest; and yet both sides of every contest are equally the road to fame; where a diftinguifhed killer of men, is fure to gain immortal honour. It is not *patriotifm*, even in that fenfe of the word which deviates the moft from general philanthropy; for a total ftranger to both parties in a war, may enter into it on either fide, as a volunteer, perform more than a vulgar fhare of the flaughter, and be for ever applauded, even by his enemies. Finally, it is not from any *pecuniary advantages* that are ordinarily attached to the profeffion of arms; for foldiers are generally poor, though part of their bufinefs be to plunder.

Indeed, I can fee but one reafon in nature, why the principal of honour fhould be felected from all human incentives, and relied on for the fupport of the military fyftem; it is becaufe it was *convenient for the governing power*; that power being in the hands of a fmall part of the community, whofe bufinefs was to fupport it by impofition. No principle of a permanent nature, whofe object is unequivocal, and whofe flighteft deviations are perceptible, would have anfwered the purpofe. Juftice, for inftance, is a principle of common ufe, of which every man can difcern the application. Should the Prince fay it was *juft*, to commence an unprovoked war with his weak neighbours, and plunder their country, the falfhood would be too glaring; all men would judge for themfelves, and give him the lie; and no man would follow his ftandard, unlefs bribed by his avarice. But honour is of another nature; it is what we all can feel, but no one can define; it is therefore whatever the Prince may choofe to name it: and fo powerful is its operation, that all the ufeful fentiments of life lofe their effect: morality is not only banifhed from political cabinets, but generally and profeſſionally from the boſoms of men, who purſue honour, in the profeſſion of arms.

It is common for a King, who wiſhes to make a thing faſhionable, to practiſe it himſelf; and in this he is ſure of general imitation and ſucceſs. As this device is extremely natural, and as the exiſtence of wars is abſolutely neceſſary to the exiſtence of Kings; to give a faſhion to the trade muſt have been a conſiderable motive to the ancient Kings, for expoſing themſelves ſo much as they uſually did in battle. They ſaid, *Let human ſlaughter be honourable*, and honourable it was.

Hence it is, that warriors have been termed heroes; and the eulogy of heroes has been the conſtant buſineſs of hiſtorians and poets, from the days of Nimrod down to the preſent century. Homer, for his aſtoniſhing variety, animation, and ſublimity, has not a warmer admirer than myſelf; he has been for three thouſand years, like a reigning ſovereign, applauded as a matter of courſe, whether from love or fear; for no man with ſafety to his own character can refuſe to join the chorus of his praiſe. I never can expreſs (and his other admirers have not done it for me) the pleaſure I receive from his poems; but in a view of philantrophy, I conſider his exiſtence as having been a ſerious misfortune to the human race. He has given to military life, a charm, which few men can reſiſt, a ſplendour which envelopes the ſcenes of carnage in a cloud of glory, which dazzles the eyes of every beholder, ſteals from us our natural ſenſibilities, in exchange for the artificial, debaſes men to brutes, under the pretext of exalting them to Gods, and obliterates, with the ſame irreſiſtable ſtroke, the moral duties of life and the true policy of nations. Alexander* is not the only human monster that has been formed after the model of Achilles; nor Persia and Egypt the only countries depopulated for no other reason than the desire of rivalling predecessors in military fame.

Another device of Princes, to render honourable the profession of arms, was to make it enviable, by depriving the lowest orders of society of the power of becoming soldiers. Excluding the helots of all nations from any part in the glory of butchering their fellow-creatures, has had the same effect as in Sparta,—it has ennobled the trade; and this is the true feudal estimation, in which this trade has descended to us, from our Gothic ancestors.

At the same time that the feudal system was furnishing Europe with a numerous body of noblesse, it became necessary, for various purposes of despotism, that they should be prevented from mingling with the common mass of society, that they should be held together by what they call *l'esprit de corps*, or the corporation spirit, and be furnished with occupations, which should leave them nothing in common with their fellow men.

---

* It is not unworthy of remark, that Aristotle was the tutor of Alexander, and the most splendid editor and commentator of Homer. As we must judge an author by his works, it is but fair to take into view the *whole* of his works. Consider, therefore, as a political school-master to the world, the forming of his pupil, and the illustrating of his poet, are the greatest fruits of the industry of that philosopher, and have had much more influence on the affairs of nations, than his treatise that bears the name of *politics*.

These occupations were offered by the church and the army ; and as the former was permanent, it was thought expedient to give permanency to the latter. Thus the military fyftem has created the nobleffe, and the nobleffe the military fyftem. They are mutually neceffary to each other's exiftence,—concurrent and reciprocal caufes and effects, generating and generated, perpetuating each other by interchangeable wants, and both indifpenfable to the governing power.

Thofe perfons, therefore, who undertake to defend the nobleffe as a neceffary order in the great community of men, ought to be apprifed of the extent of their undertaking. They muft, in the firft place, defend *ftanding armies*, and that too upon principles, not of national prudence, as relative to the circumftances of neighbours, but of internal neceffity, as relative only to the organization of fociety. They muft, at the fame time, extend their arguments to the increafe of thofe armies ; for they infallibly muft increafe to a degree beyond our ordinary calculation, or they will not anfwer the purpcfe ; both becaufe the number of the nobleffe, or " the men of the fword" (as they are properly ftyled by their friend Burke,) is conftantly augmenting, and becaufe the influence of the church is on the decline. As the light of philofophy illuminates the world, it fhines in upon the fecrets of government ; and it is neceffary to make the blind as broad as the window, or the paffengers will fee what is doing in the cabinet. The means of impofition muft be increafed in the army, in proportion as they are loft in the church.

Secondly, they muft vindicate *war*, not merely as an occurrence of fatality, and juftifiable on the defensive; but as a thing of choice, as being the moſt nutritious aliment of that kind of government, which requires privileged orders, and an army: for it is no great figure of ſpeech, to ſay that the nobility of Europe, are always fed upon human gore. They originated in war, they live by war, and without war it would be impoſſible to keep them from ſtarving. Or, to drop the figure entirely, if mankind were left to the peaceable purſuit of induſtry, the titled orders would loſe their diſtinctions, mingle with ſociety, and become reaſonable creatures.

Thirdly, they muſt defend the *honor* of the occupation which is allotted to the nobleſſe. For the age is becoming extremely ſceptical on this ſubject; there are heretics in the world (Mr. Burke calls them athiefts) who affect to diſbelieve that men were made expreſsly for the purpoſe of cutting each other's throats; and who ſay that it is not the higheſt honour that a man can arrive at, to ſell himſelf to another man for life, at a certain daily price, and to hold himſelf in readineſs, night and day, to kill individuals or nations, at home or abroad, without ever inquiring the cauſe. Theſe men ſay, that it is no compliment to the judgment or humanity of a man, to lead ſuch a life; and they do not ſee why a nobleman ſhould not poſſeſs theſe qualities as well as other people.

Fourthly, they muſt prove that all occupations, which tend to *life*, and not to *death*, are diſhonourable and infamous. Agriculture, commerce, every method of augmenting the means of ſubſiſtence, and raiſing men from the ſavage ſtate, muſt be held ignoble; or elſe men of honour will forget themſelves ſo far, as to engage in them;

and then, farewell to diſtinctions. The National Aſſembly may then create orders as faſt as it has ever uncreated them ; it is impoſſible for nobility to exiſt in France, or in any other country, unleſs the above articles are firmly defended by arguments, and fixed in the minds of mankind.

It ſeems difficult for a man of reflection to write one page on the ſubject of government, without meeting with ſome old eſtabliſhed maxims, which are not only falſe, but which are preciſely the reverſe of truth. Of this ſort is the opinion,—that inevitable wars in modern times, have given occaſion to the preſent military ſyſtem, and that ſtanding armies are the beſt means of preventing wars. This is what the people of Europe are commanded to believe. With all due deference, however, to their commanders, I would propoſe a contrary belief, which I will venture to lay down as the true ſtate of the fact : *That the preſent military ſyſtem has been the cauſe of the wars of modern times, and that ſtanding armies are the beſt, if not the only means of* PROMOTING *wars.* This poſition has, at leaſt, one advantage over thoſe that are commonly eſtabliſhed by governments, that it is believed by him, who propoſes it to the aſſent of others. Men, who cannot command the power of the ſtate, ought to enforce their doctrines by the power of reaſon.

To apply this maxim to the caſe now before us ; let us aſk, *What is war ?* and on what propenſity in human nature does it reſt ? For it is to MAN that we are to trace theſe queſtions, and not to *Princes* ; we muſt drive them up to *principle*, not ſtop ſhort at *precedent* ; and endeavour to uſe our ſenſe, inſtead of parading our learning. Among individual men, or ſavages acting in a deſultory manner, antecedent to the formation of great focieties, there may be many caufes of quarrels and affaffinations; fuch as love, jealoufy, rapine, or the revenge of private injuries. But thefe do not amount to the idea of war. War fuppofes a vaft affociation of men engaged in one caufe, actuated by one fpirit, and carrying on a bloody conteft with another affociation in a fimilar predicament. Few of the motives which actuate private men can apply at once to fuch a multitude, the greateft part of which muft be perfonal ftrangers to each other. Indeed, where the motives are clearly explained, and well underftood by the community at large, fo as to be really felt by the people, there is but one of the ordinary caufes above mentioned, which can actuate fuch a body; it is *rapine*, or the hope of enriching themfelves by plunder. There can be then but two circumftances under which a nation will commence an offenfive war: either the people at large muft be thoroughly convinced that they fhall be perfonally rewarded, not only with conqueft, but with a vaft fhare of wealth from the conquered nation, or elfe they muft be duped into the war by thofe who hold the reins of government. All motives for national offences are reduced to thefe two, and there can be no more. The fubject, like moft others, becomes extremely fimple, the moment it is confidered.

And how many of the wars of mankind originate in the firft of thefe motives? Among civilized nations, none. A people confiderably numerous, approaching towards ideas of fober policy, and beginning to tafte the fruits of induftry, require but little experience to convince themfelves of the following truths.—that no benefit can be derived to the great body of individuals from conqueft, though it were certain—that this event is always doubtful, and the decifion to be dreaded,—that nine tenths of the loffes in all wars are a *clear* lofs to both parties, being funk in expences,—that the remaining tenth neceffarily comes in the hands of the principle managers, and produces a real misfortune even to the victorious party, by giving them mafters at home, inftead of riches from abroad.

The pitiful idea of feafting ourfelves on a comparifon of fuffering, and balancing our own loffes by thofe of the enemy, is a ftratagem of government, a calculation of cabinet arithmetic. Individuals reafon not in this manner. A diftreffed mother in England, reduced from a full to a fcanty diet, and bewailing the lofs of her fon, receives no confolation from being told of a woman in France, whofe fon fell in the fame battle, and that the taxes are equally increafed in both countries by the fame war. But Kings, and minifters, and Generals, and hiftorians proclaim, as a glorious conteft, every war which appears to have been as fatal to the enemy as to their own party, though one half of each nation are flaughtered in the field, and the other half reduced to flavery. This is one of the bare-faced impofitions with which mankind are perpetually infulted, and which call upon us, in the name of humanity, to purfue this enquiry into the caufes of war.

The hiftory of ancient Rome, from beginning to end, under all its Kings, Confuls, and Emperors, furnifhes not a fingle inftance, after the conqueft of the Sabines, of what may properly be called a *popular* offenfive war; I mean a war that would have been undertaken by the people, had they enjoyed a free government, so organized as to have enabled them to deliberate before they acted, and to suffer nothing to be carried into execution but the national will.

The same may be said of modern Europe, after a corresponding period in the progress of nations; which period should be placed at the very commencement of civilization. Perhaps after the settlement of the Saracens in Spain, the Lombards in Italy, the Franks in Gaul, and the Saxons in England, we should have heard no more of offensive operations, had they depended on the uninfluenced wishes of the people. For we are not to regard as *offensive* the struggles of a nation for the recovery of liberty.

What an inconceivable mass of slaughter are we then to place to the other account; to dark, unequal government! to the magical powers, possessed by a few men, of blinding the eyes of the community, and leading the people to destruction, by those who are called their fathers and their friends! These operations could not be carried on, for a long time together, in ages tolerably enlightened, without a permanent resource. As long as the military conditions of feudal tenures remained in full vigour, they were sure to furnish the means of destruction to follow the will of the sovereign; but as the asperities of this system softened away by degrees, it seems that governments were threatened with the necessity of applying to the people at large for voluntary enlistments, and contributions in money; on which application the purpose must be declared. This would be too direct an appeal to the consciences of men on a question of offensive war, and was, if possible, to be avoided. For even the power of the church, provided there was no queſtion of hereſy, could not be always relied on, to ſtimulate the people to a quarrel with their neighbours of the ſame faith; and ſtill leſs was it ſure of inducing them to part with their money. The expedient, therefore, of ſtanding armies became neceſſary; and perhaps rather on account of the money than the men.— Thus money is required to levy armies, and armies to levy money; and foreign wars are introduced as the pretended occaſion for both.

One general character will apply to much the greater part of the wars of modern times,—they are *political*, and not *vindictive*. This alone is ſufficient to account for their real origin. They are wars of agreement,* rather than of diſſention; and the conqueſt is taxes, and not territory. To carry on this buſineſs, it is neceſſary not only to keep up the military ſpirit of the nobleſſe by titles and penſions, and to keep in pay a vaſt number of troops, who know no other God but their king; who loſe all ideas of themſelves, in contemplating their officers; and who forget the duties of a man, to practiſe thoſe of a ſoldier,—this is but half the

---

* Whenever the real ſecret hiſtory of the Engliſh and Spaniſh armaments of 1790 ſhall be publiſhed to the world, though it may not furniſh new arguments to men of reflection for diſtruſting political cabinets, it may at leaſt increaſe the number of ſuch men. But this cannot be done with ſafety during the lives of ſome of the principal actors in that aſtoniſhing piece of audacity. I am convinced, that the perſon, who at this moment ſhould do it, would not ſurvive the publication ſo long as popeGanganelli did the ſuppreſſion of the Jeſuits.

operation: an essential part of the military system is to disarm the people, to hold all the functions of war, as well the arm that executes, as the will that declares it, equally above their reach. This part of the system has a double effect, it palsies the hand and brutalizes the mind: an habitual disuse of physical forces totally destroys the moral; and men lose at once the power of protecting themselves, and of discerning the cause of their oppression.

It is almost useless to mention the conclusions which every rational mind must draw from these considerations. But though they are too obvious to be mistaken, they are still too important to be passed over in silence; for we seem to be arrived at that epoch in human affairs, when " all useful ideas, and truths the most necessary to the happiness of mankind, are no longer exclusively destined to adorn the pages of a book*." Nations, wearied out with imposture begin to provide for the safety of man, instead of pursuing his destruction.

I will mention as one conclusion, which bids fair to be a practical one, that the way to prevent wars is not merely to change the military system; for that, like the church, is a necessary part of governments as they now stand, and of society as now organized: but the *principle of government* must be completely changed; and the consequence of this will be such a total renovation of society, as to banish standing armies, overturn the military system, and exclude the possibility of war.

Only admit the original, unalterable truth, *that all men are equal in their rights*, and the foundation of every thing is laid; to build the superstructure

---

* *L'Assemblée Nationae.*

requires no effort but that of natural deduction. The firſt neceſſary deduction will be, that the people will form an equal repreſentative government; in which it will be impoſſible for *orders* or *privileges* to exiſt for a moment; and conſequently the firſt materials for ſtanding armies will be converted into peaceable members of the ſtate. Another deduction follows, That the people will be univerſally armed: they will aſſume thoſe weapons for ſecurity, which the art of war has invented for deſtruction. You will then have removed the *neceſſity* of a ſtanding army by the organization of the legiſlature, and the *poſſibility* of it by the arrangement of the militia; for it is as impoſſible for an armed ſoldiery to exiſt in an armed nation, as for a nobility to exiſt under an equal government.

It is curious to remark how ill we reaſon on human nature, from being accuſtomed to view it under the diſguiſe which the unequal governments of the world have impoſed upon it. During the American war, and eſpecially towards its cloſe, General Waſhington might be ſaid to poſſeſs the hearts of all the Americans. His recommendation was law, and he was able to command the whole power of that people for any purpoſe of defence. The philoſophers of Europe conſidered this as a dangerous criſis to the cauſe of freedom. They *knew* from the example of Cæſar, and Sylla, and Marius, and Alcibiades, and Pericles, and Cromwell, that Waſhington would never lay down his arms, till he had given his country a maſter. But after he did lay them down, then came the miracle,—his virtue was cried up to be more than human; and it is by this miracle of virtue in him, that the Americans are fuppofed to enjoy their liberty at this day.

I believe the virtue of that great man to be equal to any that has ever yet been known; but to an American eye no extraordinary portion of it could appear in that tranfaction. It would have been impoffible for the General or the army to have continued in the field after the enemy left it; for the foldiers were all *citizens*; and if it had been otherwife, their numbers were not the hundredth part of the citizens at large, who were all *foldiers*. To fay that he was wife in difcerning the impoffibility of fuccefs in an attempt to imitate the great heroes above mentioned, is to give him only the fame merit for fagacity which is common to every other perfon who knows that country, or who has well confidered the effects of equal liberty.

Though infinite praife is due to the conftituent affembly of France for the temperate refolution and manly firmnefs which mark their operations in general; yet it muft be confeffed that fome of their reforms bear the marks of too timorous a hand. Preferving an hereditary King with a tremenduous accumulation of powers, and providing an unneceffary number of priefts to be paid from the national purfe, and furnifhed with the means of rebuilding the half-deftroyed ruins of the hierarchy, are circumftances to be pardoned for reafons which I have already hinted. But the enormous military force, which they have decreed fhall remain as a permanent eftablifhment, appears to me not only unneceffary, and even dangerous to liberty, but totally and directly fubverfive of the end they had in view. Their objects were the fecurity of the frontiers and the tranquility of the state; the reverse of this will be the effect,—not perhaps that this army will be turned against the people, or involve the state in offensive wars. On the contrary, suppose that it simply and faithfully defends the frontiers and protects the people; this defence and this protection are the evils of which I complain. They tend to weaken the nation, by deadning the spirit of the people, and teaching them to look up to others for protection, instead of depending on their own invincible arm. A people that legislate for themselves ought to be in the habit of protecting themselves; or they will lose the spirit of both. A knowledge of their own *strength* preserves a temperance in their own *wisdom*, and the performance of their *duties* gives a value to their *rights*.

This is likewise the way to increase the solid domestic force of a nation, to a degree far beyond any ideas we form of a standing army; and at the same time to annihilate its capacity as well as inclination for foreign aggressive hostilities. The true guarantee of perpetual tranquility at home and abroad, in such a case, would arise from this truth, which would pass into an incontrovertible maxim, *that offensive operations would be impossible, and defensive ones infallible.*

This is undoubtedly the true and only secret of exterminating wars from the face of the earth; and it must afford no small degree of consolation to every friend of humanity, to find this unspeakable blessing resulting from that equal mode of government, which alone secures every other enjoyment for which mankind unite their interests in society. Politicians, and even sometimes honest men, are accustomed to speak of war as an uncontroulable event, falling on the human race like a concuffion of the elements,—a fcourge which admits no remedy; but for which we muft wait with trembling preparation, as for an epidemical difeafe, whofe force we may hope to lighten, but can never avoid. They fay that mankind are wicked and rapacious, and " it muft be that offences will come." This reafon applies to individuals; but not to nations deliberately fpeaking a national voice. I hope I fhall not be underftood to mean, that the nature of man is totally changed by living in a free republic. I allow that it is ftill *interefted* men and *paffionate* men, that direct the affairs of the world. But in national affemblies, paffion is loft in deliberation, and intereft balances intereft; till the good of the whole community combines the general will. Here then is a great moral entity, acting ftill from interefted motives; but whofe intereft it never can be, in any poffible combination of circumftances, to commence an offenfive war.

There is another confideration, from which we may argue the total extinction of wars, as a neceffary confequence of eftablifhing governments on the reprefentative wifdom of the people. We are all fenfible that fuperftition is a blemifh of human nature, by no means confined to fubjects connected with religion. Political fuperftition is almoft as ftrong as religious; and it is quite as univerfally ufed as an inftrument of tyranny. To enumerate the variety of ways in which this inftrument operates on the mind, would be more difficult, than to form a general idea of the refult of its operations. In monarchies, it induces men to fpill their blood for a particular family, or for a particular branch of that family, who happens to have been born firſt, or laſt, or to have been taught to repeat a certain creed, in preference to other creeds. But the effect which I am going chiefly to notice is that which reſpects the territorial boundaries of a government. For a man in Portugal or Spain to prefer belonging to one of thoſe nations rather than the other, is as much a ſuperſtition, as to prefer the houſe of Braganza to that of Bourbon, or Mary the ſecond of England to her brother. All theſe ſubjects of preference ſtand upon the ſame footing as the turban and the hat, the croſs and the creſcent, or the lily and the roſe.

The boundaries of nations have been fixed for the accommodation of the *government*, without the leaſt regard to the convenience of the people. Kings and miniſters, who make a profitable trade of governing, are intereſted in extending the limits of their dominion as far as poſſible. They have a property in the people, and in the territory that they cover. The country and its inhabitants are to them a farm ſtocked with ſheep. When they call up theſe ſheep to be ſheared, they teach them to know their names, to follow their maſter, and avoid a ſtranger. By this unaccountable impoſition it is, that men are led from one extravagant folly to another,—to adore their King, to boaſt of their nation, and to wiſh for conqueſt,—circumſtances equally ridiculous in themſelves, and equally incompatible with that rational eſtimation of things, which ariſes from the ſcience of liberty.

In America it is not ſo. Among the ſeveral ſtates, the governments are all equal in their force, and the people are all equal in their rights. Were it poſſible for one State to conquer another State, without any expence of money, or of time, or of blood,—neither of the States, nor a single individual in either of them, would be richer or poorer for the event. The people would all be upon their own lands, and engaged in their own occupations, as before; and whether the territory on which they live were called New York or Maffachufetts is a matter of total indifference, about which they have no fuperftition. For the people belong not to the government, but the government belongs to the people.

Since the independance of thofe States, many territorial difputes have been fettled, which had rifen from the interference of their ancient charters. The interference of charters is a kind of policy which, I fuppofe, every mother country obferves towards her colonies, in order to give them a fubject of contention; that fhe may have the opportunity of keeping all parties quiet by the parental bleffing of a ftanding army. But on the banifhment of foreign control, and all ideas of European policy, the enjoyment of equal liberty has taught the Americans the fecret of fettling thefe difputes, with as much calmnefs as they have formed their conftitutions. It is found, that queftions about the boundaries between free States are not matters of intereft, but merely of form and convenience. And though thefe queftions may involve a tract of country equal to an European kingdom, it alters not the cafe; they are fettled as merchants fettle the courfe of exchange between two commercial cities. Several inftances have occured, fince the revolution, of deciding in a few days, by amicable arbitration, territorial difputes, which determine the jurifdiction of larger and richer tracts of country, than have formed the objects of all the wars of the two laſt centuries between France and Germany.

It is needleſs to ſpend any time in applying this idea to the circumſtances of all countries, where the government ſhould be freely and habitually in the hands of the people. It would apply to all Europe; and will apply to it, as ſoon as a revolution ſhall take place in the principle of government. For ſuch a revolution cannot ſtop ſhort of fixing the power of the State on the baſis allotted by nature, the unalienable rights of man; which are the ſame in all countries. It will eradicate the ſuperſtitions about territorial juriſdiction; and this conſideration muſt promiſe an additional ſecurity againſt the poſſibility of war.

CHAP. IV.

THE ADMINISTRATION OF JUSTICE.

IT would be a curious ſpeculation, and perhaps as uſeful as curious, to conſider how far the moral nature of man is affected by the organization of ſociety; and to what degree his predominant qualities depend on the nature of the government under which he lives. The adage, *That men are every where the ſame*, though not wholly falſe, would doubtleſs be found to be true only in a limited ſenſe.

I love to indulge the belief, that it is true so far as to ensure permanency to institutions that are good; but not so far as to discourage us from attempting to reform those that are bad. To consider it is true in an unlimited sense, would be to serve the purposes of despotism; for which this, like a thousand other maxims, has been invented and employed. It would teach us to sit down with a gloomy satisfaction on the state of human affairs, to pronounce the race of man emphatically "fated to be curst," a community of self-tormentors and mutual assassins, bound down by the irresistible destiny of their nature to be robbed of their reason by priests, and plundered of their property by Kings. It would teach us to join with Soame Jenyns, and furnish new weapons to the oppressors, by our manner of pitying the misfortunes of the oppressed.

In confirmation of this adage, and as an apology for the existing despotisms, it is said: That all men are by nature tyrants, and will exercise their tyrannies whenever they find opportunity. Allowing this assertion to be true, it is surely cited by the wrong party. It is an apology for equal, not for unequal governments; and the weapon belongs to those who contend for the republican principle. If government be founded on the vices of mankind, its business is to restrain those vices in all, rather than to foster them in a few. The disposition to tyrannize is effectually restrained under the exercise of the equality of rights; while it is not only rewarded in the few, but invigorated in the many, under all other forms of the social connexion. But it is almost impossible to decide, among moral propensities, which of of them belong to nature, and which are the offspring of habit; how many of our vices are chargable on the permanent qualities of man, and how many refult from the mutable energies of ftate.

If it be in the power of a bad goverment to render men worfe than nature has made them, why fhould we fay it is not in the power of a good one to render them better? and if the latter be capable of producing this effect in any perceivable degree, where fhall we limit the progrefs of human wifdom, and the force of its inftitutions, in ameliorating, not only the focial condition, but the controlling principles of man?

Among the component parts of government, that, whofe operation is the moft direct on the moral habit of life, is the Adminiftration of Juftice. In this every perfon has a peculiar ifolated intereft, which is almoft detached from the common fympathies of fociety. It it this which operates with a fingular concentrated energy, collecting the whole force of the ftate from the community at large, and bringing it to act upon a fingle individual, affecting his life, reputation, or property; fo that the governing power may fay with peculiar propriety to the minifter of juftice, *divide et impera*; for, in cafe of oppreflion, the victim's cries will be too feeble to excite oppofition; his caufe having nothing in common with that of the citizens at large. If, therefore, we would obtain an idea of the condition of men on any given portion of the earth, we muft pay a particular attention to their judiciary fyftem, not in its form and theory, but in its fpirit and practice. It may be faid in general of this part of the civil polity of a nation, that, as it is a ftream flowing from the common fountain of the government, and muft be tinged with whatever impurities are found in the source from whence it descends, the only hope of cleansing the stream is by purifying the fountain.

If I were able to give an energetic sketch of the office and dignity of a rational system of jurisprudence, describe the full extent of its effects on the happiness of men, and then exhibit the perversions and corruptions attendant on this business in most of the governments of Europe, it would furnish one of the most powerful arguments in favour of a general revolution, and afford no small consolation to those persons who look forword with certainty to such an event. But my plan embraces too many subjects, to be particular on any; all that I can promise myself is to seize the rough features of systems, and mark the moral attitudes of man as placed in the necessary posture to support them.

It is generally understood, that the object of government, in this part of its administration, is merely to *restrain* the vices of men. But there is another object prior to this: an office more sacred, and equally indispensable, is to *prevent* their vices, —to correct them in their origin, or eradicate them totally from the adolescent mind. The latter is performed by instruction, the former by coercion; the one is the tender duty of a father, the other, the unrelenting drudgery of a master; but both are the business of government, and ought to be made concurrent branches of the system of jurisprudence.

The absurd and abominable doctrine, *that private vices are public benefits*, it is hoped will be blotted from the memory of man, expunged from the catalogue of human follies, with the systems of government which gave it birth. The ground of this insulting doctrine is, that advantage may be taken of the extravagant foibles of individuals to increase the revenues of the State; as if the chief end of society were, to steal money for the government's purse! to be squandered by the governors, to render them more infolent in their oppressions! it is humiliating, to answer such arguments as these; where we must lay open the most degrading retreats of prostituted logic, to discover the positions on which they are founded. But *Orders* and *Privileges* will lead to any thing: once teach a man, that *some are born to command and others to be commanded*; and after that, there is no camel too big for him to swallow.

This idea of the objects to be kept in view by the system of Justice, involving in it the business of prevention as well as of restriction, leads us to some observations on the particular subject of criminal jurisprudence. Every society, considered in itself as a moral and physical entity, has the undoubted faculty of self-preservation. It is an independent being; and, towards other beings in like circumstances of independence, it has a right to use this faculty of defending itself, without previous notice to the party; or without the observance of any duty, but that of abstaining from offensive operations. But when it acts towards the members of its own family, towards those dependent and defenceless beings that make part of itself, the *right* of coercion is preceded by the *duty* of instruction. It may be safely pronounced, *that a State has no right to punish a man, to whom it has given no previous instruction*; and consequently, any person has a right to do any action, unless he has been informed that it has an evil tendency.

It is true, that, as relative to particular cafes, the having given this information is a thing that the fociety muft fometimes *prefume*, and is not always obliged to *prove*. But thefe cafes are rare, and ought never to form a general rule. This prefumption has, however, paffed into a general rule, and is adopted as univerfal practice. With what juftice or propriety it is fo adopted, a very little reflection will enable us to decide.

The great out-lines of morality are extremely fimple and eafy to be underftood; they may be faid to be written on the heart of a man antecedent to his affociating with his fellow-creatures. As a felf-dependent being he is felf-inftructed; and as long as he fhould remain a fimple child of *nature*, he would receive from nature all the leffons neceffary to his condition. He would be a complete moral agent; and fhould he violate the rights of another independent man like himfelf, he would fin againft fufficient light, to merit any punifhment that the offended party might inflict upon him. But *fociety* opens upon us a new field of contemplation; it furnifhes man with another clafs of rights, and impofes upon him an additional fyftem of duties; it enlarges the fphere of his moral agency, and makes him a kind of artificial being, propelling and propelled by new dependencies, in which nature can no longer ferve him as a guide. Being removed from her rudimental fchool, and entered in the college of fociety, he is called to encounter problems which the elementary tables of his heart will not always enable him to folve. Society then ought to be confiftent with herfelf in her own inftitutions; if fhe fketches the lines of his duty with a variable pencil, too flight for his natural perception, fhe should lend him her optical glasses to discern them, if she takes the ferule in one hand, she is bound to use the fescue with the other.

We must observe farther,—that though society itself be a state of nature, as relative to the nation at large,—though it be a state to which mankind naturally recur to satisfy their wants and increase the sum of their happiness,—though all its laws and regulations may be perfectly reasonable, and calculated to promote the good of the whole,—yet, with regard to an individual member, his having *consented* to these laws, or even chose to live in the society, is but a *fiction?* and a rigid discipline, founded on a fiction, is surely hard upon its object. In general it may be said, that a man comes into society by birth; he neither consents nor dissents respecting his relative condition; he first opens his eyes on that state of human affairs in which the interests of his moral associates are infinitely complicated; with these his duties are so blended and intermingled, that nature can give him but little assistance in finding them out. His morality itself must be arbitrary; it must be varied at every moment, to comprehend some local and positive regulation; his science is to begin where that of preceding ages has ended; his alpha is their omega; and he is called upon to act by instinct what they have but learnt to do from the experience of all mankind. Natural reason may teach me not to strike my neighbour without a cause; but it will never forbid my sending a sack of wool from England, or printing the French constitution in Spain. These are positive prohibitions, which nature has not written in her book; she has therefore never taught them to her children.

The same may be said of all regulations that arise from the social compact.

It is a truth, I believe, not to be called in question, that every man is born with an imprescriptible claim to a portion of the elements; which portion is termed his *birth-right*. Society may vary this right, as to its form, but never can destroy it in substance. She has no control over the man, till he is born; and the right being born with him, and being necessary to his existence, she can no more annihilate the one than the other, though she has the power of new-modelling both. But on coming into the world, he finds that the ground which nature had promised him is taken up, and in the occupancy of others; society has changed the form of his birth-right; the general stock of elements, from which the lives of men are to be supported, has undergone a new modification; and his portion among the rest. He is told that he cannot claim it in its present form, as an independent inheritance; that he must draw on the stock of society, instead of the stock of nature; that he is banished from the mother and must cleave to the nurse. In this unexpected occurrence he is unprepared to act but *knowledge* is a part of the stock of society; and an indispensable part to be allotted in the portion of the claimant is *instruction* relative to the new arrangement of natural right. To withhold this instruction therefore would be, not merely the omission of a duty, but the commission of a crime; and society in this case would sin against the man, before the man could sin against society.

I should hope to meet the assent of all unprejudiced readers, in carrying this idea still farther. In cases where a person is born of poor parents, or finds himself brought into the community of men without the means of subsistence, society is bound in duty to furnish him the means. She ought not only to instruct him in the artificial laws by which property is secured, but in the artificial industry by which it is obtained. She is bound, in *justice* as well as policy, to give him some art or trade. For the reason of his incapacity is, that *she* has usurped his birth-right; and this is restoring it to him in another form, more convenient for both parties. The failure of society in this branch of her duty is the occasion of much the greater part of the evils that call for criminal jurisprudence. The individual feels that he is robbed of his natural right; he cannot bring his process to reclaim it from the great community, by which he is overpowered; he therefore feels authorized in reprisal; in taking another's goods to replace his own. And it must be confessed, that in numberless instances the conduct of society justifies him in this proceeding; she has seized upon his property, and commenced the war against him.

Some, who perceive these truths, say that it is unsafe for society to publish them; but I say it is unsafe not to publish them. For the party from which the mischief is expected to arise has the knowledge of them already, and has acted upon them in all ages. It is the wise who are ignorant of these things, and not the foolish. They are truths of nature; and in them the teachers of mankind are the only party that remains to be taught. It is a subject on which the logic of indigence is much clearer than that of opulence. The latter reasons from contrivance, the former from feeling; and God has not endowed us with false feelings, in things that so weightily concern our happiness.

None can deny that the obligation is much stronger on me, to support my life, than to support the claim that my neighbour has to his property. Nature commands the first, society the second:—in one I obey the laws of God, which are universal and eternal; in the other, the laws of man, which are local and temporary.

It has been the folly of all old governments, to begin every thing at the wrong end, and to erect their institutions on an inversion of principle. This is more sadly the case in their systems of jurisprudence, than is commonly imagined. *Compelling* justice is always mistaken for *rendering* justice. But this important branch of administration consists not merely in compelling men to be just to each other, and individuals to society,—this is not the whole, nor is it the principal part, nor even the beginning, of the operation. The source of power is said to be the source of justice; but it does not answer this description, as long as it contents itself with *compulsion*. Justice must begin by flowing from its source; and the first as well as the most important object is, to open its channels from society to all the individual members. This part of the administration being well devised and diligently executed, the other parts would lessen away by degrees to matters of inferior consideration.

It is an undoubted truth, that our duty is inseparably connected with our happiness. And why should we despair of convincing every member of society of a truth so important for him to know? Should any person object, by saying, that nothing like this, has ever yet been done; I anſwer, that nothing like this has ever yet been tried. Society has hitherto been curſt with governments, whoſe exiſtence depended on the extinction of truth. Every moral light has been ſmothered under the buſhel of perpetual impoſition; from whence it emits but faint and glimmering rays, always inſufficient to form any luminous ſyſtem on any of the civil concerns of men. But theſe covers are crumbling to the duſt, with the governments which they ſupport; and the probability becomes more apparent, the more it is confidered, that ſociety is capable of curing all the evils to which it has given birth.

It ſeems that men, to diminiſh the phyſical evils that ſurround them, connect themſelves in ſociety; and from this connection their moral evils ariſe. But the *immediate* occaſion of the moral evils is nothing more than the *remainder* of the phyſical, that ſtill exiſt even under the regulations that ſociety makes to baniſh them. The direct object therefore of the government ought to be, to deſtroy as far as poſſible the remaining quantity of phyſical evils: and the moral would ſo far follow their deſtruction. But the miſtake that is always made on this ſubject is, that governments, inſtead of laying the axe at the root of the tree, aim their ſtrokes at the branches; they attack the moral evils *directly* by vindictive juſtice, inſtead of removing the phyſical by diſtributive juſtice.

There are two diſtinct kinds of phyſical evils; one ariſes from want, or the apprehenſion of want; the other from bodily diſeaſe. The former ſeems capable of being removed by ſociety; the latter is inevitable. But the latter gives no occaſion to moral diſorders; it being the common lot of all, we all bear our part in silence, without complaining of each other, or revenging ourselves on the community. As it is out of the power of our neighbour's goods to relieve us, we do not covet them for this purpose. The former is the only kind from which moral evils arise; and to this the energies of government ought to be chiefly directed; especially that part which is called the administration of justice.

No nation is yet so numerous, nor any country so populous, as it is capable of becoming. Europe, taken together, would support at least five times its present number, even on its present system of cultivation; and how many times this increased population may be multiplied by new discoveries in the infinite science of subsistence, no man will pretend to calculate. This of itself is sufficient to prove, that society at present has the means of rendering all its members happy in every respect, except the removal of bodily disease. The common stock of the community appears abundantly sufficient for this purpose. By common stock, I would not be understood to mean the goods exclusively appropriated to individuals. Exclusive property is not only consistent with good order among men, but it is conceived by some to be necessary to the existence of society. But the common stock of which I speak consists, first, in *knowledge*, or the improvement which men have made in the means of acquiring a support; and secondly, in the *contributions* which it is necessary should be collected from individuals, and applied to the maintenance of tranquillity in the State. The property exclusively belonging to individuals can only be the surplusage remaining in their hands, after deducting what is neceslary to the real wants of fociety. Society is the firft proprieter; as fhe is the original caufe of the appropriation of wealth, and its indifpenfable guardian in the hands of the individual.

Society then is bound, in the firft place, to diftribute knowledge to every perfon according to his wants, to enable him to be ufeful and happy; fo far as to difpofe him to take an active intereft in the welfare of the State. *Secondly*, where the faculties of the individual are naturally defective, fo that he remains unable to provide for himfelf, fhe is bound ftill to fupport and render him happy. It is her duty in all cafes to induce every human creature, by rational motives, to place his happinefs in the tranquillity of the public, and in the fecurity of individual peace and property. But *thirdly*, in cafes where thefe precautions fhall fail of their effect, fhe is driven indeed to the laft extremity,—fhe is to ufe the rod of correction. Thefe inftances would doubtlefs be rare; and if we could fuppofe a long continuance of wife adminiftration, fuch as a well-organized government would enfure to every nation in the world, we may almoft perfuade ourfelves to believe that the neceffity for punifhment would be reduced to nothing.

Proceeding however on the fuppofition of the exiftence of crimes, it muft ftill remain an object of legiflative wifdom, to difcriminate between their different claffes, and apply to each its proper remedy, in the quantity and mode of punifhment. It is no part of my fubject to enter into this inquiry, any farther than fimply to obferve, that it is the characteriftic of arbitrary governments to be jealous of their power. And, as jealoufy is, of all human paffions, the moft vindictive and the least rational, these governments seek the revenge of injuries in the most absurd and tremenduous punishments that their fury can invent. As far as any rule can be discovered in their gradation of punishments, it appears to be this, That the severity of the penalty is in proportion to the injustice of the law. The reason of this is simple, —the laws which counteract nature the most, are the most likely to be violated.

The publication, within the last half century, of a great number of excellent treatises on the subject of penal laws, without producing the least effect in any part of Europe, is a proof that no reform is to be expected in the general system of criminal jurisprudence, but from a radical change in the principle of government*.

A method of communicating instruction to every member of society is not difficult to discover, and would not be expensive in practice. The government generally establishes ministers of justice in every part of the dominion. The first object of these ministers ought to be, to see that every person is well instructed in his duties and in his rights; that he is rendered perfectly acquainted with every law, in its true spirit and tendency, in order that he may know the reason of his obedience, and the manner of obtaining redress, in case

---

* The compassionate little treatise of Beccaria, *dei delitti e delle pene*, is getting to be a manual in all languages. It has already served as an introduction to many luminous essays on the policy and right of punishment, in which the spirit of inquiry is pursued much farther than that benevolent philosopher, surrounded as he is by the united fabres of feudal and ecclesiastical tyranny, has dared to pursue it.

he should deem it unjust; that he is taught to feel the cares and interests of an active citizen, to consider himself as a real member of the state, know that the government is his own, that the society is his friend, and that the officers of the state are the servants of the people. A person possessing these ideas will never violate the laws, unless it be from necessity; and such necessity is to be prevented by means which are equally obvious.

For the purposes of compulsive justice it is not enough that the laws be rendered familiar to the people; but the tribunals ought to be near at hand, easy of access, and equally open to the poor as to the rich; the means of coming at justice should be cheap, expeditious, and certain; the mode of process should be simple and perfectly intelligible to the meanest capacity, unclouded with mysteries and unperplexed with forms. In short, justice should familiarise itself as the well-known friend of every man; and the consequence seems natural, that every man would be a friend to justice.

After considering what is the duty of society, and what *would be* the practice of a well-organized government, relative to the subject of this chapter, it is almost useless to inquire, what *is* the practice of all the old governments of Europe. We may be sure beforehand, that it is directly the contrary,—that, like all other parts of the system, it is the inversion of every thing that is right and reasonable. The pyramid is every where placed on the little end, and all sorts of extraneous rubbish are constantly brought to prop it up.

Unequal governments are necessarily founded in ignorance, and they must be supported by ignorance; to deviate from their principle would be voluntary fuicide. The firft great object of their policy is to perpetuate that undifturbed ignorance of the people, which is the companion of poverty, the parent of crimes, and the pillar of the State.

In England, the people at large are as perfectly ignorant of the acts of parliament after they are made, as they poffibly can be before. They are printed by one man only, who is called the King's printer,—in the old German character, which few men can read,—and fold at a price that few can afford to pay. But left fome fcraps or comments upon them fhould come to the people through the medium of public newfpapers, every fuch paper is ftamped with a heavy duty ; and an act of parliament is made to prevent men from letting their papers to read* ; fo that not one perfon in a hundred fees a newfpaper once in a year. If a man at the bottom of Yorkfhire difcovers by inftinct that a law is made, which is interefting for him to know, he has only to make a journey to London, find out the King's printer, pay a halfpenny a page for the law, and learn the Ger-

---

* As this work may chance to fall into the hands of fome people who never fee the acts of parliament (the fame precautions not being taken to prevent its circulation), it is out of compaffion to that clafs of readers, that I give this information. It is a duty of humanity to fave our fellow-creatures from falling into fnares, even thofe that are fpread for them by the government. Therefore : Notice is hereby given to all perfons, to whom thefe prefents fhall come, that the penalty for letting a newfpaper, within the Kingdom of Great-Britain, is fifty pounds.

man alphabet. He is then prepared to spell out his duty.

As to the general system of the laws of the land, on which all property depends, no man in the kingdom knows them, and no man pretends to know them. They are a fathomless abyss, that exceeds all human faculties to found. They are studied, not to be understood, but to be disputed; not to give information, but to breed confusion. The man, whose property is depending on a suit at law, dares not look into the gulph that separates him from the wished-for decision; he has no confidence in himself, nor in reason, nor in justice; he mounts on the back of a lawyer, like one of Mr. Burke's heroes of chivalry between the wings of a griffin, and trusts the pilotage of a man, who is superior to himself only in the confidence which results from having nothing at stake.

To penetrate into what are called the courts of justice on the continent, and expose the general system of their administration in those points which are common to most countries in Europe, would be to lay open an inconcievable scene of iniquity; it would be,

"To pour in light on Pluto's drear abodes,
"Abhorr'd by men, and dreadful e'en to gods."

What are we to do with our sensibility, with our honest instinct of propriety, how refrain from exclamations of horror, while we contemplate a set of men, assuming the sacred garb of justice, for the uniform and well-known purpose of selling their decisions to the highest bidder! For a judge to receive a bribe, we should think an indelible stain upon his character as a *man*; but what shall we say of the state of human nature, where it is no disgrace to him as a *judge?* where it is not only expected as a matter of courfe, and practifed without difguife, but is made almoft a neceffary part of the judiciary fyftem?

Whether the practice of receiving bribes was the original idea on which is founded the *venality of offices* in modern governments, it is not to our purpofe to inquire. But certain it is, they are concomitant ideas, and co-extenfive practices; and it is defigned that they fhould be fo. In France, before the revolution, the office of judge was not indeed hereditary, like that of king; but it was worfe; it was held up for fale by the king, and put at auction by the minifter. As a part of the king's revenue arofe from the fale of juftice, the government fold all the offices in that department at fixed prices; but the minifter made the bargains with thofe who would give him moft. Thus the feats of the judges became objects of fpeculation, open to all the world; and the man, whofe confcience was the beft fitted to make a profitable trade of deciding caufes, could afford to give the higheft price, and was confequently fure to be judge.

Juftice then was a commodity which neceffarily gave a profit to three fets of men, before it could be purchafed by the fuitor; even fuppofing it might have flowed to him in a direct channel. But this was a thing impoffible; there were other defcriptions of men, more numerous, if not more greedy, than thofe of whom we have fpoken, through whofe hands it muft pafs and repafs, before it could arrive at the client, who had paid his money to the judge. Thefe men, who infefted the tribunals in all ftages of the bufinefs, were divided in France, into about fix claffes. For want of the precife names in Englifh to defignate all their official diftinctions, we fhall rank the whole under the great appellation of Lawyers*. But though we here confound them together, as we often do objects at a distance; yet they were not to be so treated by the client. He must address them all distinctly and respectfully, with the same *argumentum ad patronum*, with which he had addressed the judge: as one or more of each class had a necessary part in bringing forward and putting backward every cause that came into court.

Lawyers in France served two important purposes, which it is supposed they do not serve in England: they added considerably to the revenues of the crown by the purchase of their places; and they covered the iniquity of the judges under the impenetrable vail of their own. In a cause of ordinary consequence, there was more writing to be done in France than there is even in England, perhaps by a hundred and fifty pages. The reason of this was, that it was more necessary to involve the question in mysteries and perplexities that should be absolutely inscrutable. For it must never be known, either at the time of trial or ever after, on what point or principle the cause was decided. To answer this end, the multiplying of the different orders of the managers, as well as encreasing the quantity of writing, had an admirable effect; it removed the possibility of fixing a

* *To avoid any suspicion of exaggeration, I will mention by their original names such of these classes as occur to me. There were the* counseiller, avocat, procureur, secretaire, du judge, greffier, huissier-priseur, huissier-audiencier, *with all their clerks, who must likewise all be paid, or the cause would stop in any stage of its progress.*

charge of fraud or mifmanagement on any one of the great fraternity, or of difcovering, among the formidable piles of papers and parchments that enveloped the myfteries of the trial, in what ftage the iniquity was introduced.

To call this whole fyftem of operations a folemn farce, is to give no utterance to our feelings; to fay it is a fplendid mockery of juftice by which individuals are robbed of their property, is almoft to fpeak its praife.—The reflecting mind cannot reft upon it a moment, without glancing over fociety, and bewailing the terrible inroads made upon morals public and private, the devaftation of principle, the outrage upon nature, the degradation of the laft particle of dignity by which we recognize our own refemblance in man.

Its obvious tendency is, by its enormous expence, to bar the door of juftice againft the poor, who in fuch countries are fure to form the great body of mankind,—to render them enemies to fociety, by teaching that fociety is an enemy to them,—to ftimulate them to crimes both from their own neceffities, and from the example of their mafters,—and to fpread over the people at large an incruftation of ignorance, which excluding all ideas of their duties and their rights, compels them to forget their relation to the human race.

Are thefe to be ranked among the circumftances which call for a change in the governments of Europe? Or are we to join with Mr. Burke, and lament as an evil of the French revolution, That the ancient fyftem " of jurifprudence will no more be ftudied?" The whining of that good gentleman on this idea, is about as rational, as it would be to lament that the noble fcience of Heraldry was in danger of being forgotten; or that men had loft the myftical meaning of *Abracadabra*. This word, ferving as a charm, anfwered the fame purpofe in Medicine, as heraldry does in honour; or the old jurifprudence, in juftice: it rendered men fuperftitious; and confequently, immoral and unhappy.

It is fo fafhionable in Europe, efpecially among Englifhmen, to fpeak in praife of the Englifh jurifprudence, and to confider it as a model of perfection, that it may feem neceffary for a perfon to begin with an apology for offering his ideas on that fubject, if he means to deviate from the opinion fo generally eftablifhed. But inftead of doing this, I will begin by apologizing for thofe who at this day fupport the eftablifhed opinion: Your faireft apology, Gentleman, is, that you underftand nothing of the matter. To affign any other, would be lefs favourable to your characters as honeft men.

Exclufive of the rules by which the merits of a caufe are to be decided (and which, if they could be afcertained, would be the *law*), the mere *form* of bringing a queftion before a court is of itfelf a fcience, an art, lefs underftood, and more difficult to learn, than the conftruction and ufe of the moft complicated machine, or even the motions of the heavenly bodies. It is not enough, that the adminiftration of juftice (which ought to be as fimple as poffible) is fo involved in perplexity, that none but men of profeffional fkill can pretend to underftand it; but the profeffors are divided, as in France, into feveral diftinct claffes; each of which is abfolutely neceffary to lend a helping hand in every ftep of the progrefs of a caufe. This dark multiplicity of form has not only removed the knowledge of law from the generality of men, but has created such an expence in obtaining justice, that very few ever make the attempt. The courts are effectually shut against the great body of the people, and justice as much out of their reach, as if no laws existed*.

Those who have attempted to purchase justice through the necessary forms have never been known to pronounce eulogies on the courts. But their number has always been so small, that, had they uttered the anathemas that the system deserves, their feeble voice could scarcely have been heard. No man, whose eyes are not blinded by fees or by prejudice, can look upon the enormous mass of writings which accumulate in a cause, without reflecting with indignation on the expence; one hundredth part of which would have been

---

* *The provision made in the English law, enabling a person to bring his suit in forma pauperis, is rather an insult than a real advantage. Certainly, not one person in a hundred, who is deprived of justice in the ordinary course, would ever seek it in this; as, in order to be entitled to it, he must go into court and swear that he has not property enough to prosecute his claim. A young tradesman, and in general every person who wishes to carry on business, or has spirit enough to seek for justice, has a higher interest in establishing a credit among his connexions in business, than in prosecuting ordinary suit at law. He knows, that to expose his own poverty, especially in a commercial country, would be irretrievable ruin; it would be a positive injury; while sitting down with the loss of his right, without bringing his suit, is only a negative injury.*

more than sufficient for every purpose of obtaining justice between the parties. A writer who should give the names and descriptions of the various parts of a process, with the expences annexed to each part, would scarcely gain credit, except with professional men. Several hundred pounds are expended only in writing Bills, Subpœnas, Pleas, Demurrers, Answers, Petitions, Orders, Motions, Amendments, Notices, Reports, &c. in a single cause, where no witness is called.

Let us trace a few of the windings, and see where some of the paths lead which are laid down as necessary to obtaining a decision in Chancery; we shall there find how hundreds, and sometimes thousands of pounds are expended in a cause, before any defence is set up, and where no defence is ever intended to be set up. The suitor begins his incomprehensible operation, by stating his claim, in what is called a *Bill*, which he leaves at a certain office belonging to the court, and obtains an order, called a subpœna, for summoning the defendant. This being done, the court requires the defendant to send an Attorney to write his name at another office of the court. This writing the name, is called an *appearance*; it answers no possible purpose, but that of increasing expences and fees of office, for which it is a powerful engine. For if the defendant does not comply, an expence of thousands of pounds may be made, to compel him. A *capias*, a process for *outlawry*, a commission of *rebellion*, and an order and commission of *sequestration*, are pursued in their proper routine, till he consents to write his name.

If the plaintiff has property to go through this process, he may be said to be able just to keep his ground; and his cause is in every respect precisely where it was at first. If he has not sufficient property, the cause is lost for want of fees; and he is no better than if he had never been able to have begun the suit.

We will, however, suppose, that the defendant very good-naturedly writes his name; he is then entitled to a certain delay, during which, the court informs him, he must plead, demur, or answer to the bill. When this time expires, he is intitled to a farther delay of four weeks. But though he is *entitled* to this farther delay, and neither the plaintiff nor the court can refuse it, still he must employ a solicitor to make a brief for counsel; and this solicitor must attend the counsel, and give him and his clerk their fees, for moving the court for this delay, which cannot be refused. The counsel must attend the court and make the motion; the solicitor must attend the court, and pay for the order, entry, and copy; and then must cause it to be served.

At the end of this term of four weeks, the defendant is *entitled* to a farther delay of three weeks; which again cannot be refused. But he must pay his solicitor for drawing and engrossing a petition for that purpose, and the petition must be presented, and answered for which he must pay; he must also pay for order, entry, copy and service. At the end of these three weeks, he is in the same manner *entitled* to a farther delay of two weeks; but the same farce must be acted over again to obtain it. And a very solemn farce it is to the parties, a very pleasant farce to the officers of the court, and a very ridiculous farce to every body else.

If, during all this time, the defendant had stopt paying, or the solicitor had stopt writing, the same process, which was ufed to compel his appearance, muft have been repeated, to wit, *capias, outlawry*, commiffion of *rebellion*, and *fequeftration*. But we have arrived at the time when the defendant is in duty bound to anfwer to the bill ; and here, if he does not anfwer, then *capias, outlawry, rebellion*, and *fequeftration* again.

Thefe terms muft be explained to the reader ; and this is the beft opportunity to do it. For the caufe ftill remaining precifely where it was at firft, we may fuppofe it fufficiently at reft, not to move during the explanation. A *capias* is an order, to take the man, and hold him in gaol till he obeys the order of the court ; whether it be to write his name, or any thing elfe. The word *outlawry* explains, of itfelf, this horrid engine of the court. A commiffion of *rebellion* is an order iffued, after the officer with the capias has fearched and cannot find the man, and after an outlawry has taken place. It is directed to other perfons, requiring them to take up the man who was guilty of rebellion in refufing to write his name. But as the officer with the capias, before outlawry, could not find the man, the iffuing the commiffion of rebellion *now*, has no other meaning but *fees*. A *fequeftration* is taking the whole property of the defendant into the hands of the court. And when this is done, the caufe is foon done alfo ; for no eftate could laft long there. When the money is gone the proceedings ceafe.

But let us fuppofe that the defendant has complied with all orders thus far, and has put in a good and fufficient anfwer. Let us leave out of our account all motions, petitions, decrees, orders, &c. for amending the bill, for referring to Mafters the infufficiency of anfwers, reports upon thofe anfwers, and farther anfwers, and exceptions to Masters' reports, and orders and decisions relative to them ; and, instead of inquiring into the expence of these, let us go back and ask what is the use of all, or of any part of this procefs? Thirty thousand Lawyers (this is said to be the number in the kingdom) are now living on just such stuff as the procefs here described ; and I call on them all, to point out the purpose that any of it ever served, or ever can serve to their clients.

It must be remembered, that all the proceedings thus far were to end in three pretended objects,—to compel an appearance ; to obtain the *ufual* and *legal* time for the defendant to prepare his answer ; and to compel him to give his answer. For the *appearance*, which is the solemn appellation given to the action of writing a name, it would be an insult to the understanding of a child, to tell him that this could be of any service towards forwarding justice. Next comes the succession of applications and orders, for time to answer the bill. The practice of the court, which is the law in this case, allows the defendant, first a short term, and then the delay of four weeks, three weeks, and two weeks ; which in all reckonings, unlefs it be in law, make nine weeks. And if that be a reasonable time, when divided into three parts, why is it not so before it is divided ? And if neither the party, nor the court, nor any body elfe, has a right to refuse that term of time, why might not the defendant take it, without the expence of afking three times ? The remainder of the procefs goes to compel the defendant to give in an answer to the bill. And what is the importance of an answer ? To solve this queftion, let us confider the object of the bill, to which the anfwer is required.

The bill expreffes the claim of the plaintiff, and points out the nature of the decree, which he prays may be made in his favour againft the defendant. Notice is given to the defendant that fuch a fuit is pending, and that he may appear and fhow caufe why the decree fhould not be made. Having given this notice, it is not only cruel, but abfurd, to think of forcing him to defend himfelf whether he will or no. One would fuppofe it little to the purpofe, to make the attempt. Why may not the fubpœna, which gives notice to the defendant, point out the day, beyond which he cannot give an anfwer? then, if he choofes to defend, hear him candidly; but if he refufes to come, and does not choofe to defend,—proceed in the caufe; he is willing that the decree fhould pafs. Can it be reafonable,—can it be any thing fhort of flat contradiction and nonfenfe, to compel him to appear, to compel him to afk for a delay, and to compel him to defend? Can his defence be neceffary in doing juftice to the plaintiff? and, if he will not defend himfelf, can you make him? Can any one of the whole hoft of all the profeffions of the law fhow the leaft fhadow of ufe in all this flourifh of procefs thus far, but *fees* on the one hand, and *oppreffion* on the other?

To proceed through all the forms, to the end of a fuit in chancery, would be to write a commentary on many volumes of practice, and would be calling the patience of the reader to a trial, from which it would certainly fhrink. but there are parts as much worfe than what we have defcribed, as this is worfe than common fenfe. Strip from the adminiftration of juftice the forms that are perfectly useless and oppressive, and counsellors will have much less to do; while the whole order of attornies and solicitors will fall to the ground. If the mysteries of nonsense were out of the way, a counsellor, who was called upon to hazard his reputation on the manner of conducting his clients cause, would no more have it prepared and brought forward by an attorney, than a man of business would hazard his fortune by doing that business through an ignorant agent, which he could more easily do himself. The quantity of writing, really necessary, in a simple and dignified system of practice, is so small, as to be perhaps incredible to those who are acquainted only with the English process.

I have seen the mode of conducting this business in a country, where the common law of England is the general rule of decision, and where the adjudications of Westminster-hall are authorities, as much as they are in Great-Britan. But the laws of that country have stripped legal process of its principal follies, and the consequence is, that the whole profession of attornies and solicitors has vanished, the counsellor does the whole business of his client; and so simple is the operation, that a man may with ease commence and carry through every stage, to final judgment and execution, five hundred causes in a year. And the whole proceedings in all these shall not afford writing enough to employ a single clerk one hour in twenty four. The proceedings and judgments in five hundred causes, in this country, would fill a warehouse. And yet in that country, every allegation is necessary in their declarations and pleadings, which are necessary in Westminster-hall. As they are not paid by the line their declarations have but one count, and in that count there is no tautology. And so little is the expence of suits, where no more is done than is necessary for justice, that judgment, in a cause where there is no defence, may be obtained for less than ten shillings; and every person employed be fully paid for his service*.

Men who are habituated to the expenses incurred in law-suits in England, will scarcely be persuaded of the extent to which a reform would be carried, on a general destruction of abuses. But let them reflect, that when law proceedings are stripped of every thing, but what the nature of the

* As this may awaken the curiosity of some of my readers, I will give the details. Suppose a suit to recover money due on Note or Bond: The writ and declaration are incorporated in one instrument; that is, the declaration is contained in the writ. The sheriff is ordered to read this to the defendant, or leave a copy at his dwelling, at least twelve days previous to the sitting of the court. This writ is usually filled up in a well known form, in a printed blank; of which a man may with ease fill a hundred a day. For this the court taxes one shilling and six pence. The sheriff, if he has no travel to the defendant, is paid six-pence for reading the writ to him, and delivering it to the clerk of the court. It is then the duty of the plaintiff, or of his lawyer, (who is both counsellor and solicitor) to attend the court on the first day of the sitting; and then the parties in all causes are called by the crier. For this attendance the court will tax three shillings and four-pence halfpenny: and if the defendant intends to make no defence he will not answer when called; and the clerk thereupon, on the third day after

I

subject requires, there is no myſtery left. The rational part that remains is ſoon comprehended, and eaſily retained in memory. This would doubtleſs augment the number of ſuits; for it would open the courts to vaſt multitudes of people, againſt whom they are now effectually ſhut. But in proportion as it increaſed the number of law-ſuits, it would diminiſh the quantity of *law-buſi-neſs*; and the number of lawyers would dwindle to one tenth of what it is at preſent. In the State above alluded to, the number of men ſupported by this profeſſion is to the whole population, as one to 4600. Reduce the lawyers here to that proportion, and there would be left about three thouſand in the kingdom. It is aſſerted, (I know not on what ground) that the preſent number is thirty thouſand. Allowing it to be true, an army of twenty-ſeven thouſand lawyers, on this reform, would find ſome other employment. But whether the reduction would amount to the number here ſuppoſed, or to half of it, is a queſtion of little mo-

calling, if no motion is made by the defendant, enters judgment for the plaintiff; for which he has about two ſhillings; one ſhilling more is paid for a writ of execution, which is in form and effect a fieri facias, *a* capias ad fatistaciendum, *and an* elegit: *that is, it goes againſt the goods and chattels of the debtor; and if the ſheriff cannot find thoſe he is to take the body, or the land. Added to theſe coſts, there is a duty of* 1s. 6d. *to government. Theſe ſeveral charges are an ample reward for all ſervices rendered.*

Note of the Editor.

When our author obſerves, that *the laws of that country have ſtripped legal proceſs of its principal follies,* he muſt be underſtood as referring

ment. Saving the expence of maintaining twenty or thirty thousand men in an useless occupation, and sending them to profitable business, however important the object may appear, bears no proportion to the advantage of opening the door of justice to the people, and habituating them to an easy and well-known method of demanding their right.

to the New-England States. In New-York, Pennsylvania, and almost every other State of the union, justice is nearly as expensive as in Great Britain. The common law of the mother country has been universally adopted, and the statute books of the British Parliament blindly and servilely copied. When this is the case, and it cannot be controverted, have we reason to look for less expensive litigation in those States than in the island of Great Britain? Can it be expected that the channels of justice will be less corrupt; and that the social rights of individuals will be better protected and defended? In the courts of common pleas, particularly those of New-York, the bill of the plaintiffs attorney alone is seldom less than eight pounds. In the supreme court of the same State, it often times stretches beyond thirty pounds. We have purified the exterior of society; but its interior economy is fraught with injustice, and to every discerning mind must appear as harbouring the principles of moral destruction. Let us not delude the world, by impressing an opinion, that we have arrived at the summit of perfection in government and laws,—when so many glaring evils are profusely scattered around,—when the laws' delay—the expence of justice—and the in-

There is a strange idea prevalent in England, (it has had its day in America) that it is good policy to raise the expences of legal proceedings above the reach of the lower classes of people; as it lessens the number of suits. This kind of reasoning appears too absurd to support its own weight for a moment; and it would be beneath our serious notice, were it not for the reflection, that men of superficial research are perpetually caught by it. The human mind is fitted, from its own indolence, to be dazzled by the glare of a proposition; and to receive and utter for truth, what it never gives itself the trouble to examine. There is no paradox among all the enormities of despotism, but what finds its advocates from this very circumstance. We must not therefore scorn to encounter an argument because it is foolish. The business of sober philosophy is often a task of drudgery; it must sometimes listen to the most incoherent clamours, which would be unworthy of its attention, did they not form a part of the general din, by which mankind are deafened and misled.

For a man to bring into court a suit that is manifestly unjust, is a crime against the state; to hinder him from bringing one that is just, is a crime of the state against him. It is a poor compliment to the wisdom of a nation, to suppose that no method can be devised for preventing the first of these evils, without running into the last; and the last is ten times the greatest of the two. The French, who appear to have been destined to give lessons to the world by the wisdom of their new

---

solence of office, are as much to be complained of, in most of the American States, as under the much execrated systems of Europe.

PRIVILEGED ORDERS.

inftitutions, as well as by the folly of their old, have found the fecret of impofing a fmall fine on a vexatious plaintiff; and of eftablifhing many other regulations on this fubject, which effectually fhut the door of the tribunal againft the oppreffor, while it eafily opens to the feebleft cry of the oppreffed.

They have likewife eftablifhed a method of communicating the knowledge of the laws to every human creature in the kingdom, however ignorant he may be in other refpects. They are printed and pafted up on public buildings in every town and village, and read and explained by the curate from the pulpit in every parifh. It is in contemplation likewife to inftitute a general fyftem of public inftruction, on a more ufeful and extenfive plan than has ever yet been devifed. Several enlightened philofophers are bufied in thefe refearches; and feveral focieties are formed, whofe object is to difcover and bring forward the beft concerted plan for this important purpofe. In their whole fyftem of diftributing *knowledge* and *juftice*, they feem to be aiming at a degree of perfection which promifes great fuccefs. With all my partiality for the inftitutions of the United States, I fhould quote them (in comparifon to thofe of France) with lefs confidence on the fubject of this chapter, than of any other.

In the adminiftration of juftice the American States in general, are too much attached to the Englifh forms; which ferve to increafe the expence and to myfticife the bufinefs, to a degree that is manifeftly inconfiftent with the dignity of a true republic. But in refpect to Public Inftruction, there are fome circumftances which deferve

to be mentioned to their praise. I am going to
speak only of the particular State with which I am
best acquainted. How many of the others are
better regulated in this respect, and how many
are worse, I am not accurately informed. This
state, (which contains less than 240,000 inhabitants) is divided into about one hundred towns.
These are sub-divided into small portions, called
school-districts, suitable for the support of small
schools. Each of these districts has a drawback
on the state treasury for a sum, which bears a
proportion to the public taxes paid by the inhabitants of the district, and which is about half
equal to the support of a school-master. But this
sum can be drawn only on condition, that a school
is maintained in the district.*

The following remarkable consequences seem
to have resulted from this provision: There is
not perhaps in that state, a person of six years
old, and of common intellects, who cannot read;
and very few, of twelve, who cannot write and
cast accounts;—besides the usual books that are
found in every family, it is computed that there
are in the state about three hundred public libraries,
which have been formed by voluntary subscription
among the people of the districts and the parishes;
—till about the year 1768, which was more than
one hundred and thirty years after the settlement
of the state, no capital punishment, as I am informed, had been inflicted within its jurisdiction,
nor any person convicted of a capital offence; since

* *Besides the small schools above mentioned, there
is a considerable number of Academies and grammar-
schools in this little Republic; and there is one University*

that period, very few have been convicted, and those few are generally Europeans by birth and education;—there is no extreme poverty in the state, and no extraordinary wealth accumulated by individuals.

It would be absurd to suppose, that Public Instruction is by any means carried to the perfection that it ought to be, in this or any other State in the universe. But this experiment proves, that good morals and equal liberty are reciprocal causes and effects; and that they are both the parents of national happiness, and of great prosperity.

All governments that lay any claim to respectability or justice, have proscribed the idea of *ex-post-facto laws*, or laws made after the performance of an action, constituting that action a crime, and punishing a party for a thing that was innocent at the time of its being done. Such laws would be so flagrant a violation of natural right, that in the French and several of the American State Constitutions they are solemnly interdicted in their Declarations of Rights. This proscription is likewise considered as a fundamental article of English liberty, and almost the only one that has not been habitually violated, within the present century. But let us resort to reason and justice, and ask what is the difference between a violation of this article and the observance of that tremenduous maxim of jurisprudence, common to all the nations above mentioned,* *ignorantia legis neminem excusat?*

Most of the laws of society are positive regulations, not taught by nature. Indeed, such only

---

* *Ignorance of the law is no excuse for the breach of it.*

are applicable to the subject now in question. For *ignorantia legis* can have reference only to laws arising out of society, in which our natural feelings have no concern; and where a man is ignorant of such a law, he is in the same situation as if the law did not exist. To read it to him from the tribunal, where he stands arraigned for the breach of it, is to him precisely the same thing as it would be to originate it at the time by the same tribunal, for the express purpose of his condemnation. The law till then, as relative to him, is not in being. He is therefore in the same predicament that the society in general would be, under the operation of an *ex-post-facto* law*. Hence we ought to conclude that, as it seems difficult for a government to dispense with the maxim above-mentioned, a free people ought, in their declaration of rights, to provide for universal public instruction. If they neglect to do this, and mean to avoid the absurdity of a self-destroying policy, by adher-

* *What shocking ideas of morals those governments must have inculcated, which first invented that exemption in penal statutes, called* the benefit of clergy! *To be able to write and read, was at that time an evidence of an uncommon degree of knowledge. Out of respect to learning (as it is presumed) it was therefore enacted, that any person convicted of a felony should be pardoned, on showing that he could write his name. As this talent was then chiefly confined to the clerks, or clergy, this circumstance gave name to the law. The language of the exemption is simply this, that those persons only who know the law are at liberty to violate it. There is indeed much reason for a distinction; but it should have been the other way.*

ing to a fystem of juftice which would preferve a dignity and infpire a confidence worthy the name of liberty, they ought to reject the maxim altogether ; and infert in their declaration of rights, that inftruction alone can conftitute a duty ; and that laws can enforce no obedience, but where they are explained.

It is truly hard and fufficiently to be regretted that any part of fociety fhould be obliged to yield obedience to laws, to which they have not literally and perfonally confented. Such, however, is the ftate of things ; it is neceffary that a majority fhould govern. If it be an evil to obey a law to which we have not confented, it is at leaft a neceffary evil ; but to compel a compliance with orders which are unknown, is carrying injuftice beyond the bounds of neceffity ; it is abfurd, and even impoffible. Laws in this cafe may be avenged, but cannot be obeyed ; they may infpire terror, but can never command refpect.

CHAP. V.

REVENUE AND EXPENDITURE.

A Nation is furely in a wretched condition, when the principal object of its government is the increafe of its public revenue. Such a ftate of things is in reality a perpetual warfare between the few individuals who govern, and the great body of the people who labour. Or, to call things by their proper names, and ufe the only language that the nature of the case will justify, the real occupation of the governors is either to plunder or to steal, as will best answer their purpose; while the business of the people is to secrete their property by fraud, or to give it peaceably up, in proportion as the other party demands it; and then, as a consequence of being driven to this necessity, they slacken their industry, and become miserable through idleness; in order to avoid the mortification of labouring for those they hate.

The art of constructing governments has usually been to organize the Sate in such a manner, as that this operation could be carried on to the best advantage for the administrators; and the art of administring those governments has been, so to vary the means of seizing upon private property, as to bring the greatest possible quantity into the public coffers, without exciting insurrections. Those governments which are called despotic, deal more in open plunder; those that call themselves free, and act under the cloak of what they teach the people to reverence as a constitution, are driven to the arts of stealing. These have succeeded better by theft than the others have by plunder; and this is the principal difference by which they can be distinguished. Under these *constitutional* governments the people are more industrous, and create property faster; because they are not sensible in what manner and in what quantities it is taken from them. The administration, in this case operates by a compound movement; one is to induce the people to work, and the other to take from them their earnings.

In this view of government, it is no wonder hat it should be considered as a curious and complicated machine, too myſterious for vulgar contemplation, capable of being moved by none but experienced hands, and ſubject to fall in pieces by the ſlighteſt attempt at innovation or improvement. It is no wonder that a church and an army ſhould be deemed neceſſary for its ſupport; and that the double guilt of impiety and rebellion ſhould follow the man who offers to enter its dark ſanctuary with the profane light of reaſon. It is not ſurpriſing that kings and prieſts ſhould be ſuppoſed to have derived their authority from God, ſince it is evidently not given them by men; that they ſhould trace to a ſupernatural ſource claims which nature never has recognized, and which are at war with every principle of ſociety.

I conſtantly bear in mind, that there is a reſpectable claſs of men in every country in Europe, who, whether immediately intereſted in the adminiſtration of the governments or not, are conſcientiouſly attached to the old eſtabliſhed forms. I know not how much pain it may give them to ſee expoſed to public view the various combinations of iniquity which appear to me to compoſe the ſyſtem. But I ſhould pay a real compliment to their ſenſibility, in ſuppoſing that their anguiſh can be as great on viewing the picture, as mine has been in attempting to draw it; or, that they can ſhudder as much at the proſpect of a change, as I have done in contemplating ſociety under the diſtortions of its preſent organization. I ſee the noble nature of man ſo cruelly debaſed,—I ſee the horſe and the dog in ſo many inſtances raiſed to a rank far ſuperior to beings whom I muſt acknowledge as my fellow-creatures, and whom my heart cannot but embrace with a fraternal affection which muſt increaſe with the inſults I ſee them suffer,—I see the pride of power and of rank mounted to so ungovernable a height in those whom accident has called to direct the affairs of nations,— I see the faculty of reason so completely dormant in both these classes, and morality, the indispensible bond of union among men, so effectually banished by the unnatural combinations, which in Europe are called Society,—that I have been almost determined to relinquish the disagreeable task which I had prescribed to myself in the first part of this work, and, returning to my country, endeavour in the new world to forget the miseries of the old.

But I reflect that the contemplation of these miseries has already left an impression on my mind too deep to be easily effaced.—I am likewise convinced that all the moral evils under which we labour, may be traced without difficulty, to their proper source,—that the spirit of investigation, which the French revolution has awakened in many parts of Europe, is stimulating the people to pursue the enquiry, and will consequently lead them to apply the remedy. Under this prospect, every person who but thinks he can throw the least light upon the subject, is called upon for his assistance ; and this duty to his fellow-creatures becomes more imperious, as it is increased by the probability of success.

In considering the subject of *Revenue and Expenditure*, as in other articles that I have treated, I shall confine myself chiefly to the great outlines of the system ; only noticing its effect on the moral habits which must be considered as the vital principles of society, and which ought always to be kept in view as the first object of government, both in its original constitution and in every part of its administration. I was indeed sensible that this subject would require more details; and that it might be useful to form an estimate of the quantity of contributions necessary for any given portion of mankind united in a national interest; as we might thus be convinced how small a revenue would be sufficient for all the purposes of a rational government. But I find myself happily relieved from this part of my task, by the appearance of the second part of the *Rights of Man*, in which this branch of the subject is treated in that perspicuous manner which might be expected from its author; a man whom I consider as a luminary of the age, and one of the greatest benefactors of mankind. Neither my work, nor any other that shall be written for ages to come, will surely find a reader, who will not have read the *Rights of Man*.

Men are gregarious in their nature; they form together in society, not merely from necessity, to avoid the evils of solitude, but from inclination and mutual attachment. They find a positive pleasure in yielding assistance to each other, in communicating their thoughts and improving their faculties. This disposition in man is the source of morals; they have their foundation in nature, and receive their nourishment from society. The different portions of this society, that call themselves nations, have generally established the principle of securing to the individuals who compose a nation, the exclusive enjoyment of the fruits of their own labour; reserving however to the governing power the right to reclaim from time to time so much of the property and labour of individuals as shall be deemed necessary for the public service. This is the general bafis on which *property*, public and private, has hitherto been founded. Nations have proceeded no farther. Perhaps in a more improved ftate of fociety, the time will come, when a different fyftem may be introduced ; when it fhall be found more congenial to the focial nature of man to exclude the idea of feperate property, and with that the numerous evils which feem to be entailed upon it. But it is not my intention in this work to enter upon that enquiry.

When the feudal fyftem, with all its ferocities, was in full operation, the fuperior lord, who reprefented the power of the ftate, granted the lands to his immediate vaffals, on condition of military fervice. They engaged to ferve in the wars of the lord paramount a certain number of days in the year, at their own expence. Thus they ftipulated as to the *quantity* of fervice ; but gave up the right of private judgment, as to the *object of the war*. This is the origin of the revenue fyftem of modern Europe ; and it began by debafing the minds of the whole community ; as it hurried them into actions, of which they were not to enquire into the juftice or propriety. Then came the *focage-tenures*; which were lands granted to another clafs of vaffals, on condition of ploughing the lord's fields and performing his hufbandry. This was a more rational kind of fervice ; though, by a fhocking perversion of terms, it was called lefs honorable.

In proportion as war became lefs productive, and its profits more precarious, than thofe of hufbandry, the tenures upon knight-fervice were converted into focage-tenures ; and finally it was found convenient in moft cafes, efpecially in England, to make a commutation of the whole into money, in certain fixed sums; and this, by its subsequent modifications and extensions, has obtained the name of a land-tax. The feudal revenues of the crown, though they were supposed to be sufficient for the ordinary purposes of government, were capable of being increased on any extraordinary occasion; and such extraordinary occasions were sure to happen, as often as the government chose to draw more money from the people. It began this operation under the name of aids to the king, *subsidia regis*; and, in England (before it was found necessary to work the engine by regular parliaments) various expedients were used to raise from different classes of the community these extraordinary aids. In many cases the authority of the pope was brought in to the assistance of the king, to enable him to levy money for the court. The pope, as head of the church, received a revenue from the people of England through the English clergy; and the king, on certain occasions, agreed with him that he should double his demands; on condition that the additional sum to be raised, should be divided between themselves.*

A perpetual pretext for these additional impositions was always to be found in foreign wars.— Edward the first must subdue the Welch; a long succession of kings made the glory of the British nation to consist in the reduction of Ireland; others, in conquering the tomb of Christ; and others, the crown of France. But in common occurrencies, where the call for money could not be predicated on any national object sufficiently glaring to excite the enthusiasm or rouse the fears

* *Cunningham's History of Taxes, page* 6.

of the people, it was the policy of the king to detach some particular classes of the community from the common interest, and to extort money from them, as from a common enemy. Thus all strangers were heavily taxed on coming into the realm; thus Jews, with all the wealth they possessed, were declared to be the absolute property of the king;* thus, after the religion of the government was changed, the papists and non-jurors were taxed double to the professors of the national religion; and thus the king could take a savage advantage of the misfortunes of individuals, and seize their property, under the title of *wrecks, waifs, treasure-trove, strays, amercements,* and *forfeitures.* These, and a vast variety of other inventions, have been practised by the English government, to legalize partial robberies, and take possession of the people's money, without the trouble of asking for it. But all these means were insufficient to supply the unlimited expences of a government founded on orders, privileges, rank, and ignorance. The most effectual way to carry on the great business of revenue was found to be through the intervention of a parliament; and for this purpose the farce of representation has been acted over in this country, to much better effect than any species of fraud or violence has been in any other.

* *In one of the laws of Edward the Confessor (which was repeatedly enforced long after the conquest, and perhaps is not repealed to this day) the clause respecting the Jews is in these words:* Judæi et omnia sua sunt regis; quod in quispiam detinuerit eos, vel pecuniam eorum, perquirat rex, si vult, tanquam suum proprium.

PRIVILEGED ORDERS.

It would be an infult to the underftanding of any reader at this day, to defcribe to him a thing fo well known, as the manner in which this game is played between the different branches of the government. The fecret is out; and the friends of the fyftem, who ufed to be occupied in concealing its operation, are now engaged in defending it. The drift of their defence is to change the mode of the deception; and perfuade the people by *argument*, to fuffer to pafs before their eyes in open day-light, fcenes which have hitherto been acted only in the dark. The curtain has fallen from their hands; and they now declare that the play can go on without it. This for England, forms a new æra in cabinet politics. While the fyftem remains the fame, the fcheme for carrying it on is totally new-modelled; and, like other novelties in the courfe of human improvement, it becomes a proper fubject of our inveftigation.

I have known a juggler, who, after having for a long time excited wonder and drawn money from the multitude, by tricks which were fuppofed to be the effect of magic, would come forward with an engaging franknefs, and declare that there was really nothing fupernatural in the art; that it was only the effect of a little experience and attention to phyfical caufes, not beyond the capacity of any one in the company; that, though he had deceived them thus far, he was now ready to undeceive them; and, for another fee, he would go through the fame courfe again, with the explanations. This ingenious confeffion redoubled their curiofity; the fpectators continued their attention, and renewed their contributions.

The government of Great Britain, under king, lords and boroughs, is now defended both in and out of parliament, by arguments unknown to former politicians. As nearly as any words, except the right ones, can exprefs the full force of thefe arguments, they are ftated by their authors in the following language: " No people ever has been or ever can be capable of knowing what is for their own good, of making their own laws, or of underftanding them after they are made: as the people of England, during the time of the commonwealth, imbibed a different opinion, it has been thought beft, efpecially fince the laft revolution, to cherifh them in their error, in order to come more eafily at their money. We therefore told them that they were free; that they, as Englifhmen, ought to be free, becaufe their anceftors were fo; that Englifh liberty was the envy and admiration of the world; that the French were their natural enemies, becaufe they were flaves; and it was neceffary to make a war once in feven years, to keep up this idea; that we were forry for the increafing burthen of their taxes; but that was a circumftance not to be regarded by a free people, as they had the privilege of taxing themfelves, and their taxes were the price of their freedom in church and ftate; that, we intended to leffen their burthens as foon as the enemies to our religion and to our happy conftitution were deftroyed. But now, gentlemen, we fee you have difcovered, and we are willing to acknowledge, that this was all a deception: as to liberty, it is but a name; man gives it up on entering into fociety, in order to enjoy the benefits of being governed; it never was nor ever will be, realized by any nation under heaven; witnefs the horrors of pretended liberty in France, the daily aſſaſſinations and perpetual robberies which you ſee in Mr. Burke's book from beginning to end ; witneſs the late infatuation of the Americans ; who, already recovering their ſenſes, and ſick of their boaſted independence,* are now wiſhing to return to the protection of their mother-country, where they could purchaſe their laws ready made by us, who underſtand the buſineſs ; as to the church, we are convinced it is no matter on what ſort of religion it is founded, provided it be well connected with the ſtate. We ſhall ſay nothing in future of the *burthen of taxes,* as it has been falſly called, the phraſe itſelf has no longer any meaning; it is now clearly known that public taxes are, in themſelves, a public benefit ; every wellwiſher to his country muſt wiſh them to increaſe ; and for that purpoſe he will do all in his power to multiply the occaſions for creating them ; for it is acknowledged by all good ſubjects, that a national debt is national proſperity, and that we grow rich in proportion to the money we pay out. We are as frank to confeſs, as any caveller is to aſſert, that the Houſe of Commons is not a repreſentation of the people ; it has no connection with them, and it is no longer to our purpoſe to ſuppoſe that it has ; for the people have nothing to do with the government, except to be governed ; but the Houſe of Commons is retained in the ſtate, for the ſame reaſon that the other branches of the legiſlature, and that courts and armies are retained,

* *This is a ſerious argument, uſed by ſeveral writers as well as parliamentary and coffee-houſe orators, to prove that liberty cannot exiſt in any country.* See Dr. Tatham *and others.*

for the fake of increafing the wealth and happinefs of the people in the augmentation of the revenue."

Let any perfon look over the whole chaos of writings and fpeeches that have been publifhed within the laft year againft innovations in the government, and I believe he will fcarcely find an argument more or lefs than what are here comprized. Now this is clearly a different ground from what has heretofore been taken in this country for the fupport of the old fyftem. It ufed to be thought neceffary to flatter and deceive; but here every thing is open and candid. Mr. Burke, in a frenzy of paffion, has drawn away the veil; and ariftocracy, like a decayed proftitute, whom painting and patching will no longer embellifh, throws off her covering, to get a livelihood by difplaying her uglinefs.

It is hard to pronounce with certainty on the fuccefs of a project fo new; but it appears to me extremely improbable that the naked deformities of defpotifm can long be pleafing to a nation fo enlightened as the one to which thefe arguments are addreffed. I cannot but think they are ill addreffed, and that their authors have miffed their policy in fuffering the people to open their eyes to their true fituation. It is certain that the Cardinal de Richlieu has given them different advice. He, like moft other great men, is lefs known by his writings than his actions; but he left a pofthumous work, called a *Political Teftament*, which has been remarkably neglected by thofe for whofe good it was intended; and by none more than by the prefent friends of ariftocracy in England. That profound politician obferves, " That fub-
" jects with knowledge, fenfe or reafon, are as
" monftrous as a beaft with an hundred eyes, and

" that fuch a beaft would never bear its burthen
" peaceably The people muft be hood-winked,
" or rather blinded, if you would have them tame
" and patient drudges. In fhort, you muft treat
" them every way like pack-horfes or mules, not
" excepting the bells about their necks; which
" by their perpetual jingling, may be of ufe to
" drown their cares."

It muft be obferved, however, that in the bufinefs of taxation, which is nearly all the bufinefs of a public nature that is done by the government in England; a policy not very different from that of Richlieu has been practifed with great fuccefs. The aggregate quantity of the revenue raifed upon the people has indeed been fomewhat known; but the portion paid by each individual, and the time, manner and reafon of his paying it, are circumftances enveloped in total darknefs. To keep the fubject ignorant of thefe things is the great fecret in the modern fcience of finance. The money he pays to government being incorporated with every thing on which he lives, all that he can know of the matter is, that whether he eats, drinks or fleeps, walks or rides, fees the light or breathes the air,—whatever he does, drains from him a tax; and this tax is to fupport the luxury of thofe who tell him they are born to govern. But on which of thefe functions the tax falls the heavieft— whether the greateft proportion lies upon his bread or his beer, his fhoes or his hat, his labours or his pleafures, his virtues or his vices, it is impoffible for any man to know. As therefore he cannot difpenfe with the whole of his animal functions, without ceafing to exift, and as this expedient is not often fo eligible as fubmitting to the impofition, there is no danger but the tax will be collected.

It is difficult to defcribe, perhaps impoffible to conceive, the quantity of evils wrought in fociety from this mode of collecting revenue by deception; or laying the duty in fuch a manner, that the people fhall not be fenfible when or how it is paid. This is extremely unlike that manly principle of mutual confidence on which men unite in fociety. It is the reverfe of that conduct, which, arifing from the open integrity of our own hearts, is the guarantee of integrity in others. It is a policy that muft have originated from two contending interefts in the nation, from a jealoufy of their own power in the legiflative body, from a knowledge that fomething was wrong in themfelves or in the fyftem, and from a confcioufnefs that one or the other, or both, were unworthy of the confidence of the people by whom they were fupported.

I am aware that in the doctrine which I fhall labour to eftablifh on this fubject, I fhall have to encounter the whole weight of opinion of modern times. Men of all parties, and of all defcriptions, both the friends and the enemies of equal liberty, feem to be agreed in one point relative to public contributions: *That the tax fhould be fo far difguifed, as to render the payment imperceptible at the time of paying it.* This is almoft the only point in which the old and new fyftems agree, in thofe countries where a change of principle has taken place; it is one of thofe rare pofitions, on which theorifts themfelves have formed but one opinion. It is therefore not without much reflection, and as great a degree of caution as a ferious advocate for truth ought ever to obferve, that I fhall proceed to examine a pofition, which, refting on the accumulated experience of mankind, has not yet been fhaken by enquiry.

I will begin by acknowledging the force of two obfervations, which go to the fupport of the prefent fyftem, as it applies to moft of the exifting governments and to the prefent ftate of fociety in Europe: 1. As long as public revenues muft remain as great as they now are, and as difproportioned to the abilities of the people, it is abfolutely neceffary to difguife the taxes on which they depend; otherwife they cannot be collected. 2. As long as thefe revenues are applied to the purpofes to which they now are, it is impoffible to collect them but by fraud or violence; and violence has been found by repeated trials, efpecially in England, not to anfwer the purpofe fo well as fraud. While fociety remains divided into two parties, which are conftitutionally oppofed to each other, it is impoffible but that they muft regard each other as enemies, and their conduct muft be the dictate of mutual averfion. When the people fee that paying money to their governors, is paying it to their enemies, they certainly never can give it with a good will; and when they know that this money ferves only to ftrengthen the hands of their oppreffors in forging new weapons of oppreffion againft themfelves, they muft feel an obligation to withhold it, rather than to pay it. In this cafe, defrauding the revenue is confidered not only as juftice to themfelves, but as a duty to their children. A tax under thefe circumftances is more naturally objectionable than the *Dane-gelt*, which was formerly paid in England: that contribution was made by the people, to hire a foreign enemy to leave them in peace; and it always had a temporary good effect. But a contribution paid to the people's enemies at home, who being few in number, must soon, if unsupported, fall of themselves, cannot promise even a temporary benefit; the hand of the enemy that receives it, does not so much as lay down its weapon while it grasps the money. As long therefore as society continues in its present disordered condition, any arguments drawn from moral propriety must be overpowered by the strong voice of necessity; for reasons of nature generally fall in a conflict with reasons of state.

But as a new order of things begins to make its appearance, and principle is no longer to be borrowed from precedent, we will endeavour to discover the ground of the received doctrine relative to taxation; and enquire how far that doctrine is, in itself, an object of reform. Out of the seventeen millions sterling which are annually paid into the exchequer in England, but about two millions and a half are levied in direct taxes; that is, in taxes laid in such a manner as to be paid directly to the fiscal officers by the persons on whom the burthen falls. These are chiefly comprehended in the taxes on lands and houses. In France, before the revolution, the proportion of direct taxes was much greater. According to the statement of M. Necker, it was near eight millions sterling, out of about twenty-four millions and a half, of which the public revenue consisted. This is something less than a third; while the proportion in England is little more than a seventh. These proportions are supposed by some of the most approved reasoners on the subject, in each country, particularly M. Necker and Sir John Sinclair, to be as high as it would be prudent to go with direct taxation. The remaining portion of the immense revenues in these two countries, about sixteen millions and a half for France, and fourteen and a half for England, was raised in the former, and is still raised in the latter, by indirect taxation; by customs, excise, and inland duties of various kind, called *taxes on consumption*. The art of imposing these, so as to insure their collection, is to incorporate the sum to be raised for government with the price of every thing for which men pay their money in the course of life. It is the hook within the bait of all our pleasures, of all our conveniences, and of all our necessaries. The hook cannot be separated from the bait, nor the bait from our existence. With regard to individuals, the question is not, shall we pay the tax? but, shall we exist? The continuance of life is a continuance of the tax; and the language of the system is, pay the debt to government, or pay the debt to nature.

It is said in ethics, on the subject of *necessity*, that, supposing their is no choice of action, there can be no moral agency, and no virtue. We will not enquire into the propriety of the supposition as it respects our relation to the Deity, and our subjection to the great laws of nature; but there can be no doubt that the reasoning is just, when applied to the laws of society. Perhaps it is true, that, though I am prompted by the invisible destiny of nature, to do an action for the good of my fellow-creatures, this action is virtuous; but when the necessity for this action arises directly from the positive laws of society, in whose favour it is to be performed—when the argument derives its force from the ax held over my neck, no idea of virtue can be annexed to the action; it is merely mechanical. On this ground we may eftablifh a pofition, which I believe will not be controverted: that the exercife of *private judgment* is the foundation of *moral virtue*; and confequently, that all operations of government carry deftruction to the latter, in proportion as they deprive us of the former. An arbitrary order impofed by a mafter, whether it be upon a nation or a fimple domeftic fervant, tends to debafe the mind, and crufh that native dignity which is abfolutely neceffary to the exiftence of merit, or of felf approbation. And the effect that fuch an order produces on the mind is nearly the fame, whether the action enforced be right or wrong.

The true object of the focial compact is to improve our moral faculties, as well as to fupply our phyfical wants; and where it fails in the firft of thefe, it certainly will fail in the laft. But where the moral purpofe is attained, there can be no fear but that the phyfical one will be the infeparable confequence; place fociety on this footing, and there will be no aid or duty that the general intereft can require from individuals, but what every individual will underftand. His duties, when firft propofed, will all be voluntary, and being clearly underftood to be founded on the good of the whole community, he will find a greater perfonal intereft in the performance than he would in the violation. There is no pofition more undeniable in my apprehenfion, than that this would always be the cafe with a great majority of any people; and if we fuppofe a fmall portion of refractory perfons, who, from want of original confent, or from a fubfequent change of opinion, fhould refufe to perform their duties; in this cafe, the opinions of the great majority affume the fhape of government, and procure a compliance by compulsion and restraint. This is the only sure foundation on which we can ever build the real dignity of society, or the corresponding energy of government. It is establishing the moral relations of men on the moral sense of men; and it is this union alone that can cherish our esteem or command our respect.

On this plan, it is of the utmost importance that the wants of the state should never be disguised, and that the duty of the individual, in supplying those wants, should never be performed by deception. If the state be properly organized, such disguise and deception will be unnecessary; and if we wish to preserve it from degeneration, they will be extremely dangerous; as, by attacking the moral sense of the people, they sap the foundation of the state.

When a company of merchants, or other private men, engage in an enterprise that requires contributions in money, we hear of no difficulties in raising the stipulated sums among the different partners in the company. Every partner makes it his business to understand the nature of the concern; he expects an advantage from the enterprise, and pays his money with the same willingness, as he would pay it in his private business. He would feel himself insulted, if any disguise were thrown upon the subject, to cheat him into his duty. Indeed, when the enterprise has come to an end, or when there is an apprehension of loss, or a suspicion of mismanagement in the agents, it is natural to expect a reluctance in payment, which is only to be overcome by the arts of deception or the compulsion of law. But this is not the case while the company is in a prosperous condition, and while its members are united by mutual confidence in purfuit of a common intereft. A nation, whofe government fhould be habitually in the hands of the whole community, would always be a company in this profperous condition; its concerns would be a perpetual and promifing enterprife, in which every individual would find his intereft and repofe his confidence. Perfonal protection and public happinefs would be the objects aimed at in the adminiftration; and thefe would be infallibly attained, becaufe no human accidents could prevent it. There could be no fufpicion of mifmanagement in the agents, they being perpetually under the control of the whole people. Every reafon, therefore, which could induce individuals to with-hold their pecuniary contributions, would be entirely removed; and the fame motives which influence a man to give his attention and pay his money in his own perfonal concerns, would engage him to do the fame things in the concerns of the public.

If thefe pofitions are not true, then have I mifconceived the character of the human heart, and the real effects to be wrought on fociety by a rational fyftem of government; but if they are acknowledged to be true, it ought to be an indifpenfible maxim to abolifh and avoid every veftige of indirect taxation. It muft appear evident, that to raife money from the people by any other method, than by openly affigning to every one his portion, and then demanding that portion as a direct contribution, is unneceffary to the object of revenue, and deftructive to the firft principles of fociety. It has long been complained of in England (fo long that the complaint has almoft ceafed to make any impreffion even on the minds of thofe who repeat it) that *the Excife is an odious tax* The reafon on which the complaint is founded is what the principle of government would naturally fuggeft; but it is not the reafon which I fhould affign. The tax is faid to be odious, chiefly becaufe it throws a vexatious power into the hands of the revenue officers, to fearch the houfes and infpect the affairs of individuals. As long as the government and the people are two oppofite parties in the ftate, at continual enmity with each other, it is natural that each party fhould wifh to conceal its operations, the better to fucceed in their mutual hoftility and defence; for fecrecy is one of the weapons of war. But if the ftate confifted of nothing more than one great fociety compofed of all the people, if the government was their will, and its object their happinefs, the reafons for fecrecy would ceafe, the inteftine war would ceafe, the parties would ceafe.

The bufinefs of the ftate and the bufinefs of individuals might be fafely expofed to all the world. An open generofity of conduct, the reciprocal fign and guarantee of integrity, would mark the character of every member of fociety, whether acting as a public agent, or as a private citizen.

But the great objection which ought to be made againft the excife, is the fame as will apply to cuftoms, duties, and all other tricks of a fimilar kind, by which the money is drained from the people without their knowledge or confent. The whole fyftem of indirect taxation, fo univerfal in Europe, fo much extolled by the ableft financiers, as neceffary in compofing their enormous maffes of extorted revenue, is wrong from its foundation, and muft be vicious in its practice. It is built on the great aristocratical principle, that men must be governed by fraud ; and it can be only necessary to that system of management which divides the nation into two permanent parties, the party that receives and the party that pays.

The wretched resource that governments have found in lotteries,* tontines, and annuities upon separate lives, merits the severest censure, and ought to be held up to the execration of mankind, the moment we are ready to resort to the real principles of our nature, in managing the affairs of nations. A tontine partakes at once of the nature of lotteries and of simple life-annuities, and involves in itself the principal vices of both. Like a lottery it is founded in the spirit of gambling ; and like a life-annuity, it detaches a man from the feelings and interests of his friends, of society and of all mankind, except those of the particular class of the tontine to which he belongs ; and to them he is rendered, in a literal sense, a mortal enemy.

Borrowing money upon *life-annuities*, as an

---

* *It was my intention in this place to have noticed, somewhat more at large, the pernicious tendency of public lotteries. But the late crisis in the government of France, when the people found it necessary to revise their Constitution, offered an occasion for making some remarks which I thought might be useful to them on the business then lying before them, for which the the Convention was about to be assembled. I therefore published a short Treatise on the defects of their Constitution in "* A Letter to the National Convention,*" in which are particularly treated the subject of lotteries, that of public salaries, and several other matters, which otherwise would have come into this Essay on Revenue.*

operation of government, has been much more practised in France than in England. The reason of this is well explained by Adam Smith.* It was owing to the superior influence, in that country, of those unnatural distinctions among families, which prevent them from associating with each other on the principles of mutual attachment; principles congenial to the human heart, and no less necessary to individual happiness, than to the good order of society and the prosperity of the state. The pride of birth and the jealousy of rank operate on society like congelation and concussion on a body of water: they freeze up the whole mass, and break it into a thousand pieces; which refuse to unite among themselves, or to answer the purposes which nature has assigned to that element. The genius of aristocracy, by the distinctions of birth, had established in France almost as many ranks as there were families. These were perpetually repelling and repelled, tormented by jealousies, and kept asunder by artificial aversions, which silenced the voice of nature, and counteracted every object of society. A man in this frozen, and repulsive state of things, becomes a proper object for the government to seduce into a selfish hostility against the generous duties of life, by the temptation of life-annuities. An elegant French author describes the annuitant as having subdued every sentiment most dear to the human heart: " He amasses his whole capital upon his own head, makes the king his universal legatee, sells his own posterity at the rate of ten per cent. disinherits his brothers, nephews, friends, and sometimes his own children. He never marries;

* *Wealth of Nations*, Book V. Chap. III.

he vegetates, till the return of the quarter day, and enquires with eagerness in the morning whether he is still alive; his whole exercise of body and mind consists in going once in three months to the notary at the corner of the street to sign his receipt, and obtain a certificate, that he is not yet dead." The officers of government know very well the advantages derived from long humid winters and epidemical diseases; and they must delight in the winnings of the game thus played by the public treasury in partnership with death.*

I am sensible that all these maxims, which go to a change of system in the collection of revenue, are destined to rest merely in speculation, in all

---

For a more lively and affecting picture than I should be able to give, of the evils arising from this system, the reader is referred to the short sketch, drawn by the above author, Mr. Mercier; the following is a part of it:—

"*But how is it possible that a wise government could throw open the gate to those numerous and incredible disorders, which are the offspring of annuities on lives? The bands between parents and children broken, idleness pensioned, celibacy authorised, selfishness triumphant, cruelty reduced into system and practice; such are the smallest evils which arise from these annuities. Is it not from these personal and exclusive enjoyments, these additional incentives to self-love, that parents, friends and citizens are no longer known? Friendship, love, tenderness, paternal affection, all are sacrificed to annuities!*

The young women who have passed the age of being marriageable, are, in Paris, innumerable; they have signed contracts on annuities, and that prevents their signing contracts of marriage; for the first re-

countries still afflicted with unnatural plans of government; for so they must rest, till a total change of principle shall have taken place. But let it not be said that, on this account, the hints here given, are useless. If they are founded in truth and reason, the French Republic will soon be able to adopt them. By the time that its government shall be permanently settled, its public debt will doubtless be very considerably reduced. Its necessary revenue will then be so small, compared with what it hitherto has been, the people will be so far elevated to the dignity of freemen, and accustomed to the duties of citizens, that they will find a sensible pleasure, rather than a servile task, in paying their contributions to the state. This reasoning may likewise be thought worthy of consideration in the United States of America; where perhaps it may be followed by the same effects. With respect to other countries, we must wait. A reformation of so deep a nature must be preceded by a perfect regeneration of society; such as can only be expected from a radical change of principle in the government.

I am sensible that men, whose experience in the management of public affairs has taught them to judge with severity on the various perversities of human nature, will find many obvious objections to a theory so different from that on which their practise has been founded. If I do not an-

flection which they can make must be on the inevitable misery of the children, who might be the offspring of such a knot.

A contract on annuities always isolates an individual, and prevents the fulfilment of the duties of citizenship."

ticipate all their arguments in form, I certainly mean to do it in substance; for I am not unapprised of their weight. Where the revenue is to be raised only for *honest* purposes, and where it is to be kept within a moderate compass, so that the taxes are to be no more than what a well-organized community would be willing to lay upon itself, all arguments against raising the whole by direct taxation are reducible to these two points: the *improvident* temper of one class of men, and the unreasonable *selfishness* of others, have always rendered it difficult to obtain from them their contributions by direct and open means. The first of these classes comprehends many of the poor labouring people in the great towns. These people are in the habit of spending all they can earn, if not for the necessaries of life, at least for superfluous or vicious gratifications. They never provide for a future want, even their own; much less would they think of providing for the wants of the state. As it is vain to ask for money where it does not exist, no tax can be collected by applying directly to that class of men. It is therefore thought best to mingle the tax with their meat and drink; and, since they will spend all their money for these, let a part of it go to the state.

To this argument several answers may be offered: *first*, it is in a great measure owing to the inherent defects of the government, that such a class of improvident men is found in any society. That men of good intellects and sound constitutions should be inattentive to the means of procuring happiness, is certainly contrary to the analogy of nature. Indeed we overlook the cause when we go back to nature for it; there is no doubt but it is always to be found in their relative situation in the focial ftate. It is the want of early inftruction, or the want of proper objects of emulation to ftimulate the mind to a fenfe of its own dignity, as relative to the fociety in which it has to act. When the man is taught to know and feel that he never can rife above the condition of a beaft of burthen, he acts at leaft a confiftent part, perhaps even a wife part, in blunting his feelings, and beating down his mind to the level of his deftination. But it is not neceffary to fuppofe that perfons in general, who are found in the clafs above defcribed, have to go through the fame procefs of reafoning, and then of killing their reafon, in order to arrive at this condition. Such indeed muft have been the origin of the bufinefs in the firft inftance; but afterwards, the greater part are *born* in this element of apathy; they are furrounded all their lives by no other examples but beings of this fort; and they never have a thought or a wifh beyond their prefent fituation. Their only object is to banifh all thought and ftifle every wifh; and whether they perifh under the walls of an alehoufe, or in a king's fhip, or on the king's gallows, is to them a matter of perfect indifference.

Such is the deplorable condition of a numerous clafs of beings whom monarchs and minifters muft recognize as their fellow-creatures; and if they are called more *vitious* than their rulers, it is becaufe we have perverted the meaning of the word. But I am not finding fault with *men* of any particular defcription whatever. In this drama of human mifery, in which fo many diftorted characters are acted, our moral faculties are warped and fitted to the part affigned us; and we perform it without fcruple or enquiry. The judge upon the bench is fcarcely more to blame, than the ftupid felon he condemns. The oppressors and the oppressed, of every denomination, are in general, just as wicked and just as absurd as the system of government requires. In mercy to them all, let the system be changed, let society be restored, and human nature retrieved.

Those who compose the middle classes of mankind, the classes in which the semblance of nature most resides, are called upon to perform this task. It is true that, as reason is slow in returning to the mind from which it has been so fatally banished, it will require some time to bring the men, who now fill the two extremes in the wretched scale of rank, to a proper view of their new station of citizens. Minds that have long been crushed under the weight of privilege and pride, or of misery and dispair, are equally distant from all rational ideas of the dignity of man. But even these classes may be brought back by degrees to be useful members of the state; and there would soon be no individual, but would find himself happier from the change. Place government on the wisdom of the whole people, and they will always have wisdom enough to conduct it.

Second, under this natural organization of the state, should there remain a small number of improvident men, unable to perform the duties of active citizens, there would be many reasons for excusing them from any part of the public burthen. It is probable that very few instances would be found, where the inability did not arise from mental or bodily defects; in which case, their claim on society for support, would take place of any claim that society could have upon them for the payment of a tax. In addition to these, we may suppose a few others, who, from accidental losses, or other misfortunes to which separate property is liable, might be unable to answer the demand of the collector; these the government would naturally excuse. If, after these, there should remain another class, who, wantonly regardless of their own happiness and of their social duties, should be found without the means of payment, (which is a supposition I admit only for the sake of argument) the loss to the state would be very trifling in omitting to collect from them. It would bear no comparison to the infinite mischiefs that proceed from the system of disguise.

As to the other point of objection, arising from the unreasonable *selfishness* of some sorts of people, which makes it difficult to come at their money by any direct application to their persons, it deserves a farther consideration. But to give it a full discussion would lead to a new range of speculation into human nature, extending to a length which I fear would be disproportionate to the limits assined to this chapter. I cannot be satisfied with the common opinions we have entertained in regard to the effect that *property* would naturally have upon the human mind. I say *naturally*, not in contradiction to the *social* state, but in contradiction to the *unnatural* state, in which government, founded on conquest or accident, has hitherto placed mankind. A natural state of society, or a nation organized as human reason would dictate, for the purpose of supplying the greatest quantity of our physical wants, with the corresponding improvement of our moral faculties, has never yet been thoroughly tried. It must be confessed therefore that the opinions we have formed of the human heart stand a chance of being eroneous; as they have been formed under the disguise of impressions which do not belong to its nature. The picture of man could not have been fairly drawn while he sat with a veil upon his face. These facts being premised, if we wish to come at his genuine character, the history of his actions must be received with particular caution; as but little reliance can be had upon their testimony. The labyrinths of error in which he has been forced to wander, the delusive tapers with which he has been conducted, and the load of abuses under which he has had to struggle, must have dimmed his understanding and debased his moral powers, to a degree that cannot yet be accurately known. He rises into light, astonished at what he is, ashamed at what he has been, and unable to conjecture at what he may arrive.

Some general traits, however, may be discovered in his character, and recognized as the genuine stamp of nature. Among these may be reckoned a certain desire in every individual of obtaining the good opinion of his fellow-creatures.— Some degree of distinction, at least so far as to acquire an individuality of character among his equals, and merit their respect and confidence, is doubtless natural to man; and whatever, in a true sense, is natural, is, in the same sense, laudable. A man, without the artificial aid that society gives him, has but two resources on which he can rely for obtaining this respect; these are his *physical* and his *moral powers*. By the cultivation of one or both of these, he renders himself useful, and merits the distinction that he wishes. Property, which is called, perhaps with sufficient accuracy, the creature of society, is secured to individuals, only for their private benefit; or at most as a pledge of their attachment to the community, by

which it is guaranteed. It is not expected, on
the true principles of fociety, that an individual
fhould difpofe of any part of his own property to
the benefit of the public. So much of it as the
public requires in contributions, is demanded as a
right; it belongs to the ftate by the nature of the
focial contract, in return for the guarantee of the
reft. It cannot be intended therefore that this
fhould be the way in which a man fhould ufe his
property, to procure to himfelf refpect; neither
is it fo in fact. The reliance he has upon it, for
the purpofe of refpect, is founded on a different principle. Except fuch proportion as is neceffary in fupplying his perfonal wants, the pof-
feffor makes ufe of his property as a fign, or as a
fubftitute, for perfonal merit. Indeed fo far as
his property is the fruit of his own exertions, it
is not an unnatural indication of abilities; and
even where it has defcended to him from his anceftors, it is not a more unreafonable ground of
pretenfion, than hereditary titles of any other defcription.

On this principle, it is eafy to trace the beginnings of a deviation from a rational eftimate of
things, in our attachment to property. A government which had been founded in violence, and
was to be carried on for the exclufive benefit of a
fmall proportion of the community, muft have
been under the neceffity, at all times, of fupport-
ing itfelf by impofition. This circumftance goes
at once to the difcouragement and the difufe of the
moral powers of individuals; as they muft ceafe to
be cultivated, the moment they ceafe to be refpected. As the nation, at the fame time, grew
more numerous, and the fuccefs of war and other
great operations were found to depend lefs on *bod:-*

ly strength, this too began to lose its estimation, and could no longer be relied on, as a title to respect. A natural resource therefore, by which to escape from these unnatural restrictions, was found in a veneration for external and fallacious signs of merit, appropriated to individuals. This was the origin of all hereditary titles of honour; and it must likewise have been the origin, at least in a great measure, of our excessive attachment to property.

There is another point of view in which this theory may be placed, that will show it to be still more probable. In the same proportion as this veneration for property offered a resource to individuals, on their giving up the natural right of cultivating their personal talents, it also became a necessary engine in the hands of the government. It is easy to perceive, that, in a system where every thing depends on hereditary rank, the person placed at the head ought always to be entitled to the greatest share of respect. And where should a king seek for this, but in exterior pomp? Neither wisdom nor strength can be made hereditary, but titles and property may. It was absolutely requisite that those qualities, in which the king might be rivalled or surpassed by his subjects, should be brought into disrepute; and that all mankind should fix their admiration on those in which he could excel. Governments of this kind are sure to be administered in such a manner, that the king shall always be the richest man in the nation; and they generally go farther, and make other men rich in proportion to their servility to him. It is thus that the order of nature is inverted, and names are substituted for things. The simple uses of *property* are converted into the splendid magnificence of *wealth.* This becomes the great and almoſt univerſal object of human ambition; it excites the gaze and veneration of all claſſes of men. Individuals are really not to be blamed, nor their judgment to be called in queſtion, for this manner of eſtimating things. Exterior pomp is, in fact, more uſeful to them, than perſonal qualifications. It indeed often takes place of all the ſolid enjoyments of life; and it never can be ſtrange that it ſhould do ſo, as long as it procures that reſpect, the deſire of which is doubtleſs among the ſtrongeſt paſſions of our nature. We never hear of a man committing ſuicide for the want of bread, but it is often done for the want of a coach.

Such is the paſſion, and ſuch, I believe, is the *origin* of the inordinate paſſion for property, in the preſent ſtate of manners. The greater part of rational men agree that theſe things are wrong; they agree that the general taſte and ſentiments of mankind, on this ſubject, are erroneous; and they wiſh they could be changed. The only point in which I differ from theſe men in opinion is, that I have no doubt but theſe things *will* be changed. I think we diſcern the radical cauſe of the evil; I think that cauſe will ſoon be removed; and the remedy will inevitably follow; becauſe it is nothing more than a ſimple operation of nature, recovering herſelf from reſtraint. I am not preaching a moral lecture on the uſe of riches, or the duty of charity; I am endeavouring to point out the means by which the neceſſity for ſuch lectures may be ſuperceded. A duty that runs contrary to habit, is hard to be enforced, either by perſuaſion or by law. Rectify our habits, and our duties will rarely be omitted.

Good men in all civilized nations, have taken unwearied pains, and given themselves real grief of heart, in censuring the vices and recommending the duties of mankind, relative to the use and abuse of property. Their labours have doubtless done some good; for we may readily conceive that the quantity of misery in the world is not so great as it might have been without them. But these men have not penetrated to the root of the evil; or rather, they have overlooked it; and the remedies they have proposed have always been partial, unpromising, and without success. They lay the blame to the natural propensities of the human heart, and call upon individuals for reformation. Whereas, the fault lies not so deep, nor is the cure to be looked from individuals, even with respect to themselves. Habit is the ape of nature; it assumes her appearance, and palms its vices upon her. And as the universal habit with respect to the subject now in question has arisen out of unnatural and degrading systems of government, a reformation can be expected, only from referring back to nature for a change of those systems; and there is no doubt but this remedy will be effectual.

Establish government universally on the individual wishes and collected wisdom of the people, and it will give a spring to the moral faculties of every human creature; because every human creature must find an interest in its welfare. It must afford an ample subject for contemplation and exertion; which cannot fail to give a perpetual improvement to the mind, and elevate the man to a more exalted view of himself, as an active member of that social state, where virtue has a scope for expansion, and merit is sure to be rewarded.

Being thus restored to nature, every thing is easy and progressive; the individual looks to himself for his title to respect, the moment he becomes habituated to believe and know that this is the only title that will answer his purpose. The idea of relying on the glare of exterior pomp, whether it be of wealth or hereditary rank, must be regarded as what it really is in fact, the effort of a weak mind to cover its own weakness. Such efforts being resented by the people, as attempts to impose upon their understanding, they must fall into disrepute and be laid aside. They cannot be useful, they cannot be kept in countenance, in a society founded on the basis of human reason.

It is difficult to conceive to what an extent this circumstance would operate on the character of the human mind, with respect to its attachment to property. If the present systems of government are unnatural, I am convinced that this part of the human character is unnatural; and a change in the former must produce a change in the latter. One of the uses of property, that of procuring respect would be entirely cut off. And it must be considered that this is the use that has generally had the most powerful effect upon the mind; because it is immoderate and unbounded. It is well known that rivals in the display of wealth are among the most jealous rivals in the world; and that there is usually no limit to the desires of a man on this subject, when they once pass the limit of his real or expected wants.

One simple fact, with respect to the French nation, is almost sufficient of itself to support the opinion I here advance. But I thought it necessary, before adducing that fact, to recur to theoretical principles; in order to shew that both the fact and the opinion are founded in nature, and therefore may be trusted, so far as they go, as the foundation of a practical system. It is well known that the national character of that people within four years has undergone almost a total change, with regard to the estimation of exterior marks of distinction, of every kind. What is called rank, arising from hereditary titles, had formerly as great an influence in the country, as at court; it was held as sacred in the most sequestered walks of life, where actions obey the impulses of the heart, as in the most brilliant assembly, where they are regulated by a Master of Ceremonies. It is impossible for wealth itself in any nation to be more respected than titles were in France among all classes and descriptions of people. Their veneration for king was proverbial through the world; and this was only a sample of their universal respect for every thing that bore the name of hereditary tokens of rank. Their adoration of these distinctions could scarcely be considered as the effect of habit; it had so far wound itself into the native character and soul of a Frenchman, that it could not be distinguished from an element of his nature. But the change of government, like a chymical analysis, has separated the dross of habit from the gold of nature; it has melted off the courtier and shewed us the man.

This is not all. *The brilliance of wealth* has likewise in that country lost its former value; it being no longer considered, either by the proprietors or by others, as capable of commanding respect. I know it will be said, in answer to this, That it is owing to a temporary circumstance; that the great body of the people, who have taken the government into their own hands, are envious towards the rich, and are aiming to reduce all men to a level in regard to property. The plainest reply to this assertion which has often been repeated is, *that it is not true.* No people ever shewed a more sacred regard to private property than the French have uniformly done, during the whole revolution. And, as if to put calumny to the blush, and baffle all theories of sophistry against a popular reclamotion of rights, this regard to private property has been in proportion to the irregularity of their movements, and the opportunity for pillage. It is to be wished that governments themselves would learn a lesson of honour from these examples of anarchy instead of employing venal writers to abuse them.

It cannot be denied, that in all other parts of Europe there are two distinct purposes to which property is applied—a resource against physical wants, and a resource for personal respect. It cannot be denied, that in France it has already ceased, in a great measure, to answer the last of these purposes, The cause of this is perfectly natural, and I have no doubt that it must be permanent. The same effect will be produced in other countries, by placing the government on the solid basis of reason, instead of propping it up on the tottering foot-stool of imposition.

I am aware that my argument is still exposed to one objection, from those readers who are acquainted with the present state of society in *America.* It will be said, that the people of the United States manifest a great attatchment to property, considered as *wealth*, and merely for the purpose of parade; that, though their government is American, their manners are European. To this I reply, in the first place, that the charge is true only in a limited sense. The influence of riches in that country, even on the minds of those who possess them, is by no means so great as it is in Europe. But this answer will not be completely satisfactory to the objector, neither is it so to me. We must acknowledge the fact to exist, at least in a considerable degree, and endeavour to search out the cause. The people of that country have been always accustomed to borrow their maxims, as well as their manners, from the various nations of Europe, from which they emigrated; in the trading towns, many of the present inhabitants are really Europeans, having been in the country but a short time; and emigration is perpetually supplying all parts of the States with new adventures; fashions, and a taste for expensive modes of living, are imported with other merchandise. In the article of public salaries, the governments themselves have been too much guided by European ideas; which suppose it necessary that public officers should envelope themselves in pomp and splendor, in order to inspire a veneration for the laws. For though salaries in general were fixed at the revolution on a scale so low as to bear little proportion to what was common in Europe, and though in some instances they have been since reduced, yet they are still so high as to bear little proportion to what they ought to be. These things have a great effect on the general maxims of life in that country. But these things can never apply to Europe: and, on a change of government and manners in the old world, they will cease to apply to the new.

The Americans cannot be said as yet to have formed a national character. The political part of their revolution, aside from the military, was not of that violent and convulsive nature that shakes the whole fabric of human opinions, and enables men to decide which are to be retained as congenial to their situation, and which should be rejected as the offspring of unnatural connections. Happily, the weight of oppression there had never been so great, nor of so long a duration, as to have distorted in any extravagant degree the moral features of man. He recognized himself as the same being, under the new system as the old; for the change of form had not been so perceptible as to require a great change of principle. Under these circumstances, the people continued most of their ancient maxims, though they were a mixture of foreign and domestic; and, as habit is a coin current in all countries, it is not surprising that whatever had received the stamp of authority in polished nations of Europe, should be adopted without scruple by the offspring of those nations in America.

The circumstance of their not being invested with what is called national character, though hitherto a subject of regret, will in future be much in their favour. The public mind being open to receive impressions from abroad, they will be able to profit by the practical lessons which will now be afforded them from the change of system in this quarter of the world. It will be found there, as it is now found in France, that the display of wealth will cease to be challenged as an emblem or substitute for personal talents; and it will be coveted every where, in a less degree than at present; as it will fail to gratify the passion for respect. It may be farther remarked, that this is not the only circumstance in which the state of society in America will be essentially benefited by a change of manners in Europe.

But it muſt be confeſſed, after all, that this is a theory to which it is hard to gain proſelytes; eſpecially among that claſs of men, whoſe knowledge of the world has taught them a caution which ſhuns the allurements of audacious ſpeculation. And, ſince it muſt be referred to experience, to that I truſt the argument. I profeſs nothing more in this work, than to contemplate the *effects* that a general revolution will produce on the affairs of nations. But in contemplating theſe, it is eſſential that we ſhould be appriſed of the correſponding change that will neceſſarily be wrought on the character of man; in order that, being prepared for the event, he may think of ſuch arrangements as ſhall be likely to prevent his relapſing into the errors which have coſt him ſo much miſery.

A chapter which treats on the ſyſtem of abuſes ſo generally adopted in *raiſing* a revenue, can ſcarcely be cloſed with ſatisfaction to the reader, without ſome reflections on the correſponding abuſes which are found in the *application*. I ſhall ſay nothing of high ſalaries, civil liſt, peace eſtabliſhment, and the other enormities on which privileged orders and ſenſeleſs places depend. Theſe will ſo ſoon fall, with the wretched plans of government they ſupport, that it really ſeems like an ungenerous triumph, to wiſh to haſten their fate. When the buſineſs of government ſhall be conducted, like other buſineſs, on the principles of common ſenſe, it will be paid for, like other buſineſs, in proportion to the ſervice performed. And unleſs this proportion be ſtrictly obſerved in the payment, theſe principles will not long be obſerved in the ſervice. But our obſervations in this place, on the application of revenue, will chiefly be confined to the subject of Public Debts. This subject becomes more important at this time, not merely on account of the present magnitude of those debts in most of the states of Europe, but as relative to the principle on which they are contracted and supported. Should this principle be found to be dangerous to liberty, and suitable only to a vicious form of government, it will furnish matter of deep reflection to a nation that wishes to establish its affairs on the basis of reason and nature.

Here we must take a review of that mode of anticipation, which is common to most of the modern governments of Europe, and known by the name of the *funding system*. This invention (for so the art of funding is sometimes called) has received from the hands of different writers, a considerable degree of censure, as well as much unqualified and injudicious praise. Indeed, when considered with reference to its wide sweep of attending circumstances, it presents itself to the mind under a variety of aspects, and forms altogether a stupendous object of meditation; having produced effects that have far surpassed the limits of previous calculation or belief. In politics and war, it has changed the face of Europe. With regard to other concerns, both of nations and individuals, its effects have been various, contradictory, delusive, and incapable of accurate estimation. It has astonishingly multiplied the force and activity of trade; but it has increased in an equal degree the quantity of useless and destructive speculation. It has converted commerce into a weapon of war; and it has made of that tremendous calamity an alluring instrument of commerce. It has brought these two occupations, so extremely oppofite in their nature, to a cordial coalition and mutual fupport; and thus by the aid of both, it facilitates every project of ambition in the government; till it familiarifes the public mind to a ferious acquiefcence in a paradox, which muft have excited the ridicule of any age accuftomed only to common calculation, That the more a nation is debilitated and exhaufted, the more fplendid and powerful it grows. Indeed the fyftem is replete with fo much apparent good, attended with its folid weight of evils, that we may be thought to incur the guilt of partiality or inattention, fhould we fail to qualify our cenfure with fome degree of approbation.

But the queftion, Whether the fyftem of funding ought to be admitted in all its latitude, can be decided only by ftriking the balance of good and evil in the effects that it muft from its nature produce. And I think, on confidering the fubject as relative to a free republic, the balance will be found much more on the fide of the evil, than it is when applied to the old plans of government.

The benefits, to be derived from the fyftem, are of two kinds;—*commercial*, as it facilitates the bufinefs of individuals, and *political*, as it aids the government in the great operations of war. It is well known, or it is univerfally believed, that the public debt in England, being funded on the bafis of mortgaging the national revenue for its intereft, has created a prodigious mafs of capital in the hands of trade. By furnifhing men with a kind of ftock, which they are fure of turning into money at any moment they choofe, it enables them to vary their operations with fuch facility, as to feize many advantages in domeftic and foreign markets, which muft otherwife pafs without effect. It is in a great measure to this circumstance, that many persons (perhaps without a due consideration of causes) have attributed the flourishing state of commerce in this kingdom. Indeed, since it is found that commerce has increased with the augmentation of taxes, the argument in favour of unlimited funding has become so seducing, that the paradox has arisen almost to a solecism; it is said that public insolvency is public wealth, and the national debt is itself a national benefit.

The advantages of a *political* nature, which are derived from the principle of funding, consist in establishing such an unquestionable credit, that the government can at all times borrow, without the means or the intention, or even the promise of payment. This credit answers all the purpose of an inexhaustible treasury, on which the government may draw at any moment, and to any amount. It is easy to conceive the immense facility thus given to the measures of administration. It enables them to begin, on the shortest notice and with the greatest secrecy, the most expensive operations, and then to pursue them to any extent; and this without consulting the wishes of the nation. It precludes the necessity of accumulating a national treasure by previous taxation and œconomy; a measure which must always be attended with the disadvantage of losing the use of the money, from the time it is hoarded, until it is expended. It likewise avoids the necessity of another operation no less to be dreaded by officers of government in general; I mean a sudden augmentation of taxes, by which the people should be called upon to support the expences of the year, within the year. A measure which, if not sometimes impossible, would often be hazardous to the reputation of ministers, and to the success of extraordinary enterprises.

Such is the general summary of the advantages derived from the Funding System; and this opens to our view the train of evils with which they are contrasted. These I fear will be too numerous to be particularly noticed, and too great to be readily conceived. In the hands of an administration, I will not say *corrupt*, but an administration whose interest is in any measure different from that of the nation at large, this system is the most dangerous instrument that can be imagined: as it is an instrument of incalculable force, and may be always wielded without opposition. This from the nature of the subject must be the case; because the expences of any projected enterprise being charged on posterity, the party most interested in making the opposition, is not in being at the time, and cannot be heard in its remonstrance. Thus, in the business of war, which is the principal object in the funding system, it enables governments to hire men to slaughter each other with more than their own swords. They wring out of the hard earnings of future generations the means of destroying the present. Here is a double violence which the generation, that goes to war by the aid of funding, commits on the age that is to follow. It precludes the existence of one part of society, by destroying those who should have been their progenitors; and it charges the portion of posterity, that escapes into existence, with the expences of killing the fellows of their ancestors. And these expences they must pay under the cruel disadvantages of being deprived of half their natural resources, by a diminution of their natural numbers.

PRIVILEGED ORDERS. 149

As military operations are now conducted, every man killed or destroyed in war, costs to the nation upwards of a thousand pounds sterling. This calculation is taken from a view of the last war in which England was engaged. The nation expended in that war, as stated by Sir John Sinclair,* something more than 139 millions. No financier has calculated with any accuracy *the number of lives* that it cost on the part of Great Britain, in battles, hospitals, and prisons; probably it did not exceed 139 thousand. So that the people of this country are now consoling themselves for the loss of their friends and relations, by paying for their execution at the rate of a thousand pounds a head. Other jobs performed in such a wholesale manner are generally charged at a cheaper rate; but this is more expensive than the business of a like nature, which is done in the formality of detail, at the Old Bailey and Newgate.

It requires but a slight observation on the character of the times in different ages, to show that the object of war, and the spirit with which it is conducted, have been altogether different, within the present century, from what they were in more remote periods of modern history. In the maritime nations of Europe, the object of war has changed from religion to commerce; from a point of honour among kings, to a point of profit among merchants, ministers and generals. These subjects have nothing in their nature sufficiently animating to rouse the enthusiasm of a whole nation to such a degree, as to render it safe for the projector of a war to apply to the people for their immediate support. Therefore, to find the means

*Hist. of the Revenue, Part III. page 95

of carrying it on, they resort to a principle congenial to the object of the war; and it becomes supported, as it is projected, in the spirit of commerce. But, as all offensive wars, in every possible circumstance, can only be maintained by deceiving the people, the government in this case recurs to a commercial deception, and induces them to undertake the burthen, on condition that the weight of it be shifted off to a future period. Such is the origin of funding; and it has evidently risen out of the necessity that governments were under, of changing the principle of deception, in order to conform to the spirit of the times.

As an engine of state, the funding system has completely taken place of religious enthusiasm; and mankind have been hurried on to their own destruction by the former, within the two last ages, with as little prudence and as much delusion, as they were by the latter, in the twelfth century. Indeed, I see no reason why a genuine crusade could not have been undertaken, even by the government of Great Britain within the last fifty years, and carried on to any extent, by the aid of the funding system. For the principle of the system is such as to prevent men from enquiring into the object of the war; as every inducement to such enquiry is almost completely taken away, with respect to every class of society. One class, by the previous operation of the same system in the increase of taxes, are rendered so wretched in their domestic condition, that they are glad to engage as soldiers in any cause, for the sake of the pay, so pitifully small as the pay of a soldier is; another class, and one that has great influence on the public opinion, is composed of generals, contractors, ministers and secretaries, with all their dependants, who are sure to make a profitable job of any war, however it be conducted, and whatever be its object; another class consists of idle speculators in the funds, whose chance of gain increases with the jostling of public affairs, and especially with the augmentation of the debt; while the rest of the community, who cannot be rendered active by the allurements of private profit, are rendered passive by deferring the payment of the loss.

From the time when the predatory spirit, which led the northern Barbarians to ravage the south of Europe, had subsided, and given place to its natural offspring, in the establishment of feudal monarchy, the history of this quarter of the world begins to assume a consistent shape; and it offers itself to our contemplation, as relative to the spirit of nations, under three successive aspects. These are the spirit of hierarchy, the spirit of chivalry, and the spirit of commerce. Out of these different materials the genius of the government has forged instruments of oppression almost equally destructive. It has never failed to cloud the minds of the nation with some kind of superstition, conformable to the temper of the times. In one age it is the superstition of religion, in another the superstition of honour, in another the superstition of public credit.

The deplorable use that has been made of the last of these, during the present century in England, and for a much longer period in some other governments, has induced many persons to regret that the spirit of commerce has ever become predominant over that of chivalry and that of the church. They see a contracted meanness in the one, which ill compares with the open enthusiasm of the other two. But before we find fault with what seems to be the order of nature in thefe events, we ought to confider the effects that it has and will produce, in the progrefs of fociety and morals. Chivalry and hierachy taught us to believe that all men who did not pay homage to the fame monarch, or ufe the fame mode of worfhip with ourfelves, were our natural enemies, and ought to be extirpated. The fpirit of commerce has brought us acquainted with thofe people; we find them to be like other men, and that they are really ufeful to us in fupplying our wants. As their exiftence and their profperity are found to be advantageous to us in a commercial point of view, we ceafe to regard them as enemies; and refufe to go and kill them, unlefs we are hired to do it. But as commerce may deal in human flaughter as well as in other things, when ever the government will offer us more money for deftroying our neighbours than we can get by other bufinefs, we are ready to make enemies of our beft friends, and to go to war, as we go to market, on a calculation of profit.

This is the true fpirit of commerce, as relative to war. But as this fpirit has made us better acquainted with all foreign nations, and with ourfelves, it has excited a difpofition for enquiry into the moral relations of men, with a view to political happinefs. The refult of this enquiry is now beginning to appear. It has already convinced us that there can be no poffible cafe in which one nation can be the *natural* enemy of another; and this leads us to difcover the caufe why they have been *factitious* enemies. The whole is found to be a fatal deception perpetually impofed upon each nation by its own government, for the private benefit of its administrators. The same spirit of enquiry is now leading the people to change the form of their governments, that society may be restored to its proper foundation, the general happiness of the great community of men.

On examining the succession of principles which mark the character of the times through these different periods, it appears that, when the spirit of commerce had become predominant, the only engine of state, which could be relied upon to excite the people to war, was the establishment of a national credit by funding the national debts. And we should not be wide from the truth in asserting, that to the funding system alone the principal commercial nations of Europe are to attribute the wars of the present century, as well as the enormous debts under which they have learned to struggle.

Such have been the effects of funding, under the old forms of governments; and having ascertained the principles on which it has operated in producing these effects, we shall be better able to determine whether it be admissible in the policy of a free republic. In this great crisis of human affairs, it behoves mankind to probe the wounds of nature to the bottom, and remove every excrescence which might prevent a perfect cure.

Men of contemplative minds, as well as those of practical knowledge, have now become so generally agreed in the necessity of the funding system, that, though they discern the evils to which it must expose a nation, I fear it is one of the last of their established maxims that they will be willing to subject to the severity of discussion. The universal opinion is that a state cannot exist without a national credit; unless it put itself to the disadvantage of hoarding up money, and keeping a treasure in reserve. And this latter measure, besides the inconvenience above-mentioned, of losing the use of the capital while it lies inactive, would throw into the hands of the executive government, the same dangerous power which is entrusted to them by the means of credit. In this respect their reasoning is just; and perhaps a full treasury would be the greatest evil of the two.

But after all, what is the advantage of a rational credit? I mean in the sense in which it is generally understood, the facility of raising a capital on long annuities, by a mortgage of revenue. Shall we not find on an investigation of this very simple question, that the advantage derived from such a credit (even supposing it never to be abused) can only be applicable to the old systems of government? Will it not appear that it is an advantage totally unnecessary to a rational and manly administration, conducted by the wishes of a free and enlightened people? I am supposing, and it is but fair to suppose, that such a people will always understand their own interest. Or, at least, if they make a mistake, it will be the mistake of the nation, not of the ministers; they will never suffer an enterprise to be undertaken, but what is agreeable to the majority of the active citizens. This people will never engage in any offensive war. Indeed, as soon as the surrounding nations adopt the same change of government, the business of war will be forgotten; but in the interval, previous to this event, a real republic cannot stand in need of funds, as a preparative for war, unless it be invaded. It is even safer without funds; because they might be a temptation to the officers of government to counteract the spirit of the republic. In cafe fuch a people be really attacked by an enemy, then it is that the force of fociety may be feen and calculated. But the calculation does not turn on the cabinet-rules of royal arithmetic; the power of the republic for the purpofe of defence does not depend on a national credit, in the fenfe above-mentioned, or the facility of borrowing money; the government, in making up its eftimate of refiftance, never afks, How many foldiers have we in pay? And how many recruits can we inlift or imprefs?—But of how many men does the nation confift? Armies ftart into being by a fpontaneous impulfe; every citizen feels the caufe to be his own, and prefents his perfon, or his provifions and his arms, not as an offering to a tyrannical mafter, of whofe intentions he would be fufpicious, but as a defence of his own family and property. The enemy being repulfed, whatever inequalities may be found to have arifen in this emulous contribution, are liquidated and fettled on a general fcale of juftice.

Even fuppofing the war to be of long continuance, and to require fums of money beyond the voluntary contributions, and beyond the power of prudent taxation for the time; (which indeed, in a wealthy and well-regulated republic, would be an extraordinary thing, and I believe never would occur) in fuch a cafe, the juftice of the caufe, and the natural magnanimity which habitual freedom infpires, would be a fufficient guarantee for loans, at home or abroad. It is true in nature, and the truth muft prove itfelf beyond contradiction to the world, as foon as it fhall have opportunity to judge, that a great people accuftomed to exercife their rights, would never violate their duties.

Injustice may be expected from governments founded in usurpation; it is their natural character, the tenure on which they hold their authority. They never can be just, unless the deviate from their principle. What is called their *penal justice*, as well as their *pecuniary justice*, is only the fruit of their fears; and ought to be regarded only as an evidence of their constitutional weakness. As every thing they do, must be done by the force of money, it is necessary that they should establish a character for mercantile punctuality, to serve as a substitue for the quality of justice, which quality the nature of their existence denies them. The reverse of this is the case with governments founded in reason and nature, where all the people have an active interest. Justice there is the first article in the social compact; and as neither policy nor principle can ever admit of a deviation from this, the event is not to be expected.

This is the kind of national credit that is proper for a free republic. It is involved in the nature of their system, and spurns those extraneous aids which artificial credits have required. I should consider it as a circumstance dangerous to the progress of society, if the new republics, which are to rise out of the ruins of these antiquated masses of error, should retain the two great principles of finance, on which much of that error has been supported. To raise the revenue by *disguising the taxes*, and to force a public credit by *dint of funding*, have been equally necessary to the ancient system; and it appears to me that they would be equally destructive to the new.

How the national debts that now exist in several countries, are to be disposed of, under a change of government, is indeed a question of serious magnitude. Probably that of France will be nearly extinguished by the sale of the national domains. That of Spain, and those of most other catholic countries, may be balanced in the same way. In some protestant nations, where the debts and the domains have lost their relative proportion, the case will be widely different. But, whatever may be the fate of the debts, I am as clear that they ought not, as I am that they will not, impede the progress of liberty.

E N D.

A LETTER

TO THE

NATIONAL CONVENTION

OF

F R A N C E,

On the defects in the Constitution of 1791, *and the extent of the amendments which ought to be applied.*

LONDON, *September* 16, 1792.

GENTLEMEN,

THE time is at last arrived, when the people of France, by resorting to their own proper dignity, feel themselves at liberty to exercise their *un*embarrassed reason, in establishing an equal government. The pesent crisis in your affairs, marked by the assembling of a National Convention, bears nearly the same relation to the last four years of your history, as your whole revolution bears to the great accumulated mass of modern improvement. Compared therefore with all that is past, it is perhaps the most interesting portion of the most important period that Europe has hitherto seen.

Under this impreſſion, and with the deepeſt ſenſe of the magnitude of the ſubject which is to engage your attention, I take a liberty which no ſlight motives could warrant in a ſtranger, the liberty of offering a few obſertions on the buſineſs that lies before you. Could I ſuppoſe however, that any apology were neceſſary for this intruſion, I ſhould not rely upon the one here mentioned. But my intentions require no apology; I demand to be heard, as a right. Your cauſe is that of human nature at large; you are the repreſentatives of mankind; and though I am not literally one of your conſtituents, yet I muſt be bound by your decrees. My happineſs will be ſeriouſly affected by your deliberations; and in them I have an intereſt which nothing can deſtroy. I not only conſider all mankind as forming but one great family, and therefore bound by a natural ſympathy to regard each other's happineſs as making part of their own; but I contemplate the French nation at this moment as ſtanding in the place of the whole. You have ſtepped forward with a gigantic ſtride to an enterprize which involves the intereſt of every ſurrounding nation; and what you began as juſtice to yourſelves, you are called upon to finiſh as a duty to the human race.

I believe no man cheriſhes a greater veneration, than I have uniformly done, for the National Aſſembly who framed the conſtitution, which I now preſume your conſtituents expect you to reviſe. Perhaps the merits of that body of men will never be properly appreciated. The greateſt part of their exertions were neceſſarily ſpent on objects which cannot be deſcribed; and which from their nature can make no figure in hiſtory. The enormous weight of abuſes they had to overturn, the quantity of prejudice with which their functions called then to contend, as well in their own minds as in thofe of all the European world, the open oppofition of interefts, the fecret weapons of corruption, and the unbridled fury of defpairing faction—thefe are fubjects which efcape our common obfervation, when we contemplate the labors of that Affembly. But the legacy they have left to their country in their deliberative capacity will remain a lafting monument to their praife; and though while fearching out the defective parts of their work, without lofing fight of the difficulties under which it was formed, we may find more occafion to admire its wifdom, than to murmur at its faults; yet this confideration ought not to deter us from the attempt.

The great leading principle, on which their conftitution was meant to be founded, is *the equality of rights*. This principle being laid down with fuch clearnefs, and afferted with fo much dignity in the beginning of the code, it is ftrange that men of clear underftandings fhould fail to be charmed with the beauty of the fyftem which nature muft have taught them to build on that foundation. It fhows a difpofition to counteract the analogy of nature, to fee them at one moment, impreffing this indelible principle on our minds, and with the next breath declaring, That France fhall remain a monarchy,—that it fhall have a king, hereditary, inviolable, clothed with all the executive, and much of the legiflative power, commander in chief of all the national force by land and fea, having the initiative of war, and the power of concluding peace;—and above all, to hear them declare that, "The nation will provide for the fplendour of the throne," granting in their legiflative capacity to that throne more than a million fterling a year, from the national purfe, befides the rents of eftates which are faid to amount to half as much more.

We muft be aftonifhed at the paradoxical organization of the minds of men who could fee no difcordance in thefe ideas. They begin with the open fimplicity of a rational republic, and immediately plunge into all the labyrinths of royalty; and a great part of the conftitutional code is a practical attempt to reconcile thefe two difcordant theories. It is a perpetual conflict between principle and precedent,—between the manly truths of nature, which we all muft feel, and the learned fubtilties of ftatefmen, about which we have been taught to reafon.

In reviewing the hiftory of human opinions, it is an unpleafant confideration to remark how flow the mind has always been in feizing the moft interefting truths; although, when difcovered, they appear to have been the moft obvious. This remark is no where verified with more circumftances of regret, than in the progrefs of your ideas in France relative to the inutility of the kingly office. It was not enough that you took your firft ftand upon the high ground of natural right; where, enlightened by the fun of reafon, you might have feen the coulds of prejudice roll far beneath your feet—it was not enough that you began by confidering royalty, with its wellknown fcourges, as being the caufe of all your evils,—that the kings of modern Europe are the authors of war and mifery, that their mutual intercourfe is a commerce of human flaughter,—that public debts and private oppreffions, with all the degrading vices that tarnifh the face of nature, had their origin in that species of government which offers a premium for wickedness, and teaches the few to trample on the many ;—it was not enough that you saw the means of a regeneration of mankind in the system of equal rights, and that in a wealthy and powerful nation you possessed the advantage of reducing that system to immediate practice, as an example to the world and a consolation to human nature. All these arguments, with a variety of others which your republican orators placed in the strongest point of light, were insufficient to raise the public mind to a proper view of the subject.

It seems that some of your own philosophers had previously taught, that royalty was necessary to a great nation. Montesquieu, among his whimsical maxims about laws and government, had informed the world that a limited monarchy was the best possible system, and that a democracy could never flourish, but in a small tract of country. How many of your legislators believed in this doctrine, how many acted from temporising motives, wishing to banish royalty by slow degrees, and how many were led by principles less pardonable than either, it is impossible to determine. Certain it is, that republican ideas gained no ground upon the monarchial in your constituent assembly, during the last six months of their deliberations. It is likewise certain that the majority of that assembly took much pains to prevent the people from discovering the cheat of royalty, and to continue their ancient veneration, at least for a while, in favour of certain principles in government which reason could not approve.

It is remarkable that all the perfidy of your king, at the time of his flight, should have had so little effect in opening the eyes of so enlightened a people as the French. His flight, and the insulting declaration which he left behind him, were sufficient not only to give the lie to the fiction, with which common sense has always been put to the blush, and to which your assembly had attempted to give a sanction, *that kings can do no wrong*, but they were sufficient to show, at least to all who would open their eyes, that the business of government required no such officer. There is no period during your revolution, if there is any to be found in the history of France, when business went on with more alacrity and good order, than during the suspension of the royal functions in the interval from the time that the king was brought back to the capital in June, till the completion of the constitution in September. Every thing went right in the kingdom, except within the walls of the assembly. A majority of that body was determined to make an experiment of a limited monarchy. The experiment has been made. Its duration has indeed been short, being less than eleven months; but, although in some respects it has been almost as fatal to the cause of liberty as any system could have been within the time, yet in other respects it has done more good than all the reasonings of all the philosophers of the age could have done in a much longer time: it has taught them a new doctrine, which no experience can shake, and which reason must confirm, *that kings can do no good*. So that, if the question were now to be agitated by the people of France, as it may be by you in their behalf, whether they will have a king or not, I should suppose the following would be the state of the calculation: A cretain quantity of evils are to be expected from the regal office; and these evils are of of two classes, *certain* and *probable*. The *certain* evils are, 1. The million and a half sterling a year drawn from the people to "support the splendour of the throne;" 2. A great variety of enormous salaries paid to ministers at home, to ambassadors abroad, and to bishops in the church; while the only business of these men and their salaries is to support the fiction, that kings can do no wrong. It will always cost more to support this fiction, than it would to support the whole national government without it. 3. The worst of all the certain evils is, that a great part of the million and a half will be spent in bribery and corruption among the members of the legislature, to increase the power of the throne, and the means of oppression. If the money, after it is extorted from the people, could be thrown into the sea, instead of being paid to the king and his satellites, the evil would be trifling; in that case the wickedness would cease with the first act of injustice; while in this it multiplies the weapons of destruction against themselves. It creates a perpetual scrambling for power, rewards knavery in the higher ranks, encourages falsehood in others, and corrupts the morals of the whole. This it is that debases and vilifies the general mass of mankind, and brings upon them the insulting remarks of many men, who even wish them well, *that the people are unfit for liberty.*

Among the *probable* evils resulting from the kingly office, the principal one, and indeed the only one that need to be mentioned, is the chance of its being held by a *weak or a wicked man.*— When the office is hereditary, it is scarcely to be expected but that this should always be the case. Considering the birth and education of princes, the change of finding one with practical common sense is hardly to be reckoned among possible events; nor is the probability less strong against their having virtue. The temptations to wickedness arising from their situation are too powerful to be resisted. The persuasive arts of all their flatterers, the companions of their youth, the ministers of their pleasures, and every person with whom they ever converse, are necessarily employed to induce them to increase their revenue, by oppressing the people, whom they are taught from their cradle to consider as beasts of burthen. And what must almost insure the triumph of wickedness is their tempers, is the idea that they act totally and forever without restraint. This is an allurement to vice that even men of sense could scarcely resist. Impress it on the mind of any man that he *can do no wrong*, and he will soon convince you of your mistake.

Take this general summary of the evils arising from hereditary monarchy, under any restrictions that can be proposed, and place it on one side of the account,—and state, on the other side, the truth which I believe no man of reflection will hereafter call in question, *that kings can do no good*, and the friends of liberty will no longer be in doubt which way you will decide the question relative to that part of your constitution.

I cannot feel easy in dismissing this part of my subject, without offering some remarks on that general vauge idea which has long been floating about in the world, that a people under certain circumstances are unfit for liberty. You know in what insulting language this observation has been perpetually applied to the French during the course of the revolution. Some have said that they were too *ignorant* to form a government of their own, others that they were too *poor*, others that they were too *numerous*, and others that they were too *vitious*. I will not defcend to the examination of the particular parts of this charge, nor of the whole as applied to the French, or to any other particular people ; I will only remark on the general obfervation, as applicable to any poffible nation exifting in a ftate of nature. By a ftate of nature I mean a ftate of peace ; where the intention is, as a nation, to live by induftry at home, not by plunder from abroad.

I think Montefquieu has faid, that virtue muft be the foundation of a republican government. His book is not now by me, or I would try to difcover what he means by virtue. If he means thofe moral habits by which men are difpofed to mutual juftice and benevolence, which is the common idea of virtue, it cannot be the foundation of a republican government, or of any government. Thefe qualities require no reftraints : the more general their influence fhould be among any people, the lefs force would be neceffary in their government; and could we fuppofe a nation in which they fhould exift in a perfect degree, that nation would require no government at all. It is the vices, not the virtues of men which are the objects of reftraint, and the foundation of government. The expreffion of the general will, operating on the mind of an individual, ferves with him as a fubftitute for virtue. This general will may always be expreffed by a nation in any poffible circumftances ; and, if the nation be in a ftate of nature, this expreffion will always be *moral virtue*, according to their ideas of the word ; and it will always *tend* to moral virtue, in the moſt extenſive ſenſe in which we have yet been able to define it.

It has been ſaid, that man differs from man, as much as man from beaſt; it is ſaid alſo to be fit, that the wiſe and virtuous ſhould make laws for the ignorant and vitious. It is not to my purpoſe to call in queſtion the firſt of theſe aſſertions; but the ſecond, plauſible as it is, I muſt totally deny; at leaſt in the ſenſe in which it is generally underſtood. That ſome men in the ſame ſociety ſhould be wiſer and better than others, is very natural; and it is as natural, that the people ſhould chooſe ſuch to repreſent them in the formation of laws. But in this caſe the laws originate from the people at large, ignorant and vitious as they are; and the repreſentatives are only the organs by which their will is declared. This is not the ſenſe in which the aſſertion is intended. It is meant, that if kings were always wiſe and good, or if a band of nobles were always wiſe and good, it would be beſt that they ſhould be the hereditary legiſlators. This is the ſenſe in which I deny the aſſertion, becauſe it is contrary to the analogy of nature. It being a ſubject on which we cannot look for experience, we muſt reaſon only from analogy; and it appears extremely evident to me, that, were a ſucceſſion of the wiſeſt and beſt men that ever have, or ever will be known, to be perpetuated in any country as independent legiſlators for the people, the happineſs and government of the nation would be greatly injured by it. I am confident that any people, whether virtuous or vitious, wiſe or ignorant, numerous or few, rich or poor, are the beſt jedges of their own wants relative to the reſtraint of laws, and would always ſupply thoſe wants better than they could be ſupplied by others.

In expressing these ideas on the peace and happiness to be expected from a free republic, I have been often accused of holding too favourable an opinion of human nature. But it appears to me, that the question, whether men, on any given portion of the earth, are able to make their own laws, does not depend in the least on their moral character. It has no relation to their state of improvement or their state of morals. The only previous enquiry is, What is the object to be aimed at in the government? If it be the good of the whole community, the whole can best know the means of pursuing it; if it be to exalt a few men at the expence of all the rest, the decision, perhaps, may take a different turn.

A republic of beavers or of monkies, I believe, could not be benefited by receiving their laws from men, any more than men could be in being governed by them. If the Algerines or the Hindoos were to shake off the yoke of despotism, and adopt ideas of equal liberty, they would that moment be in a condition to frame a better government for themselves, than could be framed for them by the most learned statesmen in the world. If the great Mr. Locke, with all his wisdom and goodness, were to attempt the task, he would probably succeed as ill as he did in his constitution for the colony of South-Carolina.

Colonies have always been teazed and tormented more or less (and probably always will be as long as colonies shall exist) by the overweening wisdom of the mother-country, in making their laws and constitutions. This is often done without any wish to tyrannize, and sometimes with the best intentions to promote the good of the people. The misfortune more frequently lies in the legiflator's not knowing the wants and wifhes of the people, than in any wanton defire to counteract them. The fure and only characteriftic of a good law is, *that it be the perfect expreſſion of the will of the nation*; its excellence is precifely in proportion to the univerfality and freedom of confent. And this definition remains the fame, whatever be the character of the nation, or the object of the law. Every man, as an individual, has a will of his own, and a manner of expreffing it. In forming thefe individuals into fociety, it is neceffary to form their wills into a government; and in doing this, we have only to find the eafieft and cleareft mode of expreffing their wills in a national manner. And no poffible difadvantages relative to their ftate of morals or civilization can render this a difficult tafk.

I have gone into thefe arguments, not merely to prove that the *French* are fit for liberty, who are certainly at this moment the moft enlightened nation in Europe, but to fhow that the calumny contained in the contrary affertion need not be repeated againft any other nation, who fhould make the like exertions, and whofe pretenfions, in this refpect, might appear more queftionable in the eye of fafhionable remark.

But it will be faid, I am too late with all thefe obfervations on the neceffity of profcribing royalty from your conftitution The caufe is already judged in the minds of the whole people of France; and their wifhes will furely be the rule of your conduct. I fuppofe that, without being reminded of your duty by a ftranger, one of your firft refolutions would be, to declare a republic, to fix a national anathema on every veftige of regal power, and endeavour to wipe out from the human character the stain which it received, with its veneration for kings and hereditary claims. But it requires much reflection to be well aware to what extent this duty should carry you. There are many vices in your constitution, which though not opparently connect·l with the king, had their origin in regal ideas. To purify the whole code from these vices, and to purge human nature from their effects, it will be necessary to resort to many principles which appear not to have struck the minds of the first assembly.

You will permit me to hint at some of the great outlines of what may be expected from you, under the peculiar advantages with which you meet to form a glorious republic. Although many of my ideas may be perfectly superfluous, being the same as will occur to every member of your body, yet it is possible that some of them may strike the mind in a new point of light, and lead to reflections which would not rise from any other quarter. Should this be the case in the smallest degree it ought to be considered, both by you and me, as an ample reward for our pains, in writing and in reading this letter.

On considering the subject of government, when the mind is once set loose from the shackles of royalty, it finds itself in a new world. It rises to a more extensive view of every circumstance of the social state. Human nature assumes a new and more elevated shape, and displays many moral features, which, from having been always disguised, were not known to exist. In this case, it is a long time before we acquire a habit of tracing effects to their proper causes, and of applying the easy and simple remedy to those vices of our nature which society requires us to restrain.

This, I apprehend, is the source of by far the greatest difficulties with which you have to contend. We are so much used, in government, to the most complicated systems, as being necessary to support those impositions, without which it has been supposed impossible for men to be governed, that it is an unusual task to conceive of the simplicity to which the business of government may be reduced, and to which it must be reduced, if we would have it answer the purpose of promoting happiness.

After proscribing royalty, with all its appendages, I suppose it will not be thought necessary in France to support any other errors and superstitions of a similar complection; but that undisguised reason in all things will be preferred to the cloak of imposition. Should this be the case, you will conceive it no longer necessary to maintain a *national church*. This establishment is so manifestly an imposition upon the judgment of mankind, that the constituent assembly must have considered it in that light. It is one of those monarchial ideas, which pay us the wretched compliment of supposing that we are not capable of being governed by our own reason. To suppose that the people of France are to learn the mode of worshipping God from the decrees of the council of Trente, is certainly as absurd as it would be to appeal to such a council to learn how to breathe, or to open their eyes. Neither is it true, as is argued by the advocates of this part of your constitution, that the preference there given to one mode of worship by the payment of the catholic priests, from the national purse, to the exclusion of others, was founded on the idea of the property supposed to have been possessed by that church, and which by the assembly was declared to be thenceforward the property of the nation.

The church, in this sense of the word, signifies nothing but a *mode of worship*; and to prove that a mode can be the proprietor of lands, requires a subtilty of logic that I shall not attempt to refute. The fact is, the church considered as an *hierarchy*, was always necessary to the support of royalty; and your assembly, with great consistency of design, wishing to preserve something of the old fabric, preserved something of this necessary prop. But as the fabric is now overturned, the prop may be safely taken away. I am confident that monarchy and hierarchy will be buried in the same grave; and that in France they will not survive the present year.

I know that it is asserted and believed by some well-wishers to society, that religion would be lost among men, if they were to banish all legal establishments with regard to the manner of exercising it. I should not be so perfectly convinced as I am of the absurdity of this opinion, were it not easy to discover how it came to be introduced. It is an idea, as I believe, purely political; and it had its origin in the supposed necessity of governing men by fraud,—of erecting their credulity into an hierarchy, in order to sustain the despotism of the state. I hold religion to be a natural propensity of the mind, as respiration is of the lungs. If this be true, there can be no danger of its being lost: and I can see no more reason for making laws to regulate the impression of Deity upon the soul, than there would be, to regulate the action of light upon the eye, or of air upon the lungs. I should presume therefore, that, on stripping this subject of all the false covering which unc-qual governments have thrown upon it, you will make no national provision for the support of any class of men, under the mock pretence of maintaining the worship of God. But you will leave every part of the community to nominate and pay their own ministers in their own way. The mode of worship which they will thus maintain, will be the most conducive to good order, because it will be that in which the people will believe.

Much has been said, since the beginning of your revolution, on the difference between the business of framing constitutions, and that of ordinary legislation. Indeed I am afraid that either too much or too little has been inculcated on this subject; because it appears to me, that the doctrine now received is not that which the subject would naturally suggest. It teaches us to consider those laws that are called *constitutions,* in a light so sacred, as to favour too much of the old leaven of veneration for precedent; and every degree of such veneration is so much taken from the chance of improvement. To suppose that our predecessors were wiser than ourselves is not an extraordinary thing, though the opinion may be ill founded; but to suppose that they can have left us a better system of political regulations than we can make for ourselves, is to ascribe to them a degree of discernment to which our own bears no comparison; it supposes them to have known our condition by prophecy better than we know it by experience.

There was not only a degree of arrogance in your first assembly, in supposing that they had framed a constitution, which for a number of years would require no amendment; but they betrayed a great degree of weakness in imagining that the ridiculous barriers with which they fenced it round would be sufficient to restrain the powerful weight of opinion, and prevent the people from exercising the irresistible right of innovation, whenever experience should discover the defects of the system. It is partly to these barriers, as well as to the inherent vices of the constitution, that we are to attribute the late insurrections in Paris. If we would trace the causes of popular commotions, we should always find them to have originated in a previous unjust restraint.

I would not however be understood to mean that there should be no distinction between the constitutional code, and other occasional laws. There is room for a considerable difference, both as to the mode of expressing them, and as to the formalities proper to be observed in repealing or amending them. I will offer some remarks on a plan for amendments towards the close of my letter. With regard to the general complection of the code, it ought to be as simply expressed and easy to be understood as possible; for it ought to serve not only as a guide to the legislative body, but as a political grammar to all the citizens. The greatest service to be expected from it is, that it should concentrate the maxims, and form the habits of thinking, for the whole community. For this purpose, it is not sufficient that it be purified from every vestige of monarchy, and hierarchy, with all the impositions and inequalities which have sprung insensibly from these ideas; but it should contemplate the whole circle of human propensities, and cut off the temptations and opportunities for degenerating into those evils which have so long afflicted mankind, and from which we are now but beginning to arise.

After laying down the great fundamental principle *that all men are equal in their rights*, it ought to be the invariable object of the social compact to insure the exercise of that equality, by rendering them as equal in all forts of enjoyments, as can possibly be consistent with good order, industry, and the reward of merit. Every individual ought to be rendered as *independent* of every other individual as possible; and at the same time as *dependent* as possible on the whole community. On this undeniable maxim, I think the following positions ought to be founded and guaranteed in the constitutional code:

First, The only basis of representation in the government should be *population*; territory and property, though absurdly stated by your first assembly as making part of the basis of representation, have no interest in it. Property, in itself, conveys no right to the possessor, but the right of enjoying it. To say that it has the right of claiming for itself the protection of society, is absurd; because it is already protected, or it would not be property. It is the *person*, not the property, that exercises the will, and is capable of enjoying happiness; it is therefore the person, for whom government is instituted, and by whom its functions are performed. The reason why property has been considered as conveying additional rights to the possessor in matters of government, is the same as has blinded the understandings of men relative to the whole order of nature in society. It is one of those appendages of monarchy and oligarchy, which teaches that the object of government is to increase the splendour of the few, and the misfortunes of the many. And every step that such governments take has a tendency to counteract the equality of rights, by deftroying the equality of enjoyments.

Second, If you take population as the only bafis of reprefentation in the departments, the next ftep will be, to declare every independent man to be an active citizen. By an independent man, I mean every man whom the laws do not place under the control of another, by reafon of nonage or domefticity. The laws of France, in my opinion, have always placed the period of majority by feveral years too late; that is, later than nature has placed it. This however, was of little confequence in a political view, as long as the government remained defpotic; but now, when the rights of man are reftored, and government is built on that foundation, it is of confequence to encreafe as far as poffible the number of active citizens. And for this purpofe I fhould fuppofe the period of majority ought to be placed at leaft as early as the age of twenty years. To make this change in France would be attended with many advantages. It would increafe the ftock of knowledge, and of induftry, by infpiring young men with early ideas of independence, and the neceffity of providing for themfelves by fome ufeful employment: it would be a great inducement to early marriages, and, by that means, increafe population, and encourage purity of morals.

I am likewife fully convinced that the affembly was wrong in fuppofing that a ftate of domefticity ought to deprive a man of the rights of a freeman. This is a relick of thofe ideas which the ancient government has infpired. Where a fervant is abfolutely dependent on the caprice of a mafter for his place, and confequently for his bread, there is indeed much force in the argument, that he can have no political will of his own; and will give his fuffrage as directed by the mafter. But when every man fhall be abfolutely free to follow any profeffion, every kind of ufeful induftry being equally encouraged and rewarded; and efpecially when every man fhall be well inftructed in his duties and his rights, which will certainly be the confequence of the fyftem you have now begun,—fuch arguments will fall to the ground with the fyftem which they fupport. The fervant and his mafter, though not equal in property or in talents, may be perfectly fo in freedom and in virtue. Wherever the fervant is more dependent on the mafter, than the mafter on the fervant, there is fomething wrong in the government. The fame remarks I believe may be repeated, with little variation, in the cafe of infolvent debtors, another clafs of men disfranchifed by the firft affembly.

Third, The manner in which citizenfhip may be acquired or loft, is a fubject which ought to be confidered by you; as your predeceffors have left in it fome room for improvement. Their regulation was indeed a liberal one, compared with what other governments have done; but not fo, when compared with what the fubject required. I am confident that when fociety fhall be placed on the right footing, the citizens of any one ftate will confider thofe of any other ftate as their brothers and fellow citizens of the world; and in this cafe, when thofe who are called foreigners come to fettle among them, a mere declaration of their intention of refidence will be fufficient to entitle them to all the rights which the natives poffefs. I was anxious that the French fhould fet the example in this fpecies of liberality, as they have done in so many other good things; and I still believe that on reviewing the subject, you will do it.

But according to your constitution there are many ways in which the rights of citizens may be lost, for one of which I can see no reason; it is naturalization in a foreign country. This is so manifestly illiberal and unjust, that I am almost sure it will be altered. It is an old feudal idea of allegiance; and goes upon the supposition that fidelity to one country is incompatible with our duty to another. When a citizen of one state is complimented with the freedom of another, it is generally an acknowledgment of his merit ; but your constituent assembly considered it as an object of punishment. Many of your citizens have been naturalized in America; but the American governments certainly did not foresee that this act of theirs would disfranchise those gentlemen at home. You have lately conferred the rights of a French citizen on George Washington. If he should accept the honour you have thus done him, and the American constitution were in this respect the same as your own, he must immediately be turned out of office, and for ever disfranchised at home.

Fourth, You will doubtless consider the important subject of the *frequency of popular elections*, as claiming a farther deliberation. It is an article on which too much reflection cannot be bestowed. It influences the habits of the people and the spirit of the government in a variety of ways, that escape our common observation. I mentioned before, that one of the first objects of society is to render every individual perfectly dependent on the whole community. The more completely this object is attained, the more perfect will be the equality of enjoyments and the happiness of the state. But of all individuals, those who are selected to be the organs of the people, in making and in executing the laws, should feel this dependence in the strongest degree. The easiest and most natural method of effecting this purpose is, to oblige them to recur frequently to the authors of their official existence, to deposit their powers, mingle with their fellows, and wait the decision of the same sovereign will which created them at first, to know whether they are again to be trusted.

There are doubtless some limits to this frequency of election, beyond which it would be hurtful to pass; as every subject has a medium between two vitious extremes. But I know of no office, in any department of state, that need to be held for more than one year, without a new election. Most men, who give in to this idea with respect to the legislative, are accustomed to make an exception with regard to the executive, and particularly with regard to that part which is called the judiciary. I am aware of all the arguments that are usually brought in support of these exceptions; but they appear to me of little weight, in comparison to those in favour of universal annual elections. Power always was, and always must be, a dangerous thing. I mean, power collected from the great mass of society, and delegated to a few hands; for it is only in this sense that it can properly be called power. The physical forces of all the individuals of a great nation cannot be brought to act at once upon a single object; and the same may be said of their moral forces. It is necessary therefore that the exercise of these should always be performed by delegation; the moral in legislation, the physical in execution. This is the proper definition of national power; and in this sense it is necessarily dangerous; because strictly speaking, it is not exercised by those whose property it is, and for whose good it is intended to operate. It is in the nature of this kind of trust to invert in some measure the order of things; it apparently sets the servant above the master, and disposes him to feel a kind of independence which ought never to be felt by any citizen, particularly one who is charged with a public function.

It has ever been the tendency of government to divide the society into two parties,—the governors and the governed. The mischiefs arising from this are almost infinite. It not only disposes each party to view the other with an eye of jealousy and distrust, which soon rise to acts of secret or open enmity, but it effectually corrupts the morals of both parties, and destroys the vital principles of society; it makes government the trade of the few, submission the drudgery of the many, and falsehood the common artifice of the whole. To prevent this, I would have no man placed in a position in which he can call himself governor, for a moment longer than while he performs the duties of his trust to the satisfaction of his fellow citizens, nor even then, but for a short period. He should feel at all times as though he were soon to change places with any one of his neighbours, whom he now sees submissive to his authority.

But to answer this purpose, the frequent return of elections is not of itself sufficient. I am fully of the opinion, that with regard to all discretionary officers, there ought to be an exclusion by rotation. Those functions that are purely ministerial, such as those of sheriffs, constables, clerks of courts, registers, &c. perhaps may form exceptions; but legislators, executive counsellors, judges

Q

and magistrates of every description, should not only feel their dependence on the people by an annual election, but should frequently mingle with them by an exclusion from office. The effect of this would be, not what is often asserted, that no one would understand government, but the contrary, that every one would understand it. This would form a prodigious stimulus to the acquisition of knowledge among all descriptions of men, in all parts of the country. Every man of ordinary ability would be not only capable of watching over his own rights, but of exercising any of the functions by which the public safety is secured. For whatever there is in the art of government, whether legislative or executive, above the capacity of the ordinary class of what are called well informed men, is superfluous and destructive, and ought to be laid aside. The man who is called a *politician*, according to the practical sense of the word in modern Europe, exercises an office infinitely more destructive to society than that of a highwayman. The same may be said, in general, of the *financier*; whose art and mystery, on the funding system of the present century, consists in making calculations to enable governments to hire mankind to butcher each other, by drawing bills on posterity for the payment.

I would therefore suggest the propriety of your reviewing the article of biennial elections, as instituted by your first assembly, and of your making them annual; and the same term, if not the same manner of election, ought to extend to all executive officers, whose functions are in any manner discretionary. I think it would likewise be essential, that no office of this description should be held by one man, more than two years in any term of four years. This would send into the departments, and into every part of the empire, at frequent periods, some thousands of men with practical knowledge of public business; it would at least be the means of doubling the number of such well-instructed men; and, by holding out the inducement to others to qualify themselves to merit the confidence of their fellow citizens, it would multiply the number of men of theoretical knowledge, at least ten fold. All these men will be watchful guardians of the public safety. But these are not all the advantages of frequent elections. They habituate the people to the *business* of election, and enable them to carry it on with order and regularity, like their daily labour; they habituate the candidates to be gratified with the public confidence, or to be disappointed in the expectation of obtaining it; so that their success or disappointment ceases to make that deep impression on their minds, which it otherwise would do. It is thus that you would cut off an infinite source of that intrigue and corruption, which are foretold with so much horror by those who have not well studied the effects of a well organized popular government. But another method, not less effectual, to prevent the arts of scrambling for power and places, will be hinted at in the following article.

Fifth, Among the fatal misconceptions of things which monarchy has entailed upon us, and which are extremely difficult to eradicate from the mind, must be reckoned that prevalent opinion, that all governments should gratify their agents with *enormous salaries*. This idea has usually been more particularly applied in favour of the executive officers of government and their dependants; and it had its origin in the antecedent principles, that government divides the people into two distinct classes, and that the same quantity of business, coming within the verge of one of these classes, must be paid for at a higher price than it would be, within that of the other; though it should be performed by the same man, and required the same exertion of talents. Your constitution is silent as to the quantity of salary that shall be paid to any particular officer; it only says that "the nation shall provide for the splendour of the throne," (which indeed is a declaration of war against the liberties of the people) but the authors of that constitution, in their legislative capacity, after providing for that splendour with a sum sufficient to purchase the majority of almost any corps of seven hundred legislators, went on to provide for the splendour of the ministers. They gave to one, if my memory does not deceive me, one hundred and fifty thousand livres, and one hundred thousand to each of the rest. This on an average is about three times more than ought to have been given, unless the object were to carry on the government by intriguing for places.

I mention this article, not on the score of œconomy. That consideration, however weighty it may appear, is one of the least that can strike the mind on the subject of public salaries. The evil of paying too much is pregnant with a thousand mischiefs. It is almost sufficient of itself to defeat all the advantages to be expected from the institution of an equal government. The general rule to be adopted in this case, (which perhaps is all that can be said of it in the constitution) appears to me this, *That so much, and no more, shall be given for the performance of any public function,*

would be otherwife. Whatever is free and mutually advantageous in trade, would be natural, and would be carried on by each party for its own intereft: whatever is unnatural and forced, muft be fecured by means that will probably leffen the quantity of the whole; but at all events, the coft of maintaining it will for ever exceed the profits. This is not only found to be true, from the experience of every nation which has maintained colonies abroad; but the nature of the fubject requires that it fhould always be the cafe. It is a theory, for the proof of which no experience could have been neceffary; and it is to the pride of kings, and the miftaken rapacity of governments, to the falfe glare of extended fovereignty, and the defire of providing predatory places for the fycophants of courts, that we are to attribute the train of calamities which has tormented the maritime nations of Europe, in maintaining colonies for the monopoly of trade. And where are we to look for reafon and reformation, but to France? The Englifh and other governments, to fupport a confiftency of character, and fill up the meafure of their fins, are faithful only to this one point, that the more they are convinced of the truth, the more obftinate is their perfeverance in error.

I cannot but think it unneceffary, if not impertinent, to enter into farther arguments to prove, that juftice, policy, and the true principles of commerce, require you to fet the example to the world, of declaring your colonies abfolutely free and independent ftates, and of inviting them to form a government of their own. The example would foon be followed by other nations; if not from reafon and from choice, at leaft from the more imperious argument of neceffity

mind with a veneration for their authority. As this pomp cannot be supported without some expence, the supposed necessity for assuming it is always offered as a reason for high salaries; and, allowing the first position to be true, the consequence is certainly reasonable and just. If we are to be governed only by deception, it is right that we should pay for this deception. But the whole argument is wrong; that is, if we allow monarchy and hierarchy to be wrong; it is a badge of that kind of government which is directly the reverse of republican principles, or the government of reason. I do not deny, that this official pomp has in a great measure the effect which is intended from it; it imposes on the unthinking part of mankind, and has a tendency to secure their obedience. This effect, however, is not so great as that of simplicity, and the native dignity of reason would be; but on the moral habits of society, its operation is more pernicious than at first view we are ready to imagine. So far as the people are caught by the imposition, it leads them to wrong ideas of themselves, of their officers, and of the real authority of laws. This is a fatal deviation from the true design of government; for its principal object certainly ought to be, to rectify our opinions, and improve our morals.

For my own part, when I see a man in private life assuming an external splendour, for the sake of gaining attention, I cannot but feel it an insult offered to my understanding; because it is saying to me, that I have not discernment enough to distinguish his merit, without this kind of *ecce signum*. And when an officer of government exhibits himself in the foppery of a puppet, and is drawn by six or eight horses, where two would be really more convenient to himself, I am grieved at the insult offered to the nation, and at their stupidity in not perceiving it. For the language of the mummery is simply this, That the officer cannot rely upon his own personal dignity as a title to respect, nor the laws be trusted to their own justice, to insure their execution. It is a full acknowledgment on his part, that the government is bad, and that he is obliged to dazzle the eyes of the people, to prevent their discovering the cheat. When a set of judges on the bench take the pains to shroud their heads and shoulders in a fleece of horse-hair, in order to resemble the bird of wisdom, it raises a strong suspicion, that they mean to palm upon us the emblem for the reality.

It is essential to the character of a free republic, that every thing should be reduced to the standard of reason; that men and laws should depend on their own intrinsic merit, and that no shadow of deception should ever be offered to the people; as it cannot fail to corrupt them, and pave the way to oppression. I make these remarks, not that they will form an article proper to enter into your constitution, but to remove every appearance of argument in favour of high salaries. And I think the constitution ought to contain a general declaration, *that every public salary should be restricted to a sum not more than sufficient to reward the officer for his labour*; which sum must, of course, be left to be fixed by the legislature.

Sixth, There appears to me to be an error of doctrine in France, with respect to the relation which ought to subsist between the representative, and his immediate constituents. It is said, that when a representative is once chosen, and sent to the assembly, he is no longer to be considered as representing the people of the particular department which sent him, but of the nation at large; and therefore, during the term for which he is chosen, he is not accountable to the people who chose him, but is to be controuled, removed or suspended, only by the national assembly. This appears to have been established, in order to get rid of a contrary doctrine, which was found to be inconvenient; which was, that a delegate should be bound at all times to follow the *instructions* of his constituents; as thereby all the advantages to be expected from discussion and deliberation would be lost. If the first of these be an error, as I believe it is, it may be easily avoided, without running into the last. When the delegate receives instructions, which prove to be contrary to the opinion which he afterwards forms, he ought to presume that his constituents, not having had the advantage of hearing the national discussion, are not well informed on the subject, and his duty is to vote according to his conscience. It is to be supposed that, for his own sake, he will explain to them his motives; but if for this, or any other circumstance, they should be dissatisfied with his conduct, they have an undoubted right at any time to recal him, and nominate another in his place. This will tend to maintain a proper relation between the representative and the people, and a due dependence of the former upon the latter. Besides, when a man has lost the confidence of his fellow-citizens of the department, he is no longer their representative; and when he ceases to be theirs, he cannot in any sense be the representative of the nation; since it is not pretended that he can derive any authority, but through his own constituents. This, however, cannot deprive the assembly of its right to expel or suspend a member for any refractory conduct, which may be deemed an offence against the state.

Seventh, The article of *inviolability*, as applied to the members of the assembly, or to any other officers of the state, is worthy of re-consideration. But before it be again decided in the affirmative, you ought to take a general view of that interesting subject of *imprisonment for debt*. It is a species of civil cruelty which all modern governments have borrowed from the Roman law, which considered a debtor as a criminal, and committed the care of his punishment into the hands of the creditor, lending the public prison as an instrument of private vengeance. It is a disgrace to the wisdom of a nation, and can never be allowed in a well regulated state. If no citizen should be arrested or deprived of his liberty, for debt, there would be no need of making an exception in favour of the officers of government; and thus you would remove a distinction which must always appear unjust.

Eighth, You will scarcely think that your duty is discharged, so as to satisfy your own minds on the establishment of a constitution, from which the friends of humanity will anticipate a total regeneration of society, until you shall have given a farther declaration on the subject of penal law. All men of reflection are agreed, that punishments in modern times have lost all proportion to the crimes to which they are annexed, even on that scale of barbarous justice by which they were introduced. Few, however, have had the wisdom to discover, or the boldness to declare, the true cause of the evil; and while we remain ignorant of the cause, it is no wonder that we fail in finding the remedy. In the glooms of meditation on the miseries of civilized life, I have been almost led to adopt this conclusion, That society itself is the cause of all crimes; and, as such, it has no right to punish them at all. But, without indulging the severity of this unqualified assertion, we may venture to say, that every punishment is a new crime; though it may not in all cases be so great as would follow from omitting to punish.

There is a manifest difference between *punishment* and *correction*; the latter, among rational beings, may always be performed by instruction; or at most by some gentle species of restraint. But punishment, on the part of the public, arises from no other source but a jealousy of power. It is a confession of the inability of society, to protect itself against an ignorant or refractory member. When there are factions in a state, contending for the supreme command, the pains inflicted by each party are summary; they often precede the crime; and the factions wreak their vengeance on each other, as a prevention of expected injuries. Something very similar to this is what perpetually takes place in every nation, in what is called a state of tranquility and order. For government has usually been nothing more than a regulated faction. The party which governs, and the party which reluctantly submits to be governed, maintain a continual conflict; and out of that conflict proceed the crimes and the punishments, or, more properly speaking, the punishments and the crimes. When we see the power of the nation seizing an individual, dragging him to a tribunal, pronouncing him worthy of death, and then going through the solemn formalities of execution, it is natural to ask, what is the meaning of all this? It certainly means, that the nation is in a state of civil war; and even in that barbarous stage of war, when it is thought necessary to put all prisoners to death. In deciding the question, whether a particular criminal should be put to death, I never would ask what is the nature of his offence; it has nothing to do with the question; I would simply enquire, what is the condition of the society. If it be in a state of internal peace, I would say it was wicked and absurd to think of inflicting such punishment. To plead that there is a necessity for that desperate remedy, proves a want of energy in the government, or of wisdom in the nation.

When men are in a state of war, with the enemy's bayonets pointed at their breasts, or when they are in the heat of a revolution, encompassed by treason, and tormented by corruption, there is an apology for human slaughter; but when you have established a wise and manly government, founded on the moral sense, and invigorated by the enlightened reason of the people, let it not be sullied by that timid vengeance, which belongs only to tyrants and usurpers. I could wish that your constitution might declare, not merely what it has already declared, that the penal code shall be reformed, but, that within a certain period after the return of peace, *the punishment of death shall be abolished.* It ought likewise to enjoin it on the legislative body to soften the rigour of punishments in general, till they shall amount to little more than a tender paternal correction. Whoever will look into the human heart, and examine the order of nature in society, must be convinced, that this is the most likely method of preventing the commission of crimes. But,

Ninth, In order to be consistent with yourselves in removing those abuses which have laid the foundation of all offences against society, both in crimes and punishments, you ought to pay a farther attention to the necessity of *public instruction*. It is your duty, as a constituent assembly to establish a system of government that shall improve the morals of mankind. In raising a people from slavery to freedom, you have called them to act on a new theatre; and it is a necessary part of your business, to teach them how to perform their parts. By discovering to a man his rights, you impose upon him a new system of duties. Every Frenchman, born to liberty, must now claim, among the first of his rights, the right of being instructed in the manner of preserving them. This the society has no authority to refuse; and to fail of enjoining it on the legislative body, as a part of its constant care, would be to counteract the principles of the revolution, and expose the whole system to be overturned.

From what the constitution has already declared on this head, and from the disposition of the two last assemblies, I have no doubt but considerable attention will be paid to it; but I wish in this place to recommend it to a more particular consideration, as a subject connected with criminal law. It is certain that no obedience can be rationally expected from any man to a law which he does not know. It is not only unjust, but absurd and even impossible, to enforce his obedience. It is therefore but half the business of legislators to make good laws; an indispensable part of their duty is to see that every person in the state shall perfectly understand them. The barbarous maxim of jurisprudence, *That ignorance of the law is no excuse to the offender,* is an insolent apology for tyranny, and ought never to disgrace the policy of a rational government. I think therefore it would do honour to your constitution, and serve as a stimulus to your legislature and to your magistrates, in the great duty of instruction, to declare, *That knowledge is the foundation of obedience, and that laws shall have no authority but where they are understood.*

Tenth, Since I am treating of morals, the great object of all political institutions, I cannot avoid bestowing some remarks on the subject of *public lotteries.* It is a shocking disgrace to modern governments, that they are driven to this pitiful piece of knavery, to draw money from the people. But no circumstance of this kind is so extraordinary, as that this policy should be continued in France, since the revolution; and that a state lottery should still be reckoned among the permanent sources of revenue. It has its origin in deception; and depends for its support, on raising and disappointing the hopes of individuals, on perpetually agitating the mind with unreasonable desires of gain, on clouding the understanding with superstitious ideas of chance, destiny, and fate, on diverting the attention from regular industry, and promoting a universal spirit of gambling, which carries all sorts of vices into all classes of people. Whatever way we look into human affairs, we shall ever find, that the bad organization of society is the cause of more disorders than could possibly arise from the natural temper of the heart. And what shall we say of a government, that avowedly steps forward with the insolence of an open enemy, and creates a new vice for the sake of loading it with a tax? What right has such a government to punish our follies?

R

And who can look without disgust on the impious figure it makes, in holding the scourge in one hand, and the temptation in the other? You cannot hesitate to declare in your constitution, that all state lotteries shall be for ever abolished.

Eleventh, As yours is the first nation in the world, that has solemnly renounced the horrid business of conquest, you ought to proceed one step farther and declare, that you will have no more to do with *colonies*. This is but a necessary consequence of your former renunciation. For colonies are an appendage of conquest; and to claim a right to the one would be claiming a perpetual, or reiterated right to the other. Supposing your colonies were to declare independence, and set up a government of their own, (which your own principles and the first laws of nature declare they have a right to do) in that case, the same pretences which you now have to hold them under your control, would certainly justify you in reconquering and subjecting them. But it would be a mere waste of argument, to prove that you have no *right* to retain a sovereignty over them; and if I could bring myself to pay so ill a compliment to your justice, as to suppose that you could wish to violate a right, for the sake of what is called *policy*, it would be easy to show, that to maintain foreign possessions, is in all cases as impolitic, as it is unjust and oppressive. Policy, in this respect, can have no other object but the advantages of trade; and it may be laid down as a universal position, that whatever solid advantages can flow to the mother-country from the trade of her colonies, would necessarily flow to her, if they were independent states. The experience of mankind has not yet enabled us even to suppose a case, in which it would be otherwife. Whatever is free and mutually advantageous in trade, would be natural, and would be carried on by each party for its own intereft : whatever is unnatural and forced, muft be fecured by means that will probably leffen the quantity of the whole ; but at all events, the coft of maintaining it will for ever exceed the profits. This is not only found to be true, from the experience of every nation which has maintained colonies abroad ; but the nature of the fubject requires that it fhould always be the cafe. It is a theory, for the proof of which no experience could have been neceffary ; and it is to the pride of kings, and the miftaken rapacity of governments, to the falfe glare of extended fovereignty, and the defire of providing predatory places for the fycophants of courts, that we are to attribute the train of calamities which has tormented the maritime nations of Europe, in maintaining colonies for the monopoly of trade. And where are we to look for reafon and reformation, but to France? The Englifh and other governments, to fupport a confiftency of character, and fill up the meafure of their fins, are faithful only to this one point, that the more they are convinced of the truth, the more obftinate is their perfeverance in error.

I cannot but think it unneceffary, if not impertinent, to enter into farther arguments to prove, that juftice, policy, and the true principles of commerce, require you to fet the example to the world, of declaring your colonies abfolutely free and independent ftates, and of inviting them to form a government of their own. The example would foon be followed by other nations ; if not from reafon and from choice, at leaft from the more imperious argument of neceffity.

Twelfth, I cannot close my letter, without some reflections on the policy of maintaining any thing like what is called *a standing army in time of peace,* which seems to have been the intention of your first assembly. Such a force would have many fatal effects on the spirit of a republican government, without answering any good purpose that can be expected from it. According to your own principles, you will have no more to do with foreign wars, unless you are invaded; and it is probable, that the present is the last invasion that will ever be formed against France. But, be that as it may, a standing military force is the worst resource that can be found for the defence of a free republic. In this case, the strength of the army is the weakness of the nation. If the army be really strong enough to be relied on for defence, it not only imposes upon the people a vast unnecessary expence, but it must be a dangerous instrument, in the hands of dangerous men; it may furnish the means of civil wars, and of the destruction of liberty. If, on the contrary, it be not sufficient for external defence, it will only serve to disappoint the people. Being taught to believe that they have an army, they will cease to trust in their own strength, and be deceived in their expectations of safety.

But the greatest objection against a standing army is, the effect it would have on the political sentiments of the people. Every citizen ought to feel himself to be a necessary part of the great community, for every purpose to which the public interest can call him to act; he should feel the habits of a citizen and the energies of a soldier, without being exclusively destined to the functions of either. His physical and moral powers should be kept in equal vigour ; as the difuse of the former would be very foon followed by the decay of the latter. If it be wrong to truft the legiflative power of the ftate for a number of years, or for life, to a fmall number of men ; it is certainly more prepofterous to do the fame thing with regard to military power. Where the wifdom refides, there ought the ftrength to refide, in the great body of the people ; and neither the one nor other ought ever to be delegated, but for fhort periods of time, and under fevere reftrictions. This is the way to preferve a temperate and manly ufe of both ; and thus, by trufting only to themfelves, the people will be fure of a perpetual defence againft the open force, and the fecret intrigues of all poffible enemies at home and abroad.

Thirteenth, After tracing the outlines of your conftitution, according to your prefent ideas, and proclaiming it in the moft folemn manner, as the foundation of law and right, it will ftill be vain to think of reftraining the people from making alterations and amendments, as often as experience fhall induce them to change their opinions. The point you have to aim at in this, is to agree upon a method in which amendments can be made, without any of thofe extraordinary exertions, which would occafion unneceffary infurrections. The more eafy and expeditious this method fhall appear, the lefs likely it will be to provoke diforders, and the better it will anfwer the purpofe, provided it always refers the fubject to the real wifhes of the people. I would propofe, therefore, (on the prefumption that your legiflative body fhall be chofen only for one year at a time) that every annual national affembly fhall have power, to *propofe*, and the next fucceeding one *adopt* and *ratify*, any amendments that they shall think proper in the constitutional code. But it should always be done under this restriction, *that the articles to be proposed by any one assembly, should be agreed to, and published to the people in every department, within the first six months of the session of that assembly.* This would give time to the people to discuss the subject fully, and to form their opinions, previous to the time of electing their members to the next assembly. The members of the new assembly, when they should come together, would thus be competent to declare the wishes of the people on the amendments proposed, and would act upon them as they should think proper. The same power of *proposing* and then of *adopting* would be continued from year to year with perfect safety to the constitution, and with the probability of improvement.

Thus, gentlemen, I have given a hasty sketch of some leading ideas, that lay with weight upon my mind, on a subject of much importance to the interests of a considerable portion of the human race. If they should be thought of no value, they will of course occupy but little of your attention, and therefore can do no injury. If I have said any thing from which a useful reflection shall be drawn, I shall feel myself happy in having rendered some service to the most glorious cause that ever engaged the attention of mankind.

JOEL BARLOW.

A
LETTER

ADDRESSED

TO THE PEOPLE OF PIEDMONT,

On the advantages of the French Revolution, and the necessity of adopting its principles in Italy.

ADVERTISEMENT.

THIS Letter was written at Chambery in Savoy, in December 1792, at the request of those members of the National Convention, who were then in that country, for the purpose of organising the department of Mont Blanc. It was printed in French at Grenoble, and in Italian at Nice, and sent from those places into Piedmont, and other parts of Italy, during that winter.

It will occur to the reader of the English copy, which now appears for the first time in print, that the defection of Dumourier, in April 1793, the violent factions which distracted the Convention, and the subsequent civil commotions in many parts of France, occupied the attention of the republicans the remainder of that year. Their operations against the league of foreign enemies (which was now augmented by the addition of England, Holland, Spain, and Naples) were confined for that campaign to the defence of the frontiers; and they were thus prevented from pushing the

ADVERTISEMENT.

extensive advantages which they had gained the year before.

This circumstance relieved the king of Sardinia from the despair in which he had been plunged. It gave him time to augment his forces and repair his fortifications. It gave him arguments against the French and the principles of the revolution, and thus enabled him in some degree to unite his people in favour of the system of despotism to which they had been accustomed; for it must be confessed, that the manner in which the French affairs were conducted that year, had a strong tendency to excite a disrelish to their cause in the minds of distant or ignorant observers. In addition to all these advantages, he received a subsidy from England, to enable him to defend his own dominions; by the aid of which he has since obtained a large body of auxiliary troops from Tirol, Milan, and Tuscany.

These unexpected events produced a remarkable change in the relative situation of the French and Piedmontese, from the close of the first campaign to the close of the second. But the third is now opened with as much advantage to the French as the most ardent republican could expect. The troops destined for the invasion of Italy this year, did not amount to more than one tenth of the military force that they now have in motion on the continent. Yet these have already passed the Alps in three different directions, and are at this time masters of a considerable part of Piedmont. It is probable that this campaign will establish the revolution in that country, but unhappily with more expence of blood than was expected from former appearances. Could the same force have been employed there the last year,

ADVERTISEMENT.

under the circumstances that then existed, we may presume it would have met but little opposition ; and the writer might have had the satisfaction of seeing that his letter had produced some effect in promoting the cause of liberty and happiness in that interesting part of the world.

July 15, 1794.

☞ *The notes in this edition were not published in the former ones.*

A
LETTER, &c.

Chambery, *December* 27, 1792.

CITIZENS OF PIEDMONT,

You occupy one of the ſtrongeſt frontiers of a country which nature ſeems to have deſtined to be the happieſt in Europe. But a number of imperious circumſtances, of which you have been rather the victims than the authors, have for many centuries inverted the order of things, and deprived you of thoſe advantages which ought to attend your ſituation. I am a ſtranger in this part of the world; Italy is known to me only from its hiſtory, and your preſent condition only from diſtant obſervation and report. It is not probable that I ſhall ever have the pleaſure of ſeeing you or any part of your country. You muſt, therefore, acquit me of entertaining any deſire to miſlead you, as I can have no poſſible intereſt in addreſſing you this letter, but the intereſt the human heart naturally takes in uttering the truth on a very important ſubject. You are my fellow-creatures; as ſuch I love you, and cheriſh the ties which ought to be mutual between us. You are in a condition which appears to me to call upon you to burſt the bands of ſlavery; in this view, I am ready to hail you as brothers, and wiſh to aid you in your work.

I preſume in the firſt place, and I think I am not deceived, that you are diſcontented with your present situation. I believe you are convinced that you cannot be happy, as a people, while the powers of your government remain as they now are, as relative to the church, the state, and the army. If this be true, you must wish for a change; provided such change can be within your power, and provided you are convinced that it would be for your advantage. Let us examine these two points: whether you are able to effect a revolution in your government; and if you are, whether you would be benefited by it.—For it is not my wish to hurry you into measures, of which you cannot see the issue, and for which you are not prepared.

I. *Are you able to effect a revolution in your government?*

The question need never be asked of any people, when considered with reference to themselves only, without regard to their neighbours. A whole people is essentially sovereign. They can at all times do as they please with their own affairs, unless they are overpowered by surrounding nations. It is the people who support the government as it now is; and the same sovereign people can at any time change its form, and support it in whatever manner it shall please them best. The question has no difficulty in it, but when viewed with reference to the interest which other governments may have in preventing a revolution in their neighbourhood.

The enquiry, pursued in this connection, becomes more extensive; especially when applied to a country of small dimensions, and to a nation less powerful than some of its neighbours. Such is Piedmont. Had you been called upon seven years ago to look into your affairs, and take the government into your own hands, you must have considered it as a dangerous experiment. Even supposing the weight of your sufferings to have been as great then as they are now, and supposing you had been possessed of the same information which you have since drawn from the progress of liberty in Europe, it would scarcely have been prudent for you to have engaged in so daring an enterprise. All the tyrants in your neighbourhood would have brought forward their armies of slaves to crush the rebellion. The French court would have been, at that time, as much your enemy as the French nation is now your friend. And the house of Austria, with all the subdivisions of its power in Italy, posted at your gates, would have united with that of Bourbon, to have guaranteed your king in every possible extent of his oppression.

Under these disadvantages your struggles for liberty might have been vain; they might even have produced a new injury, instead of relieving you from the old. But the ground is now changed; the duty you owe to yourselves is clearly pointed out by the natural current of events; and the work you have to do, in establishing a perfect and undisturbed liberty, is in my opinion much easier than you imagine. France is at this time, not only the most powerful nation in Europe, but when engaged, as she now is, in defence of liberty, she is a match for all the other powers of Europe, when united in defence of tyranny. France is now your natural friend, the friend of all people and the enemy of all tyrants. She is indeed the only friend you have as a nation in this part of the world. France has brought liberty to your doors; and she invites you, in the name of all that is dear to you as men, in the name of all that can bind you to the interests of human nature in general, to accept the blessing at her hands. She has done more; she has taught you and all other people how public happiness is to be acquired and preferved. She has addreffed herfelf to the great principles of reafon which are common to all men; fhe has cleared away the mafs of prejudice, of falfe doctrine, of fuperftition in the fcience of morals; a mafs which the complicated abufes of tyranny, continued for many centuries, had accumulated on the human mind. She has laid down and clearly defined the rights and duties of man and of citizens, explained the great doctrine of equality, the true defign of government, the nature of the truft to be repofed in public officers, as fervants of the people, by whom they are created and by whom they are paid. She has taught you a great practical truth, which is too confoling to be rejected, and too clear to be called in queftion, *that you are the fovereigns in your own country*; that you have not, that you cannot have a mafter, unlefs you choofe to give up your reafon, and renounce the character of men; that for any man to call himfelf your fovereign is a blafphemy againft God the fovereign of nature, and againft men the proprietors of the earth.

Obligations of gratitude are due to the French nation from you, and from every people in Europe. She has conquered liberty for all men, and laid the foundation for univerfal public felicity. Other nations have only to build the fuperftructure, of which the model is given them in the conftitution of this great republic.

But let us not amufe ourfelves with words, nor reft the argument on theoretical principles, however inconteftible they may be. Let us fpeak of facts that are paffing before our eyes, and call to mind the events of the great year that is now drawing to a close. You have seen the principal tyrants and the most formidable armies of Europe, combined and marching in the full career of promised victory against the liberties of France.—— These armies after sweeping over half of Europe and famishing whole countries in their way to the French frontiers, have there been cut to pieces by a handful of freemen, and driven out of their country. Liberty has marched on the heels of the fugitives; the arch tyrant of Austria, at the head of this fatal conspiracy of kings, has lost the finest part of his dominions; many of the subaltern princes of the empire have lost the whole of theirs, and are now beggars abroad among their brother brigands, who are in expectation of the same inevitable fate. The standard of liberty has reached the borders of the Rhine by the miscarriage of the same combination which has brought it to the summit of the Alps.

All the crowned heads in Europe are now covered with thorns. The man of Turin, who calls himself your king, has been forced to relinquish one half of the usurpations of his ancestors, and is now menacing you with destruction for fear you should reclaim the rest. The Dutchy of Savoy and the county of Nice, more fortunate than you, have been the first to cast off his yoke, and are now ready to assist you with their arms to follow their example. The pope and the other Italian despots, are occupied in restraining the spirit of liberty at home; so that no one of the neighbouring powers is in a condition to take any considerable part in your affairs, except the French; and the French are wishing to give you every aid that you may ask.

Under thefe circumftances, we need no longer enquire whether you are able to effect a revolution; the more natural queftion is, are you able to refift it? It is true, the French have renounced all ideas of conqueft, and have declared that they will never make war againft the liberty of any people. But you will obferve that this principle contains in itfelf a declaration of war againft all tyrants who are hoftile to the liberty of France; efpecially againft thofe whofe vicinity renders them dangerous to the internal peace of the new republic, by foftering its fugitive traitors, and being the centre of new confpiracies againft the rights of man. The court of Turin comes under this defcription. It is hoftile to the liberties of France; it has been fo from the beginning; the nature of its external connections and of its internal conftitution requires that it fhould be fo to the end. The court of Turin muft, therefore, be overturned; the government of your country muft be changed, and its powers reftored to you, to whom they naturally belong.

This is a fimple view of facts, which may ferve to indicate the prefent crifis of your affairs, of which it is proper that you fhould be apprifed; that by a due confideration of the caufes you may not be aftonifhed at the effects. I make known to you my opinion, with all the franknefs that the folemnity of the fubject demands; and it feems almoft impoffible that you fhould fail to turn the confequences to your advantage.

II. The more important queftion to be difcuffed is, *Whether you will be benefited by a revolution in your government?*

Many of you will doubtlefs confider this enquiry as fuperfluous, becaufe your condition can scarcely be rendered worse, and the means of rendering it better are so obvious that they cannot escape the slightest observation. But those of you who are accustomed to reflect on the principles of liberty will pardon the simplicity of the enquiry, in favour of the great mass of the people whom it is our duty to instruct. There has been so much falsehood and folly imposed on that class of mankind, in order to debase and brutalize their minds to the level of their condition, that their ignorance has become preter natural; it is almost necessary to begin their instruction by informing them that they are human creatures. But, citizens of Italy, descendants of Brutus and Cato, this state of degradation is not the condition designed for man. The God of equal liberty has allotted you a different birthright; you are now invited to reclaim your inheritance, to take possession of your portion among your brethren, to enjoy it in peace, and restore harmony to the great family of men.

You have been fatally misinformed with respect to the nature of the French revolution, and the events that have attended it. Your religous teachers and your political masters have an interest in deceiving you. They unite their efforts for this purpose; they blind your eyes, as you blind the eyes of a mill horse, that he may not see his harness, nor consider the weight he draws. If the mill-horse could know that he has only a feeble child for a conductor, and that he is made to go constantly round in the same small circle, so that he cannot hope to come nearer his journey's end; especially if he could look into the neighbouring fields and see the other horses enjoying their liberty, he would soon revolt against his little despot; he would grow discouraged with the same unpromising round of fatigue, and refuse to do his work. It is for this reason that you blind his eyes. My friends, the same arts are used with you. The clergy and the nobles of your country, with a man at their head whom they call a king, do nothing but live upon your labours. They cannot support their luxury by any other means than by keeping you constantly at work. They know that if you were to be informed of their weakness and of your own strength, you would refuse to be their drudges. They are sensible that the moment you open your eyes, you will see that they are but men, that all men are equal in their rights, that they have no more right or power to be kings and lords over you, than you have to be kings and lords over them; and that in consequence of this, you would immediately overturn that abominable system of public robbery which they call a government, and establish a new and equal government, which should secure to every man the fruits of his own labours, protect the innocent, punish the guilty, and instruct every member of society in his duties and his rights.

This is precisely what the people of France have done; and, the performance of this great work, so necessary to the happiness of mankind, is called the French revolution. It is the knowledge of this revolution which your court and clergy wish to conceal from you, lest you should follow the example. They prevent the French newspapers from coming into your country; they forbid the reading of all books that treat of this revolution, and all conversation on that or any other political subject; they have shut up the popular theatres at Turin, and left open none but that of the nobility, from which the citizens are excluded; they have suppressed the great university of that capital, called *the University of the Provinces*, which used to bring students from all parts of Italy, and a considerable emolument to the town; they have doubled the number of their spies, and increased the powers of the police.

All this is to keep you ignorant of the French revolution, that you may not be disposed to follow the example. Observe the insult offered to your understanding. If the example were bad, your good sense would teach you to shun it; it would need only to be known, to be despised; and it ought to be explained to all people, that they might learn to avoid such a dangerous innovation. If it be good, it ought to be taught by your teachers, and imitated by all the world. But be assured that the very caution they use to prevent your coming to the knowledge of the fact, is a proof that such a revolution would be an advantage to you and a disadvantage to them.

But this is not all; they have invented a thousand falsehoods to supply the place of truth. They have told you lies, in order to excite your enmity against your best friends, and to rouse you to war against those principles which ought to be as dear to you as to the French; because they are the principles of equal liberty and national happiness, applicable to all people. They have told you that the French nation is a race of robbers, assassins, and atheists; that they have overturned the religion of their country, waged war against all property and against the lives of its owners. These are impudent falsehoods which never could have been imposed upon you for a moment, had you been permitted to judge for yourselves.

With regard to religion, I only requeſt you to look into the firſt principles of liberty, as declared by the national aſſembly. You will find them conformable to the ſyſtem of the catholic faith, as taught by the apoſtles and recognized in your country, before the church was connected with the civil government, and before the miniſters of the altar became the tyrants of the ſtate. The French conſtitution has declared, that all men ſhall be free to worſhip God in their own way, and to follow the dictates of their conſcience. If any man ſhall tell you that this is deſtroying your religion, he is a liar, and not worthy to be your teacher. The goſpel of Jeſus Chriſt preaches to you in the ſtrongeſt language the great doctrine of equality ; that all men are equal in the ſight of God, and that you ſhall call no man your maſter upon earth.— This is the very language of the French revolution. But its authors have gone farther ; and, to ſilence all cavillers who could perſuade you or others that they have deſtroyed the catholic religion, they have done more to maintain it than any legiſlative body ever did before ; they have ordained that the prieſts and biſhops, choſen by the people, ſhall be ſalaried and paid out of the national purſe.

It is true, they have ſuppreſſed thoſe haunts of idleneſs, hypocriſy, and vice, known by the name of monaſteries and convents. This is an advantage to religion, inſtead of being againſt it ; for religion teaches men to do good, and to labour for their living ; but theſe inſtitutions teach them to do nothing, and live upon the labours of others. Be aſſured, therefore, that the French have done nothing to the diſadvantage of religion ; but, on the contrary, they have done much to maintain it in its native purity and independence. But I intreat you in the sincerity of my heart not to receive this fact on the strength of my affertion, or that of any other man ; but to look into their conduct and judge for yourfelves.

You have been likewife taught to believe that the French have violated private property. This is a malicious calumny, which every ftep of their revolution will contradict, the moment you become acquainted with it. In all the decrees of the national affembly, in all the irregular movements and infurrections of the people, whatever was the object, you will find they have paid a moft facred regard to individual property. Their conduct in this refpect has been more laudable within the laft three years than that of any other government in Europe. The fame thing may be obferved with regard to the private morals of the people ; they are effentially better than they fòrmerly were. There have been lefs inftances of theft and robbery in France fince the revolution, than at any former period ; and probably lefs, in proportion to its population, than in any of the neighbouring countries during the fame period.

With regard to the national affembly, I will give you fome inftances of their inviolable principle of preferving the property of individuals amidft the fhock of the revolution. The abufes of the ancient government had created thoufands of ufelefs offices in every department of ftate, in the *law*, the *finance*, and the *king's houfehold*,—the fame as you fee at Turin. Thefe offices were fuppofed to have been purchafed and paid for by thofe who held them ; though many of them had been given gratis through favour and intrigue. On the regeneration of the government and of the nation by the revolution, it was necessary that these destructive sinecures should be suppressed; and the assembly, considering them as the property of the holders, purchased up this property and paid the proprietors the full prices they had given or were supposed to have given for their places. This act of justice was certainly not necessary to the revolution. It must therefore be considered as a mark of that national dignity which forbids the violation of any kind of private property, however slender the title by which it is claimed.

Another instance may be observed in the public debt. It is well known that the public debt of France, as well as that of Piedmont, was contracted by a wicked and infamous court, the greater part of it for the worst of purposes. It was in part contracted to support the vices of a horde of men and women at Versailles, who were a disgrace to human nature, and whom the nation was under no obligation to maintain; it was in part contracted to carry on foreign wars and conquests, the express purpose of which was to rivet the chains of the people at home. But as the creditors in general were not to be blamed for these things, they were declared to be the proprietors of the debt; and the nation assumed upon itself the payment, without any diminution. This must ever be remembered as an act of sovereign magnanimity and of disinterested protection to the property of individuals; an act to which they were not constrained by any necessity or previous obligation. A royal bankruptcy might have been declared, without affecting the future credit of the nation; and the revolution would have suffered no delay, but would have been facilitated by proceeding on this principle. Instead of doing this, the people have voluntarily taken an immense burden on themselves, even under the humiliating circumstance of giving a sanction to all the extravagance of the two last centuries, and paying at this day, under the rigid economy of a republic, for those splendid palaces, gardens, and water-works, which insult the poverty of millions, and stare the nation in the face with the unpunished crimes of a race of execrated kings.

The act of the assembly declaring the church lands to be the property of the nation, the suppression of tithes and other feudal claims, have been often mentioned as violations of property. Those who really consider them in this light are weak men, or they have not examined the subject; those who persuade you to think so, without believing it themselves, are wicked men, and not to be trusted. As to the church lands, this act of the assembly did not change the property of them at all. They belonged to the nation before.— What the assembly did, was to change the mode of paying the clergy, equalize their salaries, and reduce the number of ecclesiastics. That laborious and more useful class of the clergy, who before were starving upon a beggarly pittance, have had their salaries raised; that idle and overgrown class, who, without doing any duty, were living in the style of princes and tyrants, have been reduced to a moderate income. All are now chosen by the people, and all paid by the nation. With regard to the feudal claims, they were founded in usurpation. The landlords and nobles, to whom they were attributed, had no right to them or property in them, any more than the king of Sardinia has property in you, or in the people of Jerusalem, of which he likewise styles himself king. These feudal claims were mere badges of servitude, which the establishment of equal liberty and the abolition of hereditary titles rendered it necessary to destroy. The nation has in all instances showed itself able to distinguish between the empty superstition of pomp, which serves only to debase mankind, and the solid principles of society on which the revolution is founded.

You have heard it likewise asserted that the French revolution has been marked with cruelty and murder. This is unfortunately true. But it has likewise been marked with treachery, with bribery, with perjury, with all the complicated wiles of expiring despotism. All the cruelty, all the crimes of every name or denomination, that have attended this revolution, have proceeded from royalty, the adherents of royalty, and the refractory priests. The court of Versailles had been for ages a school of falsehood and deceit; and the execution of the penal laws served as a public exhibition of torture, to familiarize the people with the most sanguinary punishments. If the court of Turin and the laws of Piedmont are any better, it is happier for you; you will have the less wickedness to combat in the course of your revolution. But I fear in some respects they are worse. These circumstances in France had trained up in all parts of the kingdom a numerous class of men versed in every art of treachery and perfidy. In this situation of things the great mass of the people, who are naturally honest and good, set themselves seriously to work in the business of the revolution; which might have been carried on with the greatest harmony; as it had nothing in view but the welfare of the whole. But these deceitful men, being enemies of the revolution, and finding that they could not oppose it by open force, assumed the mask of patriotism, and brought themselves into places of trust in every department of the legislative and executive power. The effect of this was that these good people found themselves deceived and betrayed in every stage of their affairs, from the beginning of the revolution in 1789, till the tenth of August, 1792. Being surrounded by traitors, and not knowing whom to trust even with the execution of their own vengeance, it was natural and sometimes necessary that they should assume this terrible task upon themselves. In some instances indeed this popular vengeance has been ill directed, and has fallen on innocent heads. But these instances are rare.*

The limits, I prescribe to my letter, will not allow of my entering into details on a subject so intricate and extensive. This, however, may be relied on as an undeniable truth, that nothing is more humane, generous and just, than the general spirit of the revolution; and whatever particular acts may seem to contravene these principles, those acts are chargeable upon its enemies, and not upon its friends.

But to arrive at the subject the most interesting for your immediate consideration, let us follow

---

* *This was written previous to the establishment of the* Revolutionary Tribunal. *It is indeed to be regretted that that institution was deferred to so late a period; as it was calculated to prevent a more tumultuous mode of exercising popular vengeance. But it is more to be regretted that such a tribunal became necessary at all, and especially that it has been sometimes used by the leaders as an instrument of party rage, without an honest regard to the good of the cause.*

the course of the revolution in a geographical sense, and pass with it from France to Piedmont. The revolution in this journey has stopped to winter in Savoy, from whence I write this letter; and before we mount the Alps, it is natural to make a pause, to contemplate the country where we are. Here is a people who lately made part of yourselves, and who are now separated from you, rather on account of their vicinity to France, than for any particular interest different from your own. For, in the great cause of liberty, the interests of all people are the same. It is the cause of tyranny that has made them enemies; it is the imposition and falsehood of those who would live on other men's labours, that have occasioned all the wars of every nation in the world. The people of Savoy were certainly under no obligation to be governed by the king of Jerusalem; though they had groaned under his yoke for many generations. Their late conduct in declaring their own sovereignty and independence, abolishing hereditary titles, and establishing a government of their own on the principles of equal liberty, is a subject which must strike your minds in a very Interesting point of view. Your tyrants will represent it as a crime which ought to excite your indignation; and they will call on you to take up arms and rush headlong into a destructive war, to assist them in reducing this country again to their obedience. They are now preparing their forces, augmenting their armies, borrowing money abroad and extorting it from the hand of industry at home, for this detestable purpose. You are to be taken from your farms and your shops, and enrolled in the regiments of death. If you are unwilling to engage in this new kind of slavery, you are to be seized upon like so many felons, dragged from your wives and children, and tortured into discipline under the lash of a military officer. Your families are to be left to perish in poverty, while you perhaps are slaughtered in the field.

But before you suffer yourselves to be driven to this desperate business, I intreat you to resort to your own reason, and exercise the right of judging for yourselves. Consider the nature of the enterprise, and the object you have in view.—Who are the people on whom you are going to let fall this terrible stroke of vengeance? What is their crime? Are they not your brothers and friends? Have they not acted as you would have done in the same situation? And ought you not rather at this moment to follow their example, than to be the instruments of their destruction and your own? Let us attend to this enquiry before it be too late.

The people of Savoy, as to their local position stand in the same relation to France as you stand in to Italy. They and you are posted in the marches of these two great fractions of the continent.—As long as this part of Europe is governed by tyrants, perpetually contending for dominion on each side of the Alps, these positions expose you both to the inroads of all parties. You cannot avoid being insulted by foreign armies in their passage through your country, although you have no interest in their quarrels. Your history is full of examples of this kind, from the days of Hannibal, down to that infamous war of the Spanish succession, which involved your country in blood and held half Europe in arms for many years together; a war in which you had no other concern, than that of being the victims of foreign disputes.

The face of your country bears the infulting marks of this unfortunate pofition in which you are placed. It is covered with fortifications. As if nature had not thrown rocks and mountains enough in your way, you have been forced to create them by the hand of art, to encompafs your towns with walls, and disfigure your fields with towers and caftles. Your agriculture has been ill-conducted, your manufactures neglected; all the ufeful arts have been forced to yield to a general fyftem of defence againft the enemies of your neighbours, when you had no enemies of your own.

In this fituation, what is to be done? You cannot change the pofition which nature has given to your country. Your only refource is to change the policy of Europe from war to peace. You are more peculiarly interefted in the perpetual peace of Europe than any other people on earth. This is a weighty confideration, a truth which your tyrants cannot deny. It is the knowledge of this truth which has influenced the people of Savoy in their late change of government. It is in this point of view that they have contemplated the French revolution; with this they have adopted it themfelves, and wifh to extend it to you, whofe fituation fo nearly refembles their own. With this view you ought to wifh to extend it to all the ftates of Italy, to Spain, and to the circles of the empire, from whence it would travel through Europe and through the world.

The principles of this revolution are thofe of univerfal peace; and it is impoffible that it fhould fail to produce the effect, becaufe it takes away every motive for national hoftility, and teaches the people of all countries to regard each other as friends and fellow-citizens of the world. Eftablish equal liberty among the people, and instruct them in the duties that arise from that situation as the French are about to do ; you will then find that the business of tyrants has ceased, and the race is forever extinct. Purge the earth of its tyrants, and it will no more be tormented with war.

The conduct of the people of Savoy in uniting themselves to the French republic deserves a farther consideration. This was a measure incidental to their geographical position on the French side of the Alps ; and the arguments which induced them to it, do not apply to you. It is probable for the purposes of civil government you will henceforward be two distinct people. But this step of theirs cannot be considered by you as an act of hostility, or a breach of friendship. They are certainly not less your friends since they have ceased to be your fellow-subjects. It is an essential quality of a French citizen to be the friend of all people, especially of those in his neighbourhood, whose peace and happiness will always be necessary to his own.

The essence of tyranny is to counteract the economy of nature, the essence of liberty is to promote it. Nature has said that the French and the Savoyards should be one people ; but tyranny has said that the Savoyards and the Piedmontese should be one people. Consult your history, and see what torrents of blood have been shed to cement this unnatural union. Come and view the condition of this unfortunate people ; possessing one of the finest countries in the world, and deprived of the means of improving it ; subjected for ages to a race of weak and impolitic princes, who, fixing their residence on the other side of the Alps, have paid no other attention to this part of their dominions, than to keep the people in poverty and ignorance, in order to secure their obedience. A military force, sent from your country, has been maintained here to insult the inhabitants, by exercising the police in every town and village. The senate of Savoy, which was formerly a legislative body, has been long since reduced to the simple functions of a judiciary tribunal, and its members appointed by the king. He has prevented the working of the mines of iron, lead, and coals, with which the country abounds; he has prevented the establishment of any one of the different manufactures to which the inhabitants are peculiarly invited by the abundance of raw materials, by their numerous currents of water, by their vicinity to France, and the convenient navigation of the Isere and the Rhone; he has discouraged their agriculture by the shackles he has laid upon their commerce, even in the interior of his own dominions; for the trade between Piedmont and Savoy has been subjected to the same pernicious regulations and impositions which exist between rival nations among the most jealous despots of Europe; he has interposed his authority between parents and the duties they owe their children, by discouraging the education of youth, so far as to oblige those who are destined for the learned professions to perform their studies at Turin.*

T 2

* *There are in Savoy six different colleges of education, which have existed for several centuries, and have been exclusively appropriated to those studies which have been known in catholic Europe by the name*

It would be tedious to recount to you all the instances of folly and cruelty exercised by your government against the people of this country.—One general complaint, which appears to be well founded, is, that all your kings, especially the one from whom they have now revolted, have shown an humiliating distinction in their treatment of you and them. The Savoyards have been treated as your slaves, as well as the slaves of your common master. Their hard earnings have been drained from them, to increase the wealth and population of Piedmont. You must observe, however, that this was not designed as an advantage to you, neither has it been so in fact. It was done to facilitate the collection of the king's revenue. You have been made the instruments of drawing money from these people, for no other reason than it was more easy to draw it immediately from you, than from them, by the tyrants of Turin.

of Theology. This was a necessary precaution of the government; as, without distributing these institutions in all the principal towns, and rendering this sort of instruction easy and cheap, it would have been impossible to have initiated a sufficient number of men to keep the people in that state of ignorance which was necessary for their continuance in slavery.

Within a few years there has been established in the college of Chambery a professorship in law, and another in medicine, but under this restriction, that two years residence here should be reckoned for one year at the university of Turin. And no man could practise law or medicine within the king's dominions, until he had taken his degrees at Turin.

The condition of these people was perhaps no worse than yours. You have in your country more wealth than they, but you have infinitely more of real indigence. You were both taxed as high as you could bear*; and your taxes were imposed in the most arbitrary manner. The king could augment or vary them any day at his pleasure. The Savoyard was poor, but he was not miserable; he was not insulted by the display of luxury passing before his eyes, though he was

---

* *The population of the principality of Piedmont is reckoned at four millions. The amount of the public revenue arising from that principality is only 22 million livres of Piedmont, equal to £1,100,000 sterling, forming an average of 5s. 6d. a head. This is exclusive of dimes and other ecclesiastical taxes, which answer to the tithes and poor-rates in England. The public taxes in England, exclusive of these, form an average of about 55s. a head. Yet the people of Piedmont are, if possible, more distressed with taxes than the people of England; although their soil is naturally more fertile, and their country more abundant in materials for manufactures. Their situation indeed is not so favourable for commerce, but it is not unfavourable. By this comparison we may judge of the cruel, uncreating influence of a government which can so completely destroy the native energy of man.*

The Dutchy of Savoy, whose population is 424,000 used to pay annually into the treasury at Turin about three million livres of Piedmont, equal to £150,000 sterling. This was the utmost that the hand of despotism could collect from a people whom it deprived of the means of improving the advantages which nature had given them.

senfible that he supported a fet of infamous courtiers beyond the mountains, who riot on the labours of mankind.

The effect of tyranny has ufually been to vitiate the morals of fociety, and deftroy that energy of mind which is natural to man in a ftate of freedom. The people of Savoy exhibit a remarkable exception to this rule. They retain a fingular purity of morals, and a firmnefs of character, which the weight of a long and complicated tyranny has not been able to debafe. They have long witneffed the vices and indured the injuftice of their mafters, without learning to be vicious or unjuft.— They have felt the inconvenience of that unnatural combination of things which cut them off from the country to which they really belonged, and bound them to a diftant lord. But almighty liberty has at laft diffolved the chain, and reftored them to nature and to France.

The moral character of this people, which renders them fo worthy of our efteem, has likewife fitted them for the enjoyment of the liberty to which they have been fo fuddenly born. No people, rifing at once from flavery to a ftate of equality and independence, ever conducted themfelves with fo much dignity and moderation.— They rofe, like the infant Hercules, to the vigour of manhood in a fingle day. They fhowed themfelves mafters of the whole fyftem of government, the moment they became mafters of themfelves. They have committed no blunders; they have taken no retrograde fteps; they have loft no time in idle difputes, and ufelefs etiquette. Their National Convention, which was the firft reprefentative body that ever was heard of in the country, and confifted of fix hunderd and fifty members, organised itself and finished its sessions in nine days; during which time it did more business than any body of men under like circumstances could be expected to perform in so many months. But there is one fact more remarkable than all the rest, a fact which history will announce to the admiration of the latest ages: the revolution in Savoy has not yet cost a single drop of blood. It has been attended with no acts of violence, no tumultuous meetings, no necessity for the intervention of military force. The force of reason has conducted the whole operation; and the sacred energy of liberty has proved itself to be the source and guarantee of the moral attributes of man.

Such is the condition of this respectable people; and such is the point of view in which you are to consider the late measures they have taken to reclaim and secure their rights. From this consideration you will naturally turn your attention to yourselves, and contemplate the duties you are called upon to perform. For the time is fast approaching when you can no longer be the idle spectators of the triumphs of liberty. Although the revolution in Savoy is hitherto free from the violence of war, it depends on you to say whether it shall continue so to the end of another year. It is in your power at this moment to declare that the Alps shall never more re-echo the sound of a cannon, nor their majestic streams be stained with human blood. Your destiny calls you either to pronounce the sentence of misery and slaughter upon thousands of yourselves and of your neighbours who will follow your example, or to declare the immediate emancipation, peace and happiness of all the states of Italy.

This is doubtless a serious commission, as it renders you responsible for the fate of so considerable a portion of your fellow-creatures. But observe the limits as well as the extent of your power. Though you hold the balance of great benefits and of great disasters, which the present state of affairs is ready to offer to your country; though you are able by the assistance of France to rise as one man and reclaim your own sovereignty; establish your own liberty and provide for the future tranquility of this part of Europe; though by a contrary conduct you may fight the battles of your tyrant against the friends of your peace; yet remember, you cannot long impede the progress of liberty. Her cause is that of reason and of God; she will not listen to any capitulation with despotism; the monster must be driven beyond the Adriatic, and banished from the face of the earth, Italy must be free; she cannot wear her chains much longer; it would be glorious for you to be the first in this regeneration of society in that ancient garden of the world. Such a measure would be an example of virtue to your children, a consolation to the shades of your ancestors, who for a long succession of ages have passed away in the clouds of prejudice, without knowing the means of happiness, or perceiving the dignity of man.

Your king has joined the coalition of despots against the people of all nations. Their arms are directed against France; but their hostility is really against their own subjects. What cause of quarrel had the king of Hungary, or the elector of Brandenburgh with the people of France? None. Their jealousy was against the people of Hungary, of Austria, of Brabant, and of Brandenburgh. They saw that these nations were about to reclaim the rights of man and to caſt off the yoke of oppreſſion, as the French had done. They, therefore, to retain their unjuſt power at home, concluded that it was beſt to ſtrike the revolution at its root, and conquer Germany in France. They knew, if they could ſubdue the French, and completely vanquiſh the ſpirit of liberty in that country, that all the people of Europe would ſhrink beneath their chains, and their maſters might probably ſleep upon their thrones for another half century.

Such was the policy of your maſter. You cannot ſuppoſe that, as king of Jeruſalem or prince of Piedmont, he had any ground or colour of diſpute with the French nation. That nation had no concern with him, nor with any part of his dominions. They were occupied in their own affairs, at peace with all the world, and declared that they meant to remain ſo. He entered into the war with them for no other purpoſe but to keep you in ſubjection. The war was againſt you, and is ſtill to be carried on againſt you the next campaign. He intends to make you his ſoldiers to fight his own battles againſt yourſelves, although he orders you to point your cannon againſt the French.

This is the true ſtate of the caſe. The whole of this war on the part of your monarch is maintained by deceiving you. Indeed the whole buſineſs of monarchy is deception; kings muſt govern by deception, as long as they govern at all; for it is impoſſible for one man to tyrannize over a whole people, but by deceiving them. I have no particular diſlike to your king, any more than to all others; he is probably no worſe than kings in general. They hold an office that is perfectly uſeleſs in ſociety, and exceedingly deſtructive to the peace and happiness of mankind. In this view they ought to be detested by every man, and rejected by every nation.

France has been forced into the field, to encounter this infamous combination of robbers, this war of all crimes against the principles of all virtue. She has undertaken the defence of human nature. She has assumed a new kind of tactique unknown to the art of war, and irresistible to the armies of kings. She has armed herself in the panoply of reason; her manifesto is the rights of man, her sword the pledge of peace. In this species of warfare we need not be astonished at her success. What people can resist the hand that comes to break their chains? The armies of liberty are every where triumphant, while their standards are scarcely stained with blood. Victory completes her work, before they arrive to celebrate the conquest; and the entrance of the French troops into the conquered country is regarded by the people rather as the procession of a civic feast, than as the dreaded violence of war. Their general, instead of punishing the new recovered citizens with confiscation, imprisonment, and death, meets them in their popular societies, and invites them to form their primary assemblies. The forts and garrisons which he erects to secure his conquests, are printing presses and reading clubs.

Such is the war in which the illustrious monarch of Turin is engaged. These are the armies he expects you to encounter in the field. If you wish to know in what manner the combat ought to be conducted, you may learn it from the people of Savoy, whose example in this respect, as in many others, is worthy to be followed by every nation. You may learn it likewise from the people of

Nice, from thofe of Hainault, Flanders, Brabant, Malines, Antwerp, Guelderland, Namur, Liege, Spires, and Mayence; all provinces, principalities, or independent ftates, conquered to liberty within the laft three months. As I have kept no complete regifter of thefe conquefts, perhaps the above lift may be incomplete. But it matters not; if it were complete for to-day, perhaps it would not be fo for to-morrow. This advice is intended for the inftruction of the people; if your king fhould deem it inconfiftent with his warlike character to follow the fame advice, he can take a leffon from the battle of Gemmappe.

The French army deftined for your deliverance will probably not pafs the Alps till the fpring. You have the remainder of the winter to deliberate on the part you have to act. You can by that time decide whether you will receive them as enemies or as friends. In the latter cafe, you have only to ftudy the principles of a republican government, fend away your tyrants, and prepare yourfelves to give leffons of liberty to all the Italian ftates. The troops of Auftria, which are now about to enter your territories from Milan and Tufcany, under pretence of aiding you againft the French, will flee before them, as they have done in the Low Countries, the moment you manifeft your intention of doing your own bufinefs in a peaceable way.

But, after a due confideration of the circumftances which I have endeavoured to detail, fhould you conclude to regard the French people as your enemies, and to meet their armies in the field, I fhall tremble for the confequences of your unfortunate decifion. Thoufands among you muft fall the victims of the infamous caufe of your ty-

U

rant, which cannot be supported. On that day, I beg you would call to mind the honest advice of a stranger, who now speaks to you the words of truth; who has been a steady observer of the rise and progress of liberty in America and in France; and, who, from these advantages is able to estimate the force of its principles, and predict the triumph of its arms.

I advise you above all things to be cautious of the troops in the pay of Austria, who are marching to join your army. You cannot be so blinded by your leaders as to suppose that this band of ruffians is brought into your country to render service to you. They are designed to keep you in subjection, and to take from you the freedom of your choice in the great question, Whether you will adopt the principles of the French revolution? They will be posted in your rear, to act against you, if you should refuse to act against the French. Your position may seem a critical one, placed in the interval between two contending powers; but, remember that one is an army of freemen, the other a horde of slaves; on one side is the permanent force of a nation, whose means are inexhaustible, on the other the accidental hirelings of a despot whose sceptre is falling from his hands; from one you have the offer of equal liberty and perpetual peace, from the other a continuance of your slavery, an augmentation of your burthens, and certainty of future wars.

Italy is destined to form one great republic. The boundaries which nature has given it are peculiarly suited to this purpose; and as long as we follow nature, in politics as well as morals, we are sure to be in the right. Politicians, who have not well considered the effects of liberty, are alarmed at the extenfion of the French republic, fearing it will become too powerful for its neighbours. For this reafon the union of Savoy is mentioned as a fubject of jealoufy to other nations. The enemies of your liberty will not fail to make ufe of this to excite your fears and provoke your refentment. Men who reafon in this manner have formed their maxims on thofe defpotic fyftems of government to which they have been accuftomed. They are maxims which can no longer apply to nations, when mafters of their own actions, and at liberty to govern themfelves by the collected wifdom of the great body of the people. A nation in this condition will never difturb the peace of its neighbours in any manner whatever. Its intereft, on the contrary, will be to promote the peace and profperity of every country in the world.

When a nation is governed by one man, like Piedmont, or by a few families, like the ancient ariftocracy of Rome, and feveral modern ones in Italy, the intereft of thofe who govern, is to extend their dominions; becaufe it augments their perfonal revenue and adds to the weight of their influence over the people, whom they confider as their property.—For this reafon they make war; for this reafon they form treaties of alliance to guarantee each other in their conquefts, and in the property which they have in the people.—In purfuance of this policy, the prince of Piedmont, in the courfe of that long Spanifh war which I have mentioned, purchafed with the blood and treafure of your nation, the title of king of Sardinia; and at the clofe of the war, he obtained from the houfes of Auftria and Bourbon, and from the king of England, a guarantee of the poffeffion.

It is easy to conceive that a system of robbery and murder of this kind, carried on through all Europe for centuries together, must be reduced to some certain rules. These rules by a misapplication of terms, are called the *law of nations*.* It is rather the law of despots, who know no law but their own fears. It has likewise been necessary to establish some general ideas of what is called the *balance of power* among the states of Europe, requiring that each state should be restrained to certain fixed limits. On this principle, when any particular power endeavours to extend its limits, it is natural to tax that power with ambitious views, and to regard it as an object of jealousy. This reasoning is perfectly just when applied to regal and aristocratical dominions; but under the reign of liberty the argument has lost its ground; dominion itself is at an end; and all the technical terms in the science of politics have changed their meaning; and as we must begin the science anew, it is to be regretted that we are not furnished with new words, to express our ideas with more precision than we can with the old.

If all the nations of Europe were as free as the French, and every individual member of society were equally independent of every other individual, the question respecting the boundaries of any particular government would become in a great measure indifferent, both to the people of that government and to all their neighbours. No person would

---

* *We may hope soon to see the* law of nations *established on different principles; that is, on principles as different from what it has been, as the interest of nations is different from that of those persons who have usually governed them.*

have any interest in extending or contracting the territorial limits of a state. They would be established purely on the principle of convenience for the administration of the interior concerns of the people, and by the free consent of all parties. And whenever it should be found more convenient to change them, they might be extended or contracted on the same principle, without injury to any person, and without exciting the jealousy of any nation.

I could cite you many instances from the United States of America, in which this theory has been carried into practice; which would prove to you that the doctrine I here advance, as one of the effects of liberty, is not chimerical. But an instance more striking to you, and which will form an epoch in the history of Europe, is the conduct of the national convention of France on the proposition of Savoy to be united to that republic. Here we see a sovereign people, uninfluenced by any fears, hopes, or connections from abroad, deliberating in the most solemn manner, whether they will extend their territorial boundaries, by the admission of seven new provinces, inhabited by four hundred thousand freemen who had sent their deputies to solicit an union.* To raise a question on a proposition of this kind is certainly a new thing in politics. Louis XIV. would have carried on a war for half a century, and sacrificed twice that number of his own subjects, to have made such

* *The seven provinces which formed the Dutchy of Savoy, now united to France, under the name of the department of* Mont Blanc, *were Savoy proper, Genevois, Carouge, Chablais, Fauchigny, Tarentaise, and Maurienne.*

an acquifition to his dominions. But the members of the convention who deliberated on this queftion had no perfonal intereft to ferve, no ambition to gratify. It was merely a queftion of national convenience, whether the frontiers of the republic fhould remain fixed on the limits of Dauphiny and Lyonnois, or be extended to the Alps which appear to be the natural boundary of France.

The latter opinion prevailed ; but it was rather on account of the prefent circumftances of Italy than of France. Italy is ftill governed by defpots ; and it is to be expected, that as long as they remain in power, they will continue the war they have undertaken againft the French. To prevent their incurfions, it was neceffary to oppofe them the barrier of the Alps. But if Italy were as free as France, all caufes of hoftility between them would be for ever removed. It would be fcarcely poffible in the courfe of human events, that they would ever more have any ground of contention. In that cafe it would be perfectly indifferent, as to perfonal intereft, both to the French and the Savoyards, whether they fhould form one people, or two, or ten.—And whatever refolution they fhould take, as moft convenient to themfelves, would never excite your jealoufy or refentment.

No people has more to gain by this pacific fyftem than thofe of Piedmont. You inhabit a fertile country, productive of all the moft neceffary articles of life ; feveral of which are in great demand among your neighbours. All that is wanting to render you happy is to be mafters of the fruits of your own labours at home, to be fecured againft war, and to have a free circulation of the objects of commerce.

These three things are now within your reach; they would follow as a neceſſary conſequence of adopting the principles of the French revolution, and eſtabliſhing the liberties of Italy.

With the moſt ardent wiſhes to render you ſervice, in the preſent ſolemn criſis of your affairs, I have written you this letter. If it ſhould anſwer no other purpoſe, it will at leaſt ſerve as a teſtimony to my conſcience, that I have endeavoured to do my duty, and to merit the title which I claim, that of your ſincere and diſintereſted friend.

JOEL BARLOW.

THE CONSPIRACY OF KINGS;

A POEM:

Addressed to the Inhabitants of Europe, from another quarter of the world.

※※※※※※※

"But they, in sooth, must *reason*. Curses light
"On the proud talent! 'twill at last undo us.
"When men are gorged with each absurdity
"Their subtil wits can frame, or we adopt,
"For every novelty they'll fly to sense,
"And we must fall before the idol, Fashion."

※※※※※※※

PREFACE.

THE following little poem was published in London, in February 1792. It happened that two of the principal conspirators, the emperor Leopold, and the king of Sweden, died in a few weeks after. The opposite effects, produced by the death of these two persons, are very remarkable. From a view of the general character of the king of Sweden, and of the particular transactions of the last year of his life, there can be no doubt but he was determined to go any lengths with the powers which were then confederating againſt the liberty of France; and it is a conſolation to human nature, that the violent death of our ſceptred mad-man has ſaved the people of Sweden from thoſe horrid ſcenes of ſlaughter which now involve moſt of the neighbouring nations.

The character of Leopold, in ſome of its leading traits, was directly the reverſe of that of Guſtavus. The latter was prodigal of wealth, and exceſſively eager for what is called military fame, without the capacity or the means of acquiring it; the former was affectedly pacific, moderate in moſt of his vices, and remarkable for nothing but his avarice. He had ſenſe enough to ſee that nothing was to be gained by a war with France; his avarice, had he lived, would have been a ſufficient guarantee againſt that event: and his death may be conſidered as the immediate cauſe of the war.

The treaty of Pilnitz was doubtleſs fabricated in the court of Paris. The emperor agreed to it, for the purpoſe of duping the king of Pruſſia into meaſures which might ſecure the obedience of the people of Brabant, whom he had pacified the year before by a cruel deception. His deſign was likewiſe to deceive the emigrant princes, who were then deceiving him; and to exhibit ſuch a menacing appearance, as, according to his calculation, would induce the French people to ſet down quietly under a limited monarchy; well knowing that, if they did this, their government would ſoon degenerate into a deſpotiſm, which would continue to give countenance to the general principle that had ſo long enſlaved the nations of Europe.

That he never intended, or had relinquiſhed the intention, of executing the conditions of the treaty of Pilnitz by going to war with France, is evident from the following confiderations: the French conftitution was ratified, and the revolution fuppofed to be finifhed, in September 1791. A war, to overturn that conftitution, certainly ought not to have been deferred beyond the infuing fpring; and as it would require an army of two or three hundred thoufand men, the winter muft have been occupied in making the preparations. Leopold died fuddenly, about the firft of March. At that time no preparation had been made for offenfive hoftilities. The number of troops fent from Auftria into the Low Countries, during the autumn and winter, was not more than was ftipulated to be maintained there, and were fcarcely fufficient to enforce the defpotifm to which he had deftined that unhappy people. Before the death of Leopold, the French emigrants at Coblentz began to defpair. The hopes they had built on the treaty of Pilnitz had nearly vanifhed; the princes had an army of forty thoufand gentlemen to maintain; Louis was carrying on too great a fyftem of corruption at home, to be able to fupply them with money from the *civil lift*; they had exhaufted their credit in all the merchantile towns in Europe; and Leopold, confidering them in the character of beggars, began to treat them as troublefome guefts; for none of the objects of their demands could be flattering to his favourite paffion. At laft, to their great fatisfaction, the emperor died; and his fyftem with regard to France was either never underftood by his own minifters, or it was laid afide, in compliance with the predominant paffions of his fon; which happened to be for war, expence, and unqualified defpotifm.

This young man began his career by a solemn declaration to all the powers of Europe, that he should follow precisely the system of his father, with respect to the affairs of France. This declaration might be understood to mean the open and avowed system, prescribed by the treaty of Pilnitz, or the secret and unexplained system, which was to avoid the war. It was universally understood, as it was doubtless meant, in favour of the avowed system; whose object, announced in the treaty, was *"to support the rights of crowns."*

From this moment, a spirit of hostility was provoked by the court of Vienna, and encouraged by the French ambassador there, who, like their other ambassadors of that day, was betraying the nation, to serve the king; till, on the 20th of April, war was declared by the National Assembly. In this war the despots of Europe will try their strength, and will probably soon be exhausted.

Paris, July 12, 1793.

THE
CONSPIRACY
OF
KINGS.

ETERNAL Truth, thy trump undaunted lend,
People, and priests, and courts, and kings, attend;
While, borne on western gales from that far shore
Where Justice reigns, and tyrants tread no more,
Th' untainted voice that no dissuasion awes,
That fears no frown, and seeks no blind applause,
Shall tell the bliss that Freedom sheds abroad,
The rights of Nature, and the gift of God.

 Think not, ye knaves, whom meanness styles the great,
Drones of the church and harpies of the state,—
Ye, whose curst fires, for blood and plunder tam'd,
Sultans, or kings, or czars, or emp'rors nam'd,
Taught the deluded world their claims to own,
And raise the crested reptiles to a throne,—
Ye, who pretend to your dark host was given
The lamp of life, the mystic keys of heaven;
Whose impious arts with magic spells began,
When shades of ign'rance veil'd the race of man;
Who change, from age to age, the sly deceit,
As science beams, and virtue learns the cheat;
Tyrants of double powers, the souls that blind,
To rob, to scourge, and brutalize mankind,—

Think not I come to croak with omen'd yell
The dire damnations of your future hell,
To bend a bigot or reform a knave,
By op'ning all the scenes beyond the grave.
I know your crusted souls: while one defies,
In sceptic scorn, the vengeance of the skies,
The other boasts,—I ken thee, power divine,
But fear thee not; th' avenging bolt is mine.
 No! 'tis the present world that promps the song,
The world we see, the world that feels the wrong,
The world of *men*, whose arguments ye know,
Of men, long curb'd to servitude and woe,
Men, rous'd from sloth, by indignation stung,
Their strong hands loos'd, and found their fearless tongue;
Whose voice of thunder, whose descending steel,
Shall speak to souls, and teach dull nerves to feel.
 Think not (ah no! the weak delusion shun,
Burke leads you wrong, the world is not his own),
Indulge not once the thought, the vap'ry dream,
The fool's repast, the mad-man's thread-bare theme,
That nations, rising in the light of truth,
Strong with new life and pure regenerate youth,
Will shrink from toils so splendidly begun,
Their bliss abandon and their glory shun,
Betray the trust by Heav'n's own hand consign'd,
The great concentred stake, the interest of mankind.
 Ye speak of kings combin'd, some league that draws
Europe's whole force, to save your sinking cause;
Of fancy'd hosts by myriads that advance
To crush the untry'd power of new-born France.
Misguided men! these idle tales despise;
Let one bright ray of reason strike your eyes;

Show me your kings, the sceptred horde parade,—
See their pomp vanish! see your visions fade!
Indignant MAN resumes the shaft he gave,
Disarms the tyrant and unbinds the slave,
Displays the unclad skeletons of kings,*
Spectres of power, and serpents without stings.
And shall mankind,—shall France, whose giant
    might
Rent the dark veil, and dragg'd them forth to light,
Heed now their threats in dying anguish tost?
And she who fell'd the monster, fear the ghost?
Bid young Alcides, in his grasp who takes,
And gripes with naked hand the twisting snakes,
Their force exhausted, bid him prostrate fall,
And dread their shadows trembling on the wall.

  But grant to kings and courts their ancient play,
Recal their splendour and revive their sway;
Can all your cant and all you cries persuade
One power to join you in your wild crusade?
In vain ye search to earth's remotest end;
No court can aid you, and no king defend.

  Not the mad knave who Sweden's sceptre stole,
Nor she, whose thunder shakes the northern pole;
Nor Frederic's widow'd sword, that scorns to tell
On whose weak brow his crown reluctant fell.
Not the tri-sceptred prince, of Austrian mould,
The ape of wisdom and the slave of gold,
Theresa's son, who, with a feeble grace,
Just mimics all the vices of his race;
For him no charm can foreign strife afford,
Too mean to spend his wealth, too wise to trust his
    sword.

    * *Ossa vides regum vacuis exhausta medullis.*
                        JUVENAL, *Sat.* 8.

Glance o'er the Pyrenees,—but you'll difdain
To break the dream that foothes the monk of
    Spain.
He counts his beads, and fpends his holy zeal
To raife once more th' inquifitorial wheel,
Prepares the faggot and the flame renews,
To roaft the French, as once the Moors and Jews;
While abler hands the bufy tafk divide,
His queen to dandle and his ftate to guide.

    Yet afk great Pitt to join your defp'rate work,—
See how his annual aid confounds the Turk!
Like a war-elephant his bulk he fhows,
And treads down friends, when frighten'd by his
    foes.

    Where then, forfaken villains, will ye turn?
Of France the outcaft and of earth the fcorn;
What new-made charm can diffipate your fears?
Can Burke's mad foam, or Calonne's houfe of
    peers?*
Can Artois' fword, that erft near Calpe's wall,
Where Crillon fought and Elliott was to fall,
Burn'd with the fire of fame, but harmlefs burn'd,
For fheath'd the fword remain'd, and in its fheath
    return'd!†

---

   * M. de Calonne, at an immenfe labour, and by the aid of his friends in England, has framed a conftitution for France, after the Englifh model; the chief ornament of which is that "Corinthian capital of polifhed fociety," a houfe of peers. It is faid that, after debates and altercations which lafted fix months, he has perfuaded the emigrant princes to agree to it. It only remains now for him and them to try on this new livery upon the French nation.

   † Among the difadvantages attending the lives of princes, muft be reckoned the fingular difficulties with

Oh Burke, degenerate slave! with grief and shame
The Muse indignant must repeat thy name.
Strange man, declare,—since, at creation's birth,
From crumbling chaos sprang this heav'n and earth,

which they have to struggle in acquiring a military reputation. A duke of Cumberland, in order to become an Alexander, had to ride all the way to Culloden, and back again to London. Louis the fourteenth was obliged to submit to the fatigue of being carried on board of a splendid barge, and rowed across the Rhine, about the same time that the French army crossed it; and all this for the simple privilege of being placed above the Macedonian in the temple of Fame, and of causing this achievement to be celebrated, as more glorious than the passing of the Granicus: as may be seen on that modest monument in the Place Vendome in Paris.

The count d'Artois has purchased, at a still dearer rate, the fame of being styled "le digne rejeton du grand Henri," and of being destined to command all the armies of Europe in re-establishing the monarchy of France. This champion of Christendom set out at the age of twenty-five, and travelled by land with a princely equipage, from Paris to Gibraltar; where he arrived just in time to see, at a convenient distance, Elliott's famous bonfire of the floating batteries. He then returned, covered with glory, by the way of Madrid; and arrived at Versailles, amidst the caresses of the court and the applauses of all Europe. The accomplishment of this arduous enterprise has deservedly placed him, in point of military fame, at the head of all the present branches of the illustrious house of Bourbon.

Since wrecks and outcast relics still remain,
Whirl'd ceaseless round confusion's dreary reign,
Declare, from all these fragments, whence you
  stole
That genius wild, that monstrous mass of-soul ;
Where spreads the widest waste of all extremes,
Full darkness frowns, and heav'n's own splendour
  beams ;
Truth, error, falsehood, rhetoric's raging tide,
And pomp and meanness, prejudice and pride,
Strain to an endless clang thy voice of fire,
Thy thoughts bewilder and thy audience tire.

   Like Phœbus' son, we see thee wing thy way,
Snatch the loose reins, and mount the car of day,
To earth now plunging plough thy wasting course,
The great sublime of weakness and of force.
But while the world's keen eye, with generous
  glance,
Thy faults could pardon and thy worth enhance,
When foes were hush'd, when justice dar'd com-
  mend,
And e'en fond freedom claim'd thee as a friend,
Why, in a gulph of baseness, sink forlorn,
And change pure praise for infamy and scorn ?

   And didst thou hope, by thy infuriate quill
To rouse mankind the blood of realms to spill ?
Then to restore, on death devoted plains,
Their scourge to tyrants, and to man his chains ?
To swell their souls with thy own bigot rage,
And blot the glories of so bright an age ?
First stretch thy arm, and, with less impious
  might,
Wipe out the stars, and quench the solar light :
" *For heav'n and earth,*" the voice of God ordains,
" *Shall pass and perish, but my word remains,*"

Th' eternal WORD, which gave, in spite of thee,
REASON to man, that bids the man be free.
   Thou could'st not hope: 'twas heav'n's return-
      ing grace,
In kind compassion to our injur'd race,
Which stripp'd that foul, ere it should flee from
      hence.
Of the last garb of decency or sense.
Left thee its own foul horrors to display
In all the blackness of its native day,
To sink at last, from earth's glad surface hurl'd,
The sordid sov'reign of the letter'd world.
   In some sad hour, ere death's dim terrors spread,
Ere seas of dark oblivion whelm thy head,
Reflect, lost man,—If those, thy kindred knaves,
O'er the broad Rhine whose flag rebellious waves,
Once draw the sword; its burning point shall
      bring
To thy quick nerves a never-ending sting;
The blood they shed thy weight of woe shall
      swell,
And their grim ghosts for ever with the dwell.*
   Learn hence, ye tyrants, ere ye learn too late,
Of all your craft th' inevitable fate.
The hour is come, the worlds inclosing eyes
Discern with rapture where its wisdom lies;
From western heav'ns th' inverted orient springs,
The morn of man, the dreadful night of kings.
Dim, like the day-struck owl, ye grope in light,
No arm for combat, no resource in flight;
If on your guards your lingering hopes repose,
Your guards are men, and men you've made your
      foes;

    * *See Note at the end.*

If to your rocky ramparts ye' repair,
* De Launay's fate can tell your fortune there.
No turn, no shift, no courtly arts avail,
Each mask is broken, all illusions fail;
Driv'n to your last retreat of shame and fear,
One counsel waits you, one relief is near:
By worth internal, rise to self-wrought fame,
Your equal rank, your human kindred claim;
'Tis reason's choice, 'tis wisdom's final plan,
To drop the monarch and assume the man.

 Hail MAN, exalted title! first and best,
On God's own image by his hand imprest,
To which at last the reas'ning race is driven,
And seeks anew what first it gain'd from heaven.
O MAN, my brother, how the cordial flame
Of all endearments kindles at the name!
In every clime, thy visage greets my eyes,
In every tongue thy kindred accents rise;
The thought expanding swells my heart with glee,
It finds a friend, and loves itself in thee.

 Say then, fraternal family divine,
Whom mutual wants and mutual aids combine,
Say from what source the dire delusion rose,
That souls like ours were ever made for foes;
Why earth's maternal bosom, where we tread,
To rear our mansions and receive our bread,

---

* *De Launay was the last governor of the Bastile. His well-known exit, serving as a warning to others, saved the lives of many commanders of fortresses in different parts of France, during the first stages of the revolution. It may probably have the same salutary effect in other countries, whenever the agents of despotism in those countries find the people are determined to be free.*

Should blufh fo often for the race fhe bore,
So long be drench'd with floods of filial gore;
Why to fmall realms for ever reft confin'd
Our great affections, meant for all mankind.
Though climes divide us ; fhall the ftream or fea,
That forms a barrier 'twixt my friend and me,
Infpire the wifh his peaceful ftate to mar,
And meet his falchion in the ranks of war ?

 Not feas, nor climes, nor wild ambition's fire
In nations' minds could e'er the wifh infpire ;
Where equal rights each fober voice fhould guide,
No blood would ftain them, and no war divide.
'Tis dark deception, 'tis the glare of ftate,
Man funk in titles, loft in fmall and great ;
'Tis rank, diftinction, all the hell that fprings
From thofe prolific monfters, courts and kings.
Thefe are the vampires nurs'd on nature's fpoils ;
For thefe with pangs the ftarving peafant toils,
For thefe the earth's broad furface teems with grain,
Theirs the dread labours of the devious main ;
And when the wafted world but dares refufe
The gifts oppreffive and extorted dues,
They bid wild flaughter fpread the gory plains,
The life-blood gufhing from a thoufand veins,
Erect their thrones amid the fanguine flood,
And dip their purple in the nation's blood.

 The gazing crowd, of glittering ftate afraid,
Adore the power their coward meannefs made ;
In war's fhort intervals, while regal fhows
Still blind their reafon and infult their woes.
What ftrange events for proud proceffions call !
See kingdoms crowding to a birth-night ball !
See the long pomp in gorgeous glare difplay'd,
The tinfel'd guards, the fquadron'd horfe parade ;

See heralds gay, with emblems on their vest,
In tissu'd robes, tall, beauteous pages drest;
Amid superior ranks of splendid slaves,
Lords, dukes and princes, titulary knaves,
Confus'dly shine their crosses, gems and stars,
Sceptres and globes and crowns and spoils of wars.
On gilded orbs see thundering chariots roll'd,
Steeds, snorting fire, and champing bitts of gold,
Prance to the trumpet's voice; while each assumes
A loftier gait, and lifts his neck of plumes.
High on a moving throne, and near the van,
The tyrant rides, the chosen scourge of man;
Clarions and flutes and drums his way prepare,
And shouting millions rend the troubled air;
Millions, whose ceaseless toils the pomp sustain,
Whose hour of stupid joy repays an age of pain.
  Of these no more. From orders, slaves and kings,
To thee, O MAN, my heart rebounding springs,
Behold th' ascending bliss that waits thy call,
Heav'n's own bequest, the heritage of all.
Awake to wisdom, seize the proffer'd prize;
From shade to light, from grief to glory rise.
Freedom at last, with reason in her train,
Extends o'er earth her everlasting reign;
See Gallia's sons, so late the tyrant's sport,
Machines in war and sycophants at court,
Start into men, expand their well-taught mind,
Lords of themselves and leaders of mankind.
On equal rights their base of empire lies,
On walls of wisdom see the structure rise;
Wide o'er the gazing world it towers sublime,
A modell'd form for each surrounding clime.
To useful toils they bend their noblest aim,
Make patriot views and moral views the same,

Renounce the wish of war, bid conquest cease,
Invite all men to happiness and peace,
To faith and justice rear the youthful race,
With strength exalt them and with science grace,
Till truth's blest banners, o'er the regions hurl'd,
Shake tyrants from their thrones, and cheer the
  waking world.

In northern climes, where feudal shades of late
Chill'd every heart and palsied every state,
Behold, illumin'd by th' instructive age,
That great phenomenon, a sceptred sage.
There Staniflaus unfurls his prudent plan,
Tears the strong bandage from the eyes of man,
Points the progressive march, and shapes the way,
That leads a realm from darkness into day.

And deign, for once, to turn a trancient eye
To that wide world that skirts the western sky;
Hail the mild morning, where the dawn began,
The full fruition of the hopes of man.
Where sage experience seals the sacred cause;
And that rare union, liberty and laws,
Speaks to the reas'ning race: to freedom rise
Like them be equal, and like them be wise.

NOTE ON Mr. BURKE.
[*Referring to page* 247.]

* SOME of the author's friends in England, although they join with him in censuring the writings of Mr. Burke on the French revolution, are of opinion that the picture here drawn of that writer is too highly coloured; or at least, that the censure is so severe as to lose the effect that it might otherwise produce. It is impossible to say what effect, or whether any, has or will be produced by this poem; but, out of respect to the opinion above stated, it may be proper to make some observations on the effect that has already followed from the writings of Mr. Burke. I speak not of what has taken place in England; where it is supposed that, contrary to his intentions and those of the government that set him at work, his malicious attack upon liberty has opened a discussion which cannot be closed until the whole system of despotism, which he meant to support, shall be overturned in that country. The present war with France is doubtless the last piece of delusion that a set of hereditary tyrants will ever be able to impose upon the people of England.

But this subject opens a field of contemplation far more serious and extensive on the continent of Europe; where, if Mr. Burke can view without horror the immensity of the mischiefs he has done, he will show himself worthy of much higher attributes of wickedness than have yet been ascribed to him. It is a painful task to traverse such a wide scene of slaughter and desolation as now involves the nations of Europe, and then to lay it all to the charge of a single individual; especially when we consider that individual as having, for a long time before, enjoyed the confidence of all good men, and having at laſt betrayed it from the worſt and vileſt motives ; as he had eſtabliſhed his previous reputation by ſpeaking the language of liberty, and profeſſing himſelf to be the friend of national felicity. But it is not from a tranſitory diſguſt at his deteſtible principles, it is from deliberate obſervation and mature conviction, that I ſtate it as an hiſtorical fact, That the preſent war, with all its train of calamities, muſt be attributed almoſt excluſively to the pen of Mr. Burke. There is a peculiar combination of circumſtances which threw this power into his hands, and which ought to be duly confidered, before we come to a deciſion on the ſubject. The people of England had enjoyed for ſeveral ages a much greater portion of liberty than any other people in Europe. This had raiſed them to a great degree of eminence in many reſpects. At the ſame time that it rendered them powerful as a nation, it made them ſober, induſtrious, and perſevering, as individuals ; it taught them to think and ſpeak with a certain air of dignity, independence, and preciſion, which was unknown in other countries. This circumſtance could not fail to gain the admiration of foreigners, and to excite a perpetual emulation among themſelves. England has therefore produced more than her proportion of the illuſtrious men of modern times, eſpecially in politics and legiſlation, as theſe affairs came within the reach of a larger claſs of men in that country than in any other.

In a nation where there is an enormous civil liſt at the diſpoſal of the crown, and a conſtitutional ſpirit of liberty kept alive in the people, we muſt neceſſarily expect to find two parties in the government. In such a case, as the king is sure to carry all the measures that he dares to propose, the party in favour of the people are called the *opposition*; and it being always a minority, it gives occasion for great exertion of talents, and is supposed to be the nurse of every public virtue. Such has been the composition of the English government ever since the last revolution. The opposition has been the school of great men; its principal disciples have been the apostles of liberty; and their exertions have made the British name respectable in every part of the world. Mr. Burke had been for many years at the head of this school; and from the brilliant talents he discovered in that conspicuous station, he rendered himself universally respected. His eloquence was of that flowery and figurative kind, which attracted great admiration in foreign countries; where it was viewed, for the most part, through the medium of a translation; so that he was considered, at least in every country out of England, as the ablest advocate of liberty that then existed in Europe. Even kings and tyrants, who hated the cause, could not withhold their veneration from the man.

Under these impressions, their attention was called to the great event of the French revolution. It was a subject which they did not understand, a business in which they had no intention to interfere; as it was evidently no concern of theirs. But viewed as a speculative point, it is as natural for kings as for other persons to wait till they learn what great men have said, before they form their opinion. Mr. Burke did not suffer them to remain long in suspense; but, to enlighten their understandings and teach them how to judge, he came forward with his " *Reflections on the Revolu-*

tion in France;" where, in his quality of the political fchool-mafter of his age, in his quality of the profeffed enemy of tyrants, the friend of the people, and the moft enlightened leader of the moft enlightened nation in Europe, he tells them that this revolution is an abominable ufurpation of a gang of beggarly tyrants; that its principle is atheifm and anarchy; that its inftruments are murders, rapes, and plunders; that its object is to hunt down religion, overturn fociety, and deluge the world in blood. Then, in the whining cant of ftate-piety, and in the cowardly infolence of perfonal fafety, he calls upon the principal fovereigns of Europe to unite in a general confederation, to march into France, to interfere in the affairs of an independent power, to make war with the principles which he himfelf had long laboured to fupport, to overturn the nobleft monument of human wifdom, and blaft the faireft hopes of public happinefs that the world had ever feen.

Copies of his book were fent in great profufion by the courts of London and Paris to the other courts of Europe; it was read by all men of letters, and by all men of ftate, with an avidity infpired by the celebrity of the author and the magnitude of the fubject; and it produced an effect which, in other circumftances, would have appeared almoft miraculous; efpecially when we confider the intrinfic character of the work. M. de Calonne, about the fame time, publifhed a book of much more internal merit; a book in which falfehood is clothed in a more decent covering; and in which there is more energy and argument, to excite the champions of defpotifm to begin the work of defolation. But Calonne wrote and appeared in his true character. It was known that he had been a robber in France, and was now an exile in England ; and, while he herded with the English robbers at St. James's, he wrote to revenge himself upon the country whose justice he had escaped. His writings, therefore, had but little weight ; perhaps as little as Mr. Burke's would have had, if his real object had been known.

But this illustrious hypocrite possessed every advantage for deception. He palmed himself upon the world as a volunteer in the general cause of philanthropy. Giving himself up to the frenzy of an unbridled imagination, he conceives himself writing tragedy, without being confined to the obvious laws of fiction ; and taking advantage of the recency of the events, and of the ignorance of those who were to read his rhapsodies, he peoples France with assassins, for the sake of raising a hue-and-cry against its peaceable inhabitants ; he paints ideal murders, that they may be avenged by the reality of a wide extended slaughter ; he transforms the mildest and most generous people in Europe into a nation of monsters and atheists, " heaping mountains upon mountains, and waging war with heaven," that he may interest the consciences of one part of his readers, and cloak the hypocrisy of another, to induce them both to renounce the character of men, while they avenge the cause of God.

Such was the first picture of the French revolution presented at once to the eyes of all the men who held the reins of government in the several states of Europe ; and such was the authority of the author by whom it was presented, that we are not to be astonished at the effect. The emigrant princes, and the agents of the court of the Thuilleries, who were then besieging the anti-chambers of ministers in every country, found a new source of impudence in this extraordinary work. They found their own invented fictions confirmed in their fullest latitude, and a rich variety of super-added falsehood, of which the most shameless sycophant of Louis or of Condé would blush to have been the author. With this book in their hands, it was easy to gain the ear of men already predisposed to listen to any project which might rivet the chains of their fellow creatures.

These arguments, detailed by proper agents, induced some of the principal sovereigns of Europe to agree to the treaty of Pilnitz; then the death of Leopold, as I have stated in the preface, unhappily removed the great obstacle to the execution of that treaty, and the war of Mr. Burke was let loose, with all the horrors he intended to excite. And what is the language proper to be used in describing the character of a man, who, in his situation, at his time of life, and for a pension of only fifteen hundred pounds a year, could sit down deliberately in his closet and call upon the powers of earth and hell to inflict such a weight of misery on the human race? When we see Alexander depopulating kingdoms and reducing great cities to ashes, we transport ourselves to the age in which he lived, when human slaughter was human glory; and we make some allowance for the ravings of ambition. If we contemplate the frightful cruelties of Cortez and Pizarro, we view their characters as a composition of avarice, and fanaticism; we see them insatiable of wealth, and mad with the idea of extending the knowledge of their religion. But here is a man who calls himself a philosopher, not remarkable for his avarice, the delight and ornament of a numerous fociety of valuable friends, refpected by all enlightened men as a friend of peace and preacher of humanity, living in an age when military madnefs has loft its charms, and men begin to unite in fearching the means of avoiding the horrors of war; this man, wearied with the happinefs that furrounds him, and difgufted at the glory that awaits him, renounces all his friends, belies the doctrines of hisformer life, bewails that the military favagenefs of the fourteenth century is paft away, and, to gratify his barbarous wifhes to call it back, conjures up a war, in which at leaft two millions of his fellow creatures muft be facrificed to his unaccountable paffion. Such is the condition of human nature, that the greateft crimes have ufually gone unpunifhed. It appears to me, that hiftory does not furnifh a greater one than this of Mr. Burke; and yet all the confolation that we can draw from the detection, is to leave the man to his own reflections, and expofe his conduct to the execration of pofterity.

E N D.